D1569285

# Holocaust Fighters

# Holocaust Fighters

## Boxers, Resisters, and Avengers

Jeffrey Sussman

ROWMAN & LITTLEFIELD
Lanham • Boulder • New York • London

Published by Rowman & Littlefield
An imprint of The Rowman & Littlefield Publishing Group, Inc.
4501 Forbes Boulevard, Suite 200, Lanham, Maryland 20706
www.rowman.com

6 Tinworth Street, London SE11 5AL, United Kingdom

British Library Cataloguing in Publication Information Available

**Library of Congress Cataloging-in-Publication Data**

Names: Sussman, Jeffrey, author.
Title: Holocaust fighters : boxers, resisters, and avengers / Jeffrey
   Sussman.
Other titles: Boxers, resisters, and avengers
Description: Lanham : Rowman & Littlefield, 2021. | Includes
   bibliographical references and index. | Summary: "This book shares the
   remarkable stories of boxers who had to fight for their lives while
   incarcerated in Nazi concentration camps. Alongside their stories are
   accounts of prisoners who resisted their captors and escaped the camps
   and those who sought revenge against the Nazis, creating a well-rounded
   portrait of those who fought against Nazi rule"—Provided by publisher.
Identifiers: LCCN 2021008401 (print) | LCCN 2021008402 (ebook) | ISBN
   9781538139820 (hardback) | ISBN 9781538139837 (ebook)
Subjects: LCSH: Holocaust survivors—Biography. | Holocaust, Jewish
   (1939–1945) | World War, 1939–1945—Prisoners and prisons, German. |
   Concentration camps—Germany. | Concentration camp
   escapes—Poland—Oświęcim. | Jewish boxers—Europe—Biography. |
   Nakam (Organization)—Biography. | Concentration camp inmates—
   Poland—Biography.
Classification: LCC D804.195 S877 2021 (print) | LCC D804.195 (ebook) |
   DDC 940.53/180922—dc23
LC record available at https://lccn.loc.gov/2021008401
LC ebook record available at https://lccn.loc.gov/2021008402

To Barbara, my wife and best friend

# Contents

# Acknowledgments

I am grateful to the following people: Stephen Spataro, East Hampton reference librarian, for his research; Morris Shapow, son of Nathan Shapow, for our conversations about his father; Alan Haft, son of Harry Haft, for our conversations about his father; Christen Karniski, for her editorial acumen and belief in this book; Barbara Sussman, for her suggestions and support; and the numerous concentration camp survivors whose stories have engaged me for many years.

# Introduction

This book provides an account of heroic people who when faced with the threat of extermination by the Nazis fought back with the best means at their disposal: exposing the reality of the death camps, carrying out armed guerrilla attacks during World War II, performing deadly acts of vengeance after the war, and boxing. They were heroes whose activities were finally capped by the successful prosecution of many Nazi war criminals.

This book begins with an account of Hitler's belief that boxing was necessary for a young Aryan man to become a warrior. The narrative then moves to the men who ran the concentration camps where Hitler's devotion to pugilism was transmogrified into brutal life-or-death boxing battles for the entertainment of the *Schutzstaffel* (SS). The lives of five boxers, who were forced to fight for their lives, are explored in five separate chapters. Of those boxers, two were murdered and three survived; one of the survivors was a psychologically damaged victim, and the others had the psychological adaptability to enjoy their freedom while optimistically looking forward to lives of fulfillment.

Not all of those imprisoned in the concentration camps accepted their fate as dealt to them by the Nazis. Of the 900 inmates who attempted to escape, 155 succeeded. Two of those, Rudi Vrba and Witold Pilecki, were able to bring to the world true accounts of the atrocities that were befalling millions of inmates. Many others joined underground military units and fought the Nazis throughout the war. After the war ended, many of those same guerrilla fighters decided that they must avenge all those who had been gassed, incinerated, starved, or beaten to death. They formed a military unit known as the Avengers, and they managed to hunt down and kill 1,500 Nazi war criminals.

The story of the Avengers is an important chapter in the history of the Holocaust fighters. The Avengers were succeeded by specially trained Mossad agents who hunted and killed another 1,500 Nazi war criminals during the years after World War II. Finally, there were the trials that brought the Nazi leaders to justice, the same leaders for whom watching Jewish boxers beat each other had been a primary source of entertainment. Those who prosecuted those criminals have gone down in history as the final heroic victors of World War II. After the war, as Germany lay in ruins, the popularity of boxing, which had never died, increased and attracted thousands of new fans.

The boxers who had been forced to fight their fellow inmates or be killed for not agreeing to entertain their captors had been popular with the public before the war. When their careers died with their imprisonment, they were generally forgotten and certainly never noted in the media. Their only popularity, while fighting in the concentration camps, was with the SS. Not since Roman times, when emperors passed death sentences on defeated gladiators, have contenders fought for their lives as did Jewish and Sinti concentration camp boxers during the time of the Holocaust.

It takes enormous courage to get into a boxing ring and face a skillful opponent whose intention is to cause you as much damage as possible and perhaps even kill you. For a professional boxer, to lose a ring battle may result in a diminution of self-confidence, embarrassment, depression, and reduced financial opportunities. Imagine then how much worse it would be for a boxer to lose a fight knowing that he will be removed from the ring then starved to death, shot, or gassed. Winning temporarily eliminated the existential threat. The winner was permitted to live, but that decision depended on the outcome of his next bout.

Boxers who were incarcerated in Nazi concentration camps lived with almost unimaginable levels of anxiety that no professional boxers experience: in the camps, one's very life often depended on winning bout after bout, week after week, month after month. And how about the less-skillful opponents who desperately fought on, knowing they would probably lose and then face the likelihood of being murdered? While the superior boxer would go on to fight another day, he would see his defeated opponent, already bloody and bruised, denied food and medical care, being carted off to be gassed then incinerated. Relieved to still be alive, the superior boxer would also feel maddening guilt about the likely death of his opponent. Some winners may have wondered if it wouldn't be better to be dead than go through such dehumanizing turmoil over and over again. But then the will to survive would reassert itself, and the dreadful bouts would continue: one man surviving by destroying another human being.

All through those matches, drunken sadistic guards would laugh, goad the fighters on, and curse the losers. For the guards, the spectacle was somewhat better than cockfights or seeing two dogs rip each other to pieces. The guards would bet not on the outcome, for much of that was assured; instead, they would bet on the length of the fight. If it ended quickly with a devastating knockout, the winner might be treated to a more-nourishing bowl of soup than the other inmates were given, for additional nourishment was necessary to maintain a boxer's strength. And since winning boxers were the property of the camps' commandants, they were kept relatively fit. For those who were entertained by the fights, the boxers were no better than wild animals who are tamed, trained, and goaded to attack each other. Once tamed and trained, they never rejected an order to enter the boxing ring. Obedience was paramount, and to resist the order to fight would be a death sentence.

It took enormous strength of character not to be warped by the concentration camp experience. Some boxers emerged with their humanity intact. Others were justifiably furious at the Nazis and at a world that remained largely silent and complicit. Their anger raged inside of them; it became part of their DNA.

So who were those gladiators whose fists won them the right to go on living?

They were four well-known Jewish boxers from different countries and one Sinti boxer who fought weekly in order to survive the gas chambers. They were Victor Perez, world flyweight and French flyweight champion; Salamo Arouch, middleweight champion of Greece; Nathan Shapow, a Latvian boxer who killed an SS officer with two quick punches; Harry Haft, a Polish boxer who went on to fight in the United States after his liberation; and Johann Trollmann, a Sinti boxer, who had to endure the same sadistic treatment meted out to Jewish concentration camp boxers, for he was regarded as a gypsy (a non-Aryan), a subhuman who had to wear a black or brown triangle denoting his inferior status.

Victor Perez, known as "Young Perez," was perhaps the most charismatic of the four Jewish concentration camp boxers. He had been a celebrity in pre-war France, the subject of numerous newspaper and magazine stories. He was reported to have had affairs with movie stars who found him devilishly handsome and sexy. He was eventually taken captive and sent to an Auschwitz subcamp called the Monowitz camp. He fought every week, winning each fight.

Salamo Arouch was short and powerful, all muscle and guts. He was a ferocious fighter who refused to ever give up. He fought 200 bouts at Auschwitz. In his civilian career, he had 238 wins, all by knockouts; he started out as a lightweight, became a welterweight, and finally a middleweight. Regardless of his weight division, he proved unbeatable in each.

Nathan Shapow's first win was scored with a pair of powerful punches that killed a sadistic SS officer. Though Shapow's professional boxing career was aborted by the start of World War II, he boxed regularly as a concentration camp inmate. Following the end of World War II, he became a soldier in the Israel Irgun and the Stern Gang, where he fought in the country's 1948 war.

Harry Haft, handsome enough to be a movie star and with a physique that Michelangelo could have used for his sculpture of David, was a heavyweight boxer who had been born in Poland in 1925. In 1941 he was arrested and sent to Auschwitz where he fought 76 times, winning each fight.

Johann Trollmann was denigrated by the Nazis as a non-productive member of society, a germ-infested Gypsy. Though despised and ridiculed by the Nazis, Trollmann developed a reputation as a superb boxer in the late 1920s and early 1930s. He was subsequently arrested by the Gestapo and sent to a concentration camp. There he was forced to fight for his life. In his last bout, he beat a hated kapo who—in revenge—snuck up on Trollmann and beat him to death with a club.

For the Jews and Sinti and Roma, simply being born was sufficient to receive a death sentence in Nazi Germany. And who carried out those death sentences? Otherwise law-abiding citizens who followed the dictates of the Nuremberg Laws and who placed obedience to the state above their individual consciences. As C. P. Snow wrote, "When you look at the long and gloomy history of man you will find more hideous crimes have been committed in the name of obedience than have ever been committed in the name of rebellion."[1]

And Hitler not only demanded complete obedience from German citizens and those of conquered and Axis countries (i.e., Italy, Japan, Hungary, Romania, Slovakia, Bulgaria, and Croatia), he was also determined to make them complicit in the destruction of what he referred to as subhumans, that is, Jews, Gypsies, homosexuals. In a speech, Hitler stated,

> Genghis Kahn had millions of women and men killed by his own will and with a gay heart. History sees him only as a great state builder. I have sent . . . my Death Head Units with the order to kill without mercy men, women and children. . . . Who after all talks nowadays of the extermination of the Armenians?[2]

Hitler was counting not only on a history of German obedience to authority but also on the growth of German anti-Semitism following the end of World War I. The term *anti-Semitism* had been introduced by a German journalist named Wilhelm Marr in 1879. He founded and led the German League of Antisemites. His was not the only party dedicated to the promulgation of anti-Semitism. There was also the German Social Anti-Semitic Party, the Christian Socialist Workers' Party, and the Anti-Semitic People's Party. They planted the seeds that Hitler watered and vehemently nurtured. He grew and ruled a jungle inhabited by vicious feral creatures who attacked and killed with impunity and without a tear of mercy.

Nourishing that malign jungle required a steady diet of conspiracy theories. Defeated countries often rely on such theories to avoid accepting blame for their defeat. Scapegoats are sought out and become the targets for revisionist fervor. The Nazis declared that responsibility for Germany's humiliating defeat in World War I and the imposition of the harsh Versailles Treaty was the fault of back-stabbing, sinister, money-grubbing Jews. They had conspired to bring Germany to its knees. Neither evidence nor contradiction mattered to those who believed that Jewish bankers and arms merchants had sold out the country; that Jewish Bolsheviks had aligned themselves with Lenin and the Communist Party to defeat a noble Germany; that Jewish capitalists had wanted to make a fortune from Germany's defeat. Such vermin could never be true Germans: they were an alien race, parasitical and cosmopolitan. From there, it was not long before the Nazi's were promulgating the ideal of the superior man: a blond, blue-eyed superman who would stamp out the germ-infested Jew and save the Aryan civilization.

The destruction of the Jews was comprehensive and systematic. It involved new laws, new technologies, and broad bureaucratic planning. The war against the Jews became a primary goal of the Nazis that was separate from its war against America, Great Britain, and Russia. Ronnie S. Landau writes,

> Ultimately, the destruction of the Jews would be so intrinsically desired by the Nazi state that even when it was clear to all but the most fanatical and self-deluded that Germany was heading inescapably for military defeat her anti-Jewish policy would be carried out with even more rigour and determination. What is even more remarkable and noteworthy is that this policy continued to be enacted with ruthless efficiency even though it worked directly against the German war interest. . . . The Holocaust cannot be explained merely as a by-product of the Second World War or as a consequence of the brutalization of

the German populace at a time of national emergency. The path to the death camps had been prepared many years before the outbreak of that war.[3]

With the passage of the Nuremberg Laws in 1935, the Jews were not merely excluded from the professions (which began in 1933), they were now stripped of their citizenship and forbidden to have sexual relations with non-Jews. (This would be a factor in the betrayal of Victor Perez.) Then in 1938, Jews had to register all of their property and assets, the first step to confiscating their material wealth. Under such onerous conditions, it is not surprising that more than 300,000 German Jews departed their homeland. What is surprising is that slightly more than 200,000 Jews remained in pre-war Germany. It has been estimated that between 160,000 and 180,000 German Jews were killed by the Nazis. By May 1943, the Nazis would declare that Germany was *Judenrein* (clean of Jews).

The vile treatment of Jews and their subsequent departure from Germany into other lands led the leaders of thirty-two nations to convene a conference in Evian, France, in July 1938. Thirty-two countries were represented at the Evian Conference. The conference was designed to give cover to government officials (especially those from the United States) who did not want to liberalize their immigration laws. They postured about the sad predicament of the Jews but said that their own countries were in the depths of the Depression and they could barely help their own citizens. How could they possibly support immigrant Jews when so many of their own countrymen were out of work? Of course, it didn't matter that many Jews were professionals who would have easily found work in their adopted country. Following the conference, a number of American Jews noted that the United States had passed a restrictive immigration law in 1924 that was designed to limit the number of Jewish immigrants. Nevertheless, more than 270,000 German Jews applied for visas to come to the United States. But by 1940, only 90,000 visas had been granted.

Arthur Morse wrote that the Evian Conference "would be months in planning, would silence the critics of apathy and if all worked well, would divert refugees from the United States to other cooperating nations."[4]

The entire conference, especially the words of the Americans and the British representatives, struck many as hypocritical and ultimately playing into the hands of Hitler and Goebbels, both of whom complained that nobody wanted Germany's Jews. When the British representative returned home, he proudly informed his colleagues that he was able to veto any denunciation of Nazi policy about Jews. Golda

Meir, who had been an observer at Evian, was distraught at what she had witnessed. She later wrote that the conference left her feeling rage and frustration.

Almost a year later, Hitler played upon the world's unwillingness to accept Jewish refugees. In May 1939, the German ship the *St. Louis* sailed from Hamburg to Havana, Cuba. On board were 937 Jewish refugees. Upon docking in Havana, the ship was denied landing permits though Cuba permitted 22 Jews with valid visas to disembark. The Cuban president then ordered the ship to leave Cuban waters. After sailing from Cuba, the ship passed close to the coast of Florida, and passengers could see the lights of Miami. Several passengers sent President Roosevelt cables asking for permission to dock and disembark in the United States. He did not respond to their pleas for help. The State Department, however, sent a cable that passengers must "await their turns on the waiting list and qualify for and obtain immigration visas before they may be admissible into the United States." In June 1939, the ship was back in European waters. Great Britain agreed to take 288 passengers; the Netherlands took 181; Belgium took 214; and France took 224. Of those who found temporary refuge in Europe, 254 died.

In the world conceived by Hitler, there was no room for subhumans. Aryans were superior in every way. Therefore they must dominate the less-civilized breeds of humanity. The Aryans were not only intellectually and artistically superior, they were also athletically superior. Athleticism was a mandatory discipline that would develop strong soldiers who could conquer other lands and defend the fatherland if necessary. For Hitler, therefore, physical fitness was integral to being a good Nazi. He was especially enamored of boxing and an admirer of Max Schmeling, who became a symbol of the strong Aryan man who represented the future of the race in Europe. For many years, boxing had been one of the most popular sports in Germany. During the Third Reich boxing seemed, along with soccer, to be a national pastime. While Max Schmeling exemplified Hitler's view of the strong man who could get in a ring and pummel an opponent, Schmeling was decidedly anti-Nazi, going so far as to refuse to fire his Jewish manager in America, Joe Jacobs, and then jeopardizing his own safety by hiding a number of Jewish teenagers in his apartment during *Kristallnacht*.

The Nazis had a difficult time reconciling their view of the Nazi boxer as an Aryan strongman with the skills of a Jewish boxer who could defeat their champion. This was especially true when partly Jewish boxer Max Baer so badly pummeled Max Schmeling that the referee had to stop the fight to prevent Baer from killing Schmeling. Max Baer's name and image were banned in Germany by Joseph Goebbels. Reality was not permitted to shatter Nazi illusions.

The Nazi love of boxing extended to the concentration camps, where Jews and Sinti were ordered to fight one another. As long as the Jews and Sinti fought one another, there was no chance of an Aryan boxer losing to a subhuman. But how to explain that Jesse Owens beat his Nazi counterparts at the 1936 Olympics?

According to Albert Speer, Hitler "was highly annoyed by the series of triumphs by the marvelous colored American runner Jesse Owens. People whose antecedents came from the jungle were primitive, Hitler said with a shrug; their physiques were stronger than those of civilized whites and hence should be excluded from future games."[5]

Strong as the boxers were, only one of them escaped the deadly clutches of the Nazis. Two prisoners who actually escaped from the barbed wire confines of Auschwitz were Witold Pilecki and Rudi Vrba. They were determined to let the world know what the Final Solution meant for Jews, Roma and Sinti, communists, homosexuals, the disabled, the sick, the mentally ill, and Jehovah's Witnesses. The heroics of these two escapees, during an otherwise depressing period in history, are inspiring stories of courage and intelligence.

Witold Pilecki was a handsome, dashing Polish cavalry officer and devout Christian who sought sustenance from the Sermon on the Mount. He treated all beings without religious, national, or racial prejudice. He was a member of the Polish Home Army and fought courageously against the Nazis and the Soviets, and after he heard stories about atrocities committed by the SS in Auschwitz, he volunteered to be taken prisoner so that he could verify those stories and report his findings to the Allied forces fighting the Nazis. After his arrest and imprisonment in Auschwitz, he organized an underground of resisters and smuggled information to the Polish Home Army and the Polish-government-in-exile in London. After more than two years in the camp, he and some colleagues made a daring escape, and on his way back to Warsaw he was shot in the shoulder by a Wehrmacht soldier, but he kept going. Back in Warsaw, he wrote a report on what he had observed of the atrocities committed at Auschwitz. It became known as Witold's Report. After the war, he remained loyal to the Polish Home Army but was declared a traitor by the newly installed communist government, severely tortured, then executed. Just prior to his execution in 1948, he stated, "I tried to live my life in such a fashion so that in my last hour, I would rather be happy than fearful. I find happiness in knowing that the fight was worth it."[6]

Pilecki would have been justified in believing, as Shakespeare wrote in *Julius Caesar*, that "the evil that men do lives after them, the good is oft interred with their bones." Today, however, his memory lives on and he is honored as a Polish patriot and Holocaust hero. Or as British historian Norman Davies, writes, "if there was an Allied hero who deserved to be remembered and celebrated, this was a person with few peers."[7]

Rudi Vrba also qualifies as a Holocaust hero. Born Walter Rosenberg in Czechoslovakia in 1924, Vrba was a brilliant Jewish biochemist who was shipped off to Auschwitz in 1942. There he befriended Alfred Wetzler. They engineered a successful escape several weeks after the Nazis invaded Hungary. They were determined to warn the Jews of Hungary what awaited them in Auschwitz. They tramped and trudged their way to Slovakia where they were given safe residence and a place to write a report about the atrocities of Auschwitz. Their report refuted the German claim that inmates were deported so that they could be comfortably resettled outside the Reich; instead it provided details of the mass killings that occurred day by day in the camp. A Romanian diplomat named Florian Manilou sent the report to George Mantello, a Jewish diplomat representing El Salvador, who was stationed in Geneva. He publicized the report in Swiss and British newspapers, and more than four hundred newspaper stories about the Vbra-Wetzler report appeared in Swiss newspapers, resulting in mass demonstrations by Swiss citizens against the Nazis. As a result, more than 200,000 Hungarian Jews were saved from extermination. Following the issuance of the report, Vrba fought alongside members of the Slovakian partisans against the Nazis. He was later honored with the Czechoslovak Medal of Bravery and years later was called upon to testify against captured Nazi war criminal Adolf Eichmann.

Informing the world of the Nazi atrocities was not sufficient for many Jews. They wanted revenge. Following the end of the war, many Jews believed that vengeance was a necessary and justified response against Nazi war criminals. They coalesced and formed a group of about fifty militants known as the Avengers (in Hebrew they were known as Nakam). They wanted to kill all the Nazis who were responsible for the murder of 6 million Jews. They were led by a charismatic poet and guerrilla fighter named Abba Kovner, who in the early days of the war had warned his neighbors in Vilna, Lithuania, that the Nazis intended to exterminate all the Jews of their country. Many did not believe him, but those who did fought alongside him during the war, committing acts of sabotage and assassinating SS men wherever they could. More than 1,500 Nazi war criminals were assassinated by Jewish vigilantes, many of whom were members of Nakam.

Whereas Nakam was an unofficial group of revenge seekers, Mossad was an arm of the Israeli government that was ordered to exact non-judicial revenge against Nazi war criminals. Its most spectacular success was the kidnapping of Adolf Eichmann, one of the major organizers of the Holocaust and who had served under the notorious Reinhard Heydrich, the man Hitler proudly said had a heart of iron. It was Eichmann who said, shortly before Germany's defeat, that he would "leap laughing into the grave because the feeling that he had five million people on his conscience would be for him a source of extraordinary satisfaction."[8]

Mossad was formed on December 13, 1949, as the Central Institute for Coordination on orders from Prime Minister David Ben-Gurion. Its motto is "For Wise Guidance You Can Wage Your War," and it has consistently waged war against Israel's many enemies, including those Nazis who had attempted to exterminate the Jews. The unit in charge of carrying out the assassinations of Nazi war criminals was known as Kidon, and its agents include a group of the world's most expert assassins. Most of its activities are highly secret, though according to Ronen Bergman, Kidon has carried out 2,700 assassinations.

Its most public assassination was of Herberts Cukurs, known as the "Butcher of Riga." Cukurs was a leader of a pro-Nazi group of Latvians known as Arajs Kommando. He was captured in South America by a Mossad agent, who shot him in the head and left his corpse in a trunk on which was a note stating the accused had been sentenced to death by those who can never forget the killing of 30,000 Jewish men, women, and children. The note was sent to local media, and Cukurs's death was reported throughout the world.

Those are highlights from the story of those who resisted the Nazis, who fought back, who sacrificed their lives to save others and sought justice for the victims of Nazi war crimes. They are inspiring Holocaust heroes. They all fought to create a better world for all of humanity.

Yet they were not naive; they knew that there is no vaccination against evil. As Bertolt Brecht in *The Resistible Rise of Arturo Ui* wrote,

> If we could learn to look instead of gawking,
> We'd see the horror in the heart of farce,
> If only we could act instead of talking,
> We wouldn't always end up on our arse.
> This was the thing that nearly had us mastered;
> Don't yet rejoice in his defeat, you men!
> Although the world stood up and stopped the bastard,
> The bitch that bore him is in heat again.

# Hitler and Boxing

Though a fan of boxing, Hitler never tied on a pair of gloves, never entered a ring. To imagine otherwise is to envision a comedic scene: the skinny arms flailing about, the eyes flashing anger and frustration, the voice gutturally screaming at his opponent. Yet the man thought boxing a necessary ingredient for becoming a successful Nazi warrior.

There have been many satirical depictions of Hitler in movies such as *The Great Dictator* and *The Producers*, but there is a silent 1915 movie titled *The Champion* in which Charlie Chaplin looks like a young ragamuffin Hitler. In fact, they were born the same year: 1889. Full of his own self-importance, the Chaplin character can only win his boxing match by hitting his opponent with a horseshoe hidden in his boxing glove. Hitler too was a man who imagined himself unbeatable but only if he could resort to lies and overwhelming force to achieve his ends.

While never engaging in fisticuffs, Hitler vicariously thrilled at the sight of German pugilists outboxing non-Aryan opponents, as when Max Schmeling beat Joe Louis in their first match. Schmeling had been invited to show Hitler the film of that bout with Louis. In his autobiography Schmeling wrote,

> At the start, the camera swept over the massive arena and the crowds of people streaming in. Hitler was captivated. This was the kind of atmosphere that he knew from his own experiences and that he clearly enjoyed. Even the first couple of fight sequences seemed to put him in a state of feverish excitement. He gave a running commentary and every time I landed a punch he slapped his thigh with delight. "Schmeling," he suddenly directed at me, "have you read what I wrote in *Mein Kampf* about the educational value of boxing? Boxing is a manly

sport. That's why I tell everyone, Schirach and Tschammer, that boxing should be introduced into the public school curriculum."[1]

Indeed, Hitler wrote in *Mein Kampf*,

Seeing that its members must undergo a good physical training, the place of chief importance must not be given to military drill but rather to the practice of sports. I have always considered boxing and ju-jitsu more important than some kind of bad, because mediocre, training in rifle-shooting. If the German nation were presented with a body of young men who had been perfectly trained in athletic sports, who were imbued with an ardent love for their country and a readiness to take the initiative in a fight, then the national State could make an army out of that body within less than two years if it were necessary, provided the cadres already existed. In the actual state of affairs only the *Reichswehr* could furnish the cadres and not a defence organization that was neither one thing nor the other. Bodily efficiency would develop in the individual a conviction of his superiority and would give him that confidence which is always based only on the consciousness of one's own powers. They must also develop that athletic agility which can be employed as a defensive weapon in the service of the Movement.[2]

And one only need look at YouTube to see scenes of hundreds of skinny young boys, all members of the Hitler Youth, wearing identical white shorts and happily flailing away at one another with their small boxing gloves. Their innocence and joy in sports hardly portend the devastation they would inflict as adult soldiers on countries and populations in conquered lands.

Hitler foresaw that the Hitler Youth League, with its emphasis on fitness and boxing, would be his training institution for a strong Nazi army. At its height, the Hitler Youth had several million members, all of whom were indoctrinated from a young age to be tough, self-sacrificing, and devoted to the fatherland. Their motto could have been "Ask not what your country can do for you, but what you can do for your country." While organizations such as the Boy Scouts were very popular in Germany and not faux military-training organizations, all those organizations were dissolved and replaced by the Hitler Youth in 1935. In addition to training its members in boxing, it also trained them in the use of military weapons as well as military tactics. The combination of athleticism and militarism was far more important than academic studies. In addition, the youthful members were indoctrinated to hate Jews and other "subhuman" enemies of the fatherland. By December 1936, membership in the Hitler Youth had become mandatory under the Hitler Youth Law, which was reaffirmed in March 1939 under the Youth Service Duty. Parents who objected to their sons being conscripted into the Hitler Youth were visited by Gestapo agents who threatened them with fines, imprisonment, and loss of employment. Young men who dropped out of the league were denied admission to universities and could not be employed. So effective was the government's coercion that by 1940, the Hitler Youth had 8 million members. According to David Williamson, "effectively, the Hitler Youth constituted the single most successful of all the mass movements in the Third Reich."[3]

In fact, historian Gerhard Rempel wrote that Nazi Germany could not have achieved its level of success without the Hitler Youth League for its members represented the "social, political, and military resiliency of the Third Reich" and were thus "the incubator that maintained the political system by replenishing the ranks of the dominant party and preventing the growth of mass opposition."[4]

Following Germany's surrender at the end of World War II, the Allies did not think it necessary for the Hitler Youth members to undergo denazification, which meant that they carried their ideology with them for the remainder of their lives. Unlike its members, the leaders of the Hitler Youth were found guilty and sent to prison for varying terms.

While the Hitler Youth trained numerous men who aspired to be professional boxers, very few of them emerged as professionals either during the war or after. Max Schmeling, the country's most famous boxer and world heavyweight champion from 1930 to 1932, was neither a graduate of the Hitler Youth nor a member of the Nazi Party. (His refusal to join the party was a particular irritant to both Hitler and Goebbels.) Yet his popularity in Germany seemed to have been pervasive, especially after he married a beautiful blonde Czech film star, Anny Ondra, in 1933. They were regularly photographed and written about not only in German magazines and newspapers, but also in Austrian, French, Italian, English, and—of course—Czechoslovakian ones. They were considered one of the glittering couples on the boulevards and in the cafes and nightclubs of Berlin and beyond.

While the Nazis hoped to use Schmeling's celebrity to their advantage, they faced several obstacles that could not be overcome. For the Nazis, Schmeling's most controversial and galling relationship was with his Jewish manager in America, Joe Jacobs. Hitler demanded that Schmeling fire Jacobs. But as diplomatically as possible, Schmeling refused. Schmeling wrote,

Hitler's face showed displeasure, Instead of giving an answer, he lifted his teacup and loudly slurped his tea. "I really need Joe Jacobs," I continued. "I owe all my success in America to him." But Hitler said nothing. In the pause that followed, I added, "Mr. Jacobs is competent, he is respectable and correct. And beyond that, you can't get anywhere in New York without a local manager." Unsettled by the still mute Hitler, I persisted somewhat senselessly with: "Besides loyalty is a German virtue."

Hitler made an angry gesture, then he again stared absently into space.[5]

Who was Joe Jacobs and why did Schmeling depend on him? According to the Jewish Virtual Library,

> he was the quintessential boxing manager of the 1920s and 1930s, a cigar-chomping, fedora-wearing, streetwise, brash, combative, argumentative, and fast-talking schmoozer who "knew nothing about boxing, but he knew how to negotiate and get his man the best deal possible," in the words of his most famous fighter, Max Schmeling. Jacobs [who was nicknamed "Yussel the Muscle"] became Schmeling's manager in 1928.[6]

Matters went from bad to dangerously bad following one of Schmeling's victories. In 1935, Jacobs went to Germany to see Schmeling fight Steve Hamas in Hamburg. Following Schmeling's victory, the crowd of more than 25,000 spectators enthusiastically rose to their feet and sang the Nazi anthem, *"Deutschlandlied,"* with its infamous opening line *"Deutschland Deutschland uber alles."* While singing, the spectators gave the stiff-armed Nazi salute. Overcome with enthusiasm, Jacobs rushed to the center of the ring to congratulate his fighter. Jacobs looked around at the crowd, not knowing how to react, and he then smiled and winked at Schmeling. Much to Schmeling's surprise, Jacobs raised his right arm in the Nazi salute. But rather than flatly stretching out his fingers, Jacob held a cigar between his folded index and middle fingers. The cigar was a prosthetic substitute for his middle finger. In the photographs that appeared in German newspapers, Jacob appears to be giving the finger to the entire audience. The Nazis were furious. Anti-Semitic epithets poured with a volcanic rush out of radios throughout the country. Newspapers editorialized against Jacobs. The Reich minister of sports, Hans von Tschammer, called Schmeling into his office and demanded that he fire Jacobs. It wouldn't happen. In America, news of the event inspired the Three Stooges to change the title of a popular song titled "I'll Never Fall in Love Again" to "I'll Never Heil Again." For their irreverence, not only were the Stooges banned from Germany by Goebbels, they were put on a list of subversives to be exterminated after the Reich conquered the United States. It is doubtful that the Stooges feared the clatter of Nazi jackboots on the pavements of U.S. cities.

Schmeling was a courageous man who endangered himself by his loyalty to the irrepressible Jacobs. Schmeling appreciated that he owed much of his success to his inventive and publicity-savvy manager. For the rest of his life, Schmeling remained grateful to Jacobs and often spoke appreciatively of all that Jacobs had done for him. When war broke out, the two were separated. During the war, when Schmeling learned that Jacobs had died, he felt that he had lost a vital friend. Jacobs was only forty-one when he keeled over from a fatal heart attack. In 1954, Schmeling came to New York and his first stop was the grave of Yosef Jacobs. At the cemetery, he was greeted by an ancient caretaker, shriveled and bent over, who wore a black yarmulke. When the caretaker learned that Schmeling was there to visit the grave of Jacobs, he acted as if he were a privileged tour guide. Upon reaching the grave, the caretaker announced to Jacobs's spirit that Schmeling hadn't forgotten him and this visit was Schmeling's first stop in America. As Schmeling touched Jacobs's gravestone, tears filled his eyes. He silently stood there for several minutes then bent over, picked up a pebble, and placed it on the gravestone of his friend. He nodded at his cemetery guide then departed in silence as he wiped a tear from his eye.

While not firing Jacobs was one act of rebellion that antagonized the Nazis, there were other instances of Schmeling not doing what the Nazis expected of him. Just prior to the outbreak of war, he was asked by a reporter if he thought Germany would go to war against the United States. Rather than stating that the Nazis would smash the Americans, Schmeling responded that such a war would be a terrible tragedy not just for the world but for him personally because he regarded America as his second home. His comments were printed in newspapers not only in Germany but also in much of Europe and the United States. Goebbels flew into a rage and demanded that Schmeling be tried as a traitor and shot. Nothing came of the demand.

In 1939, Schmeling achieved his goal of becoming European heavyweight champion, which should have made the Nazis proud. But before they could start crowing about their unbeatable Aryan pugilist, newspaper headlines undercut their arrogance. Headlines across the country announced that Schmeling had indeed become the heavyweight champion but not by knocking out his opponent, Adolf Heuser. While the headlines correctly stated Schmeling's victory and possession of the heavyweight title, they got an important aspect of the story wrong: the original headline writer led other headline writers astray by declaring, "Max Schmeling KO's Adolf Hitler in Adolf Heuser Stadium." Once again, the aggrieved Goebbels flew into a sustained fury, calling newspaper editors and threatening to shut down their papers and toss them into prison or worse. Editors turned on their typesetters, who believing that their own lives could be in danger quickly corrected their error before the Gestapo could round them up and crack their skulls with truncheons. Corrected headlines appeared in a few hours but not before Hitler had seen the misinformation and raged against subversive elements in the press. Poor Schmeling. He was becoming an embarrassment to the Nazi hierarchy. First he lost a fight to partially Jewish Max Baer, then to the Brown Bomber Joe Louis. Yet he managed to knock out Adolf Hitler to win the heavyweight championship? Impossible!

On another occasion, Schmeling was asked to be an emissary to the Vatican and help repair a relationship that had been fractured with the Church by the SS. At the Vatican, Schmeling was welcomed by Pope Pius XII, who expressed his admiration for Schmeling's athletic abilities. They drank tea together and discussed boxing. When the subject of war arose, the pope told Schmeling that he thought war was terrible and was deeply saddened by the destruction and deaths that war was causing throughout Europe. He said he would pray for peace. Before departing, Schmeling was invited to return to the Vatican whenever he was in Italy.

Following his return to Germany, Schmeling was met by a group of reporters who asked him if the pope had prayed for a German victory. No. He said the pope prays for peace. Again, Goebbels flew into a rage. For Goebbels, Schmeling was rapidly becoming insufferable and unreliable, a thorn in his side that had to be removed. He determined never again to use Schmeling to advance Nazi propaganda aims.

To no one's surprise, Goebbels cancelled production of a laudatory documentary about Schmeling. Had Goebbels known about Schmeling's opinion of Nazism and its racial credo from the time the Nazis rose to power, he would never have ventured into using Schmeling for propaganda purposes in the first place.

From the time that Schmeling learned of Hitler's racial policies, he had nothing but contempt for those policies. And Schmeling's contempt for Nazi anti-Semitism led him to take heroic action that, if discovered, would have led—at the very least—to his incarceration, but more likely to a death sentence. Schmeling selflessly acted to protect Jews. It was *Kristallnacht*, the Night of Broken Glass. On the nights of November 9 and 10, 1938, Nazi *Sturmabteilung* (SA) and mobs of violent civilians participated in a pogrom against Jews. During that organized rampage, Jewish businesses were destroyed and looted, synagogues burned, and Jews beaten and killed. Schmeling called down to the front desk from his suite in the Excelsior Hotel and said that he was ill and should not be disturbed. He didn't want anyone to know that he was hiding two Jewish boys—Henry and Werner—in his suite. The boys were the sons of Schmeling's good friend David Lewin. Following the pogrom, Schmeling helped the boys escape Germany and gain entry to the United States. The boys grew to be successful businessmen. They said that they owed their lives to Schmeling, who they believed had put his own life in danger by protecting them and then smuggling them out of Germany. In 1989, Henry Lewin wanted the world to know of Schmeling's humanitarian act and invited him and the public to toast Schmeling's act of courage and generosity at a celebration in Las Vegas. It was the beginning of Americans learning that Schmeling had never been a Nazi sympathizer or stooge.

Two years before Kristallnacht, just prior to the start of the Berlin Olympics, Schmeling urged Hitler not to harm Jewish athletes who might compete in various sports events. Schmeling need not have worried, for Jews were banned from participating. And that included the excellent German-Jewish boxing champion Eric Seelig, who had held both the middleweight and the light heavyweight titles in Germany: the middleweight title in 1931 and the light-heavyweight title in 1933. The Nazis stripped him of his titles and warned him that if he fought to regain his titles he would be killed. So Seelig and his family immigrated to France, where he fought for two years. In 1935 he immigrated to the United States and boxed until 1940. The Nazis were glad to be rid of him for they did not want a Jew to be a German boxing champion. Such an event would have made a mockery of the Nazi belief in the Aryan superman. Seelig's wife, Greta, was another athlete denied the opportunity to participate in the Berlin Olympics. She was an admired track star who could have run the hurdles and possibly won a medal. The Nazis only wanted her to run out of the country, not in its athletic competitions.

There was, however, one symbolic exception to the banning of Jewish athletes. She was Helene Mayer, a championship fencer, who had won a gold medal at the 1928 Olympics when she was seventeen years old. She was acclaimed as the greatest female fencer in the world and became a celebrity throughout Europe. Her athletic skills were not her only attraction for she was tall, elegant, beautiful, and blonde. Knowing that her path to additional athletic success had been barred in Nazi Germany, she left the country and settled in California in 1935. The Nazis, however, decided to invite her to compete in the 1936 Olympics; they did so to prevent a threatened boycott of the games. Many organizations, Jewish and non-Jewish, had urged countries not to compete in the Olympics unless the ban on Jews were lifted. By including Mayer in the games, Goebbels could declare that a Jew would participate. Yet he instructed the media not to mention that Mayer was a Jew. How does one note a single Jewish inclusion on a Nazi Olympic team while refusing to identify the Jew as a Jew? Goebbels never untangled that knot of a paradox.

Though surprised by the invitation to participate in the games, Helene decided that her competition in fencing might help relatives who were convicts in Nazi labor camps, especially if she could win a medal. And indeed she won a silver one. Following the presentation of her medal, Mayer gave the Nazi salute as a mandatory part of the awards ceremony. Though it caused consternation and anger among Jews, especially in the United States, France, and England, Mayer insisted that she did so to protect relatives. She returned to the United States, where many Jews criticized her not only for the salute but also for participating in the games. Many of those critics said that Mayer should have boycotted the games and used her boycott to further expose the Nazi treatment of Jews. Mayer did not offer further responses to the criticism other than to repeat what she had earlier stated. She went on to have a successful fencing career in the United States, winning the U.S. women's foil championship eight times from 1934 to 1946. In 1952, Mayer surprised many when she returned to Germany, where she married Erwin Falkner von Sonnenburg, whom she had known for years. They were married without fanfare in a quiet ceremony in Munich. Shortly thereafter, the couple moved to the hills above Stuttgart. From there, they moved to Heidelberg. Only a year after her return to Germany, Mayer died of breast cancer; her death occurred just two months before her forty-third birthday. *Sports Illustrated* declared her one of the 100 greatest female athletes of the twentieth century. West Germany finally honored her achievements in 1968 by issuing a stamp with an image of her handsome profile.

While never mentioning Mayer's Jewish heritage, Hitler was pleased that his athletes were proving to be examples of Aryan superiority. He was particularly pleased that German boxers won a total of five medals at the 1936 Olympics, which was more than those won by boxers representing any other country. Altogether there was a total of 179 boxers from thirty-one countries who participated in the 1936 Olympic games. From Germany there was Willy Kaiser, who won a gold medal in the flyweight division; Michael Murach, who won a silver medal in the welterweight division; Richard Vogt, who won a silver medal in the light-heavyweight division; Herbert Runge, who won a gold medal in the heavyweight division; and Josef Milner, who won a bronze in the featherweight division. Of the five, only Vogt and Runge went on to become professional boxers. Runge's career, however, was short-lived and disappointing: from 1946 to 1949, he fought in twenty-five bouts and won only five of those. Vogt had a somewhat illustrious professional career: three times he won the German light-heavyweight championship, and in 1948, he beat an over-the-hill, forty-three-year-old Max Schmeling before twenty thousand disappointed fans who still honored Schmeling as the greatest German boxer of the twentieth century. Josef Miner was killed in World War II as was Michael Murach. Willy Kaiser retired from boxing and died in 1986.

The winning boxers who fought for their lives in Auschwitz and other concentration camps for the entertainment of their guards had not been invited to exhibit their skills to the cheers of boxing fans at the 1936 Olympics. Instead, they had to endure the jeers of guards and watch helplessly as their defeated victims were led off to be worked to death or to be quickly gassed. If the winners were fortunate enough to survive their imprisonment in the camps, their lives were fraught with searing memories of brutality and guilt.

# 2

# Men of Unsurpassed Evil

The men who created the hellish conditions in the Nazi concentration camps, where a select group of men were placed in the uniquely compromised position of having to fight to save their lives, were individuals of pure evil. These bloodthirsty, power-hungry men forced other men, who had been stripped of their humanity, to engage in life-threatening gladiatorial combat. The most powerful of the evil monsters who conceived, developed, and governed the concentration camp prisoners were Heinrich Himmler, Rudolf Höss, Reinhard Heydrich, and Theodor Eicke. They were a who's-who of vicious psychopaths.

The first Nazi concentration camp, Dachau, was put into service in 1933 shortly after Hitler took over as *Führer* (leader) of Germany. Most of the initial prisoners were communists, socialists, homosexuals, Jehovah's Witnesses, and Romanis and Sintis (who are colloquially known as gypsies). By 1934, the category of those imprisoned was extended to include Jews, disabled people, and hardened criminals. The Nazis used color-coded triangles to categorize prisoners: green triangles were for criminals, red triangles for communists, pink triangles for homosexuals, yellow triangles for Jews, black triangles for those who were asocial, purple triangles for Jehovah's Witnesses, and brown triangles for Romanis and Sintis.

Heinrich Himmler, the sadistic head of the SS, took control of the concentration and extermination camps. Though he had the appearance of a mild-mannered bookkeeper, he was a cold-hearted overseer who took immense satisfaction in perpetuating genocide. He appointed Theodor Eicke, a man governed by an iron commitment to brutality and a stridently expressed need for order and control, to serve as commandant of the first concentration camp, Dachau, then as inspector of all concentration camps. According to the Jewish Virtual Library, those two men and Reinhard Heydrich established fifteen thousand camps in countries under Nazi control. They were a trio committed to the apocalyptic goal of murdering all of the Reich's enemies.

In addition to being the overseer of the concentrations camps, Himmler created the *Einsatzgruppen* (paramilitary death squads) whose purpose was to follow German soldiers into conquered Eastern European countries and massacre Jews, Soviet commissars, Slavs, Romanis, intellectuals, and even passive enemies of the Reich. They carried out their grisly work by shooting their victims with a series of shots fired by firing squads or individual officers or by machine gunning them; the victims had first to dig their own graves, either trenches or single plots. By the end of World War II, historians estimate that the *Einsatzgruppen* had slaughtered more than 2 million Jews, Romanis and Sintis, political prisoners, resistance fighters, communists, Polish intellectuals and priests, and innocent women and children. Though formed by Himmler on orders from Hitler, the *Einsatzgruppen* received their direct orders from Reinhard Heydrich, who took great pride in the number of people that had been killed. Hitler was so impressed with Heydrich's cruelty that he commented that Heydrich had a heart of iron.

Himmler also admired Heydrich, who seemed the essence of the strong, pitiless Aryan man who through brutality would control Nazi-dominated Europe. From his boyhood, Himmler had always been fascinated by strong men and Jews; the former he admired, the latter he came to despise (and in some instances to fear). His intense anti-Semitism was fed by the writings of professional anti-Semites who proselytized in books and pamphlets against Jews. One such provocateur was the originator of the term "anti-Semitism." He was Friedrich Wilhelm Adolph Marr, who wrote an 1879 pamphlet, *The Way to Victory of Judaism over Germanism*, in which he asserted that Germans and Jews were locked in a historical conflict based on race. He complained that self-defeating liberal ideals had resulted in Jewish emancipation, and as a result Jews controlled German finance and industries. A resolution of the problem could only be attained by the victory of Germans and the death of the Jews. To further promulgate his ideas, he founded the *League of Antisemites*, which was the first German organization committed to combating the alleged threat that Jews posed to Germany. Short of killing off all the Jews, Marr advocated their forced emigration to other countries. For Himmler, Marr's writings as well as those of other professional anti-Semites were building blocks that would result in the creation of concentration camps.

At the university, Himmler participated in a fencing club, the League of Apollo, whose president was Jewish. There may be nothing more injurious to an aspiring athlete's dreams of glory than to be surpassed by the athletic skills of a member of a hated minority. Himmler's envy and malevolent hatred of a Jew's skills further fueled his feverish anti-Semitism.

His hatred of Jews even led him to disavow his allegiance to Catholicism. For Himmler, there was nothing as wrong-headed as the Jewish Christ's Sermon on the Mount. In place of Catholicism, Himmler embraced an exotic German mythology of heroes that included a belief in the occult and in the evil doings of Jews. He was well on his way to being a perfect Nazi ideologue. His need for a superman was fulfilled by the dictatorial leadership of Hitler. Himmler—like millions of others—came to regard Hitler as the embodiment of the ideal of the powerful leader, a person of nearly god-like abilities who would lead the German people to their glorious destiny. Himmler so profoundly believed in the idea of the Aryan superman that he created a criteria based on that idea for those who wanted to join the SS. It was a racial entrance exam that proved one's Aryan ancestry and established the necessary physical attributes of blue eyes, blond hair, and an athletic physique. Himmler commented that "like a nursery gardener trying to reproduce a good old strain which has been adulterated and debased, we started from the principles of plant selection and then proceeded quite unashamedly to weed out the men whom we did not think we could use for the build-up of the SS."[1]

Not only would Himmler not have qualified as an SS superman, neither would have Goebbels, who had a club foot, nor Goring, who was obese. And Hitler, who closely resembled Charlie Chaplin's Little Tramp, was not exactly a blond athletic god. Nevertheless, Himmler attempted to generate a new race of supermen, though not from his own genes. Instead, he urged his SS members to marry Aryan women whose ancestry had been thoroughly researched and who would give birth to the new race of supermen. Himmler said that each of the SS men should father at least four children. However, he was sorely disappointed that 40 percent of the SS remained unmarried, and those who did marry had—on average—only one child.

While Himmler tried to turn his puerile myth of Aryan supermen into a reality, he regarded the prisoners of the concentration camps as abhorrent, diseased scum. In a mind such as his, Jews were viewed as carriers of something more dangerous and infectious than the Black Plague. As one would exterminate disease-carrying rats, so one had an obligation to exterminate Jews whose contagious germs should not be permitted to infect and destroy the race of Aryans.

In a speech at Posen in Poland, Himmler spoke not only of the need to exterminate the Jews but also of the need to never speak publicly about it. He explicitly told his SS officers about the Reich's plan to exterminate Jews so that the officers could not later claim they had been ignorant of the plan. Their complicity would cause them to be circumspect, if not silent. Here is what Himmler said:

> I also want to refer here very frankly to a very difficult matter. We can now very openly talk about this among ourselves, and yet we will never discuss this publicly. Just as we did not hesitate on 30 June 1934 [the Night of the Long Knives, when hundreds of SA troops were murdered] to perform our duty as ordered and put comrades who had failed up against the wall and execute them, we also never spoke about it, nor will we ever speak about it. Let us thank God that we had within us enough self-evident fortitude never to discuss it among us, and we never talked about it. I am talking about the "Jewish evacuation": the extermination of the Jewish people. It is one of those things that is easily said. "The Jewish people is being exterminated," every Party member will tell you, "perfectly clear, it's part of our plans, we're eliminating the Jews, exterminating them, ha!, a small matter" . . . because we know how difficult it would be for us if we still had Jews as secret saboteurs, agitators and rabble-rousers in every city, what with the bombings, with the burden and with the hardships of the war. If the Jews were still part of the German nation, we would most likely arrive now at the state we were at in 1916 and '17.[2]

Himmler not only expected all of the SS to be his loyal and obedient subjects, he also looked for particular individuals who would enthusiastically carry out his policies while remaining as loyal to him as he was to Hitler. One such person was Rudolf Höss, who turned out to be one of Himmler's most devoted epigones. In fact, he was so ardent in his devotion that he kept a photo of Himmler on his desk rather than one of Hitler. As a reward for his devotion and his hard work carrying out anti-Jewish policies, Höss was appointed commandant of Auschwitz in 1940. This followed his successful role running Dachau.

Beyond the barbed wire of the Auschwitz camp, Höss spent his leisure time in a stately mansion with his wife and five children. No luxury was too good for them. As the bodies of gassed little children were shoveled into ovens from where their incinerated remains went up in smoke, the happy-go-lucky Höss children laughingly played games, enjoyed their toys, and remained ignorant of their condemned neighbors whose only hope was either survival or a quick death. For the Höss family, there was no sense that their world was on a path to Armageddon at the hands of a monomaniacal psychopath.

Höss's reputation as a brilliant manager of death continued to impress Himmler, Hitler, and others in the Nazi hierarchy, so in June 1941 Höss was summoned to a meeting in Berlin. There Himmler informed him that Hitler wanted him to exterminate all the Jews, but he should not speak about it. It must be kept secret. Back in Auschwitz on September 3, 1941, Höss set about finding the most efficient and rapid manner for disposing of Jewish prisoners. Having learned about Zyklon B from one of his subordinates, Höss began using the deadly chemical. He was pleased at the pace he was able to kill prisoners. He said that it only took three to fifteen minutes for victims to perish, and he knew that they were dead because they had stopped screaming.

Following his capture and interrogation, Höss was hardly the relaxed and smiling SS man frequently pictured in his elegantly tailored uniform. Shortly after being taken prisoner by the British, he was beaten, leaving him with a bloodied face and dressed in a beggar's uniform of torn and crumpled clothes. He was a man whose pride had been shattered and made feeble, leaving him nothing but his newly adopted religious faith and a look of stark confusion. He was put on trial in Nuremberg on April 5, 1946. He made the following statement as part of his confession.

> I commanded Auschwitz until 1 December 1943, and estimate that at least 2,500,000 victims were executed and exterminated there by gassing and burning, and at least another half million succumbed to starvation and disease, making a total of about 3,000,000 dead. This figure represents about 70% or 80% of all persons sent to Auschwitz as prisoners, the remainder having been selected and used for slave labor in the concentration camp industries. Included among the executed and burnt were approximately 20,000 Russian prisoners of war (previously screened out of Prisoner of War cages by the Gestapo) who were delivered at Auschwitz in *Wehrmacht* transports operated by regular *Wehrmacht* officers and men. The remainder of the total number of victims included about 100,000 German Jews, and great numbers of citizens (mostly Jewish) from The Netherlands, France, Belgium, Poland, Hungary, Czechoslovakia, Greece, or other countries. We executed about 400,000 Hungarian Jews alone at Auschwitz in the summer of 1944.[3]

When he was accused of murdering three and a half million people, Höss replied, "No. Only two and one-half million—the rest died from disease and starvation."[4]

Found guilty and sentenced to death, Höss (who had returned to his Catholic faith) wrote,

> My conscience compels me to make the following declaration. In the solitude of my prison cell, I have come to the bitter recognition that I have sinned gravely against humanity. As Commandant of Auschwitz, I was responsible for carrying out part of the cruel plans of the "Third Reich" for human destruction. In so doing I have inflicted terrible wounds on humanity. . . . May the Lord God forgive one day what I have done. . . . May the facts which are now coming out about the horrible crimes against humanity make the repetition of such cruel acts impossible for all time.[5]

However, such a confession does not wash away his casual attitude to the death of millions that he expressed at his trial.

> At Auschwitz we endeavored to fool the victims into thinking that they were to go through a delousing process. Of course, frequently they realized our true intentions and we sometimes had riots and difficulties due to that fact. Very frequently women would hide their children under their clothes, but of course when we found them we would send the children in to be exterminated. We were required to carry out these exterminations in secrecy but of course the foul and nauseating stench from the continuous burning of bodies permeated the entire area and all of the people living in the surrounding communities knew that exterminations were going on at Auschwitz.[6]

Höss also noted that it had been easy to exterminate large numbers of prisoners. Two thousand bodies could be disposed on in half an hour. And he didn't need guards to force the prisoners into the gas chambers because the prisoners thought they were entering showers. Of course, instead of water washing over their bodies, poison entered and filled their lungs, killing them. Höss expressed pride in the success of his technical accomplishments.

Following his trial and subsequent death sentence, he was taken to be hanged. In his crumpled outfit, hands tied behind his back, he shuffled to the gallows; there, he was hoisted onto a stool. Standing before the hooded hangman, he blankly stared ahead, his lips sternly set. The rope was placed over his head, tightly looped around his neck, and the stool that he stood on was kicked out from under hm. He suddenly dropped to his death. The once fiercely sadistic overseer of mass exterminations, his neck broken, dangled from a rope of vengeance and justice.

Though Höss had authority over only one concentration camp, there was another brutal henchman who wielded far greater power. Along with Himmler that man exercised murderous power over millions of prisoners. He was Reinhard Tristan Eugen Heydrich. But unlike Himmler, whose background was modest and unimportant, Heydrich came from a highly cultured and talented family. His father, Richard Bruno Heydrich, was an admired composer and opera singer who founded the Halle Conservatory of Music, Theater, and Teaching. Reinhard's mother was a popular piano teacher at the conservatory. His family was wealthy and socially prominent.

His parents named him Reinhard after the tragic hero in Richard's opera *Amen*, and he was named Tristan in honor of Wagner's opera *Tristan und Isolde*. The name Eugen was bestowed on him in honor of his grandfather, Professor Eugen Krantz, who had been director of the Dresden Royal Conservatory. Coming from such a background, Reinhard naturally developed a strong interest in music and rigorously studied the violin. Discriminating listeners were impressed by his musical talent, and wherever Reinhard went, he carried his violin. He could be heard playing outside concentration camps, in his office, at home. How such a man could become one of the primary architects of the Holocaust has been a question asked by many. But perhaps Hitler had the answer when he said that Reinhard had a heart of iron. He was a man full of inordinate self-regard who prided himself on his erect posture, his invulnerability, his adherence to discipline, and his lack of sympathy for the victims of the Holocaust. Psychologists have classified him as an extreme case of narcissistic sociopathology. In other words, he was a perfect administrator for mass murder.

Robert Gerwath, the author of *Hitler's Hangman*, stated that Heydrich was one of the most terrible figures within the Nazi regime, a regime that was notorious for the large number of people who committed or were complicit in war crimes.[7]

He was also intensely ambitious and rose to numerous positions of authority from which he could put his murderous plans into effect— one of the most far reaching was chief of the Reich Main Security Office which controlled the Gestapo, the *Kriminalpolizei* (criminal police), and the *Sicherheitsdienst* (secret police). In addition, he was chief of what would become Interpol, which gave him an international reach against his enemies.

In addition to his police roles, he was assigned to carry out the propaganda aims of the Nazi regime regarding the 1936 Olympics. He made sure that anti-Jewish acts were suppressed before the Olympics and certainly during the games. He did not want the world to see the Nazi regime as brutal and inhumane. After all, Germany was the country that gave the world Goethe and Beethoven, among various other luminaries. For his success in painting a benevolent picture of Nazism, Heydrich was awarded the Olympic Games Decoration. His suppression of anti-Jewish acts was short-lived, however, for two years later he helped organize the pogrom known as Kristallnacht. To make sure that the Reich's goals were reached, he instructed the attackers to burn Jewish businesses and synagogues and to arrest affluent Jews. Arrested Jews were first beaten then thrown into local prisons. From there, they were sent, like herds of cattle, to slaughterhouses euphemistically called concentration camps. It has been estimated that more than twenty thousand Jews were arrested during Kristallnacht, and the event presaged the savagery of the Holocaust. By the time Germany went to war, Heydrich had organized the *Einsatzgruppen*, which was to follow the army into conquered lands and shoot all Jews between the ages of fifteen and forty-five. However, Heydrich expanded his order so that Jewish women and children and the elderly would also be murdered. Not satisfied that some Jews would escape execution, he finally decided that all Jews had to be killed. The *Einsatzgruppen* in their savagery not only shot thousands of Jewish women, they often gang raped them. If a woman was pregnant, she was shot in her belly to make sure that no Jewish infant would survive, grow to adulthood, and procreate.

The meeting at which Heydrich determined that all the Jews in conquered lands had to be exterminated was held at the Wannsee Conference on January 20, 1942. The conference was held to carry out the Final Solution to the Jewish Question (*Endlösung der Judenfrage*), as Hitler called it. Heydrich made it clear to the fifteen attending Nazi officials (eight of whom held PhDs) that all Jews would be deported to concentration camps in Poland and there they would be killed. Heydrich prepared and distributed minutes of the conference, thus making all attendees complicit in the Final Solution. By war's end, Heydrich believed, there wouldn't be a Jew alive in all of Europe.

This psychopathic man who loved beautiful music and was totally devoted to carrying out the Holocaust was also a lover of sports, a highly competitive athlete who enjoyed tennis, fencing, skiing, and boxing. He was an excellent fencer and a competent tennis player and skier, but he was an awkward boxer as seen in brief film clips made in the 1930s. Yet he loved putting on boxing gloves with one of his young sons and letting the little boy pummel him. Seen with his family, Heydrich appears to be a happy man, untroubled by all the murders he oversaw. His conscience never troubled him because he believed fanatically in the righteousness of his deeds. Or it may have been that Heydrich, the narcissist, did not have a conscience. He was a man who could as casually order mass murders as order dinner in an expensive restaurant. He was a devoted father, a loving husband, and the blood on his hands washed over his entire being like a summer breeze. Not only did he look like a happy family man, he also looked like the perfect Aryan according to Himmler and Hitler. But unlike Hitler, Goebbels, Göring, and Himmler, who were short, dark haired, and unattractive, Heydrich was tall, blond, and blue eyed. In uniform, he looked officious and cold. His tiny porcine eyes seemed to convey his coldness.

Yet there were rumors swirling around Berlin and Munich that could have ignominiously ended Heydrich's career. What was the nature of those rumors? It was stated in whispers that Heydrich had Jewish ancestors. When the whispers reached the ears of Hitler (who had also endured such rumors) and those of Himmler, they could not believe that such a fine Aryan specimen was diseased with Jewish blood. To show his disregard for the rumors and support of Heydrich, Himmler decided to promote him. He stated to Hitler and the Nazi hierarchy that Heydrich would become an even more zealous instrument for carrying out the extermination of Jews just to prove that he had no Jewish blood.

Heydrich, much to the pleasure of his enemies, came to a bloody end. On May 27, 1942, while riding in his convertible Mercedes-Benz, he was the victim of two assassins who had been trained in England for just such a mission. The mission was code named Operation Anthropoid. The assassins had been trained by the British and sent by the Czechoslovak government-in-exile to kill the man they referred to as the Butcher of Prague. Heydrich had previously killed numerous Czech partisans and other enemies of the Reich. And hatred of him in Prague was epidemic. The assassins were armed with a gun, which jammed at the time of their attack, but they had several handgrenades, which they flung with the accuracy of major league baseball pitchers. A single grenade landed against one rear wheel of Heydrich's car. When it exploded it sent shrapnel into Heydrich's body, damaging his spleen, diaphragm, and one lung. He suffered from the pain of metal particles splintering numerous organs, especially his spleen and liver. Heydrich was rushed to a hospital, and upon hearing the news, Hitler dispatched his personal physician to care for the wounded man. A doctor wanted to give Heydrich medicine to prevent the onset of a blood infection, but his suggestion was vetoed by Hitler's doctor. An infection set in, and a week after the attack Heydrich went into a coma and died. Czech partisans cheered, but their good cheer turned to solemn anguish: Hitler ordered that two Czech villages (Lidice and Lezaky) suspected of hiding the two assassins be destroyed, their men and boys shot, and their women sent to concentration camps. So incensed was Himmler by the assassination of Heydrich, now raised to the status of a martyr, that he created Operation Reinhard to accelerate the extermination of Jews. He ordered that three extermination camps be constructed. They were Sobibor, Belzec, and Treblinka.

Another key figure in the lineup of criminals who developed the concentration camps and pursued the goal of complete extermination of a race was Theodore Eiche. Having been put in charge of Dachau, he ambitiously made it a prototype for all other Nazi concentration camps, and as commander of the SS Division *Totenkopf* of the *Waffen–SS*, he continued to expand the number of concentration camps in conquered lands. Eiche not only enjoyed overseeing the torture and terror he inflicted on prisoners, he also enjoyed killing prominent enemies of the Reich such as Ernst Rohm, Nazi head of the SA (*Sturmabteilung*, or Storm Detachment, an original Nazi paramilitary organization), and Gregor Strasser, an important Nazi organizer. Excessively proud, arrogant, and cruel, Eiche believed that only an important Nazi, such as himself, should be permitted to kill other important personages. A famous man should be killed by another famous man, he said. A common soldier should not be permitted to kill a general or a political leader, for example.

Like many early devotees of Nazism, Eiche had a history of failure in all that he had attempted. (Hitler was a failed painter; Goebbels was a failed novelist.) He dropped out of school, was fired from jobs in several police departments, was hired by the German firm BASF but fired after being found guilty in an attempted bombing plot, and was sent to prison but escaped to Italy. Upon his return to Germany he participated in additional criminal activities and was arrested, then sent to prison where he went on a hunger strike. He was then placed in the Psychiatric Clinic of Wurzburg. His friend and admirer Heinrich Himmler ordered Eiche's release. Himmler then appointed Eiche commandant of Dachau, informing him that he could redeem himself in that position and impress the Nazi hierarchy with his management skills and liberal use of punishment.

At Dachau, Eicke brought organization to what had been a chaotically run institution. While punishments had often been meted out impetuously, Eicke set up rules and a list of specific offenses that resulted in varied punishments ranging from beating to execution. While prisoners had been dressed in the deteriorating clothes in which they had arrived, they now found themselves wearing the notorious blue-and-white-striped pajamas that further diminished their individuality. The guards were put in different uniforms, each of which had death's head insignias on the collars. Eiche trained not only the guards at Dachau but also the guards who would be assigned to camps that Eicke subsequently developed. In addition to teaching guards when and how to use punishment, especially torture and murder, he taught them how to keep the work of the camps secret from surrounding communities. Eiche's work at Dachau proved successful. Himmler thus considered Eiche redeemed and reported the successful results to Hitler. In 1934, Himmler put Eicke in charge of all concentration camps in Germany. Eicke organized each camp based on what he had accomplished at Dachau. He was promoted to inspector of the concentration camps (*Inspekteur der Konzentrationslager und SS–Wachverbande*) and a week later he was promoted to a group leadership position in the SS (*SS–Gruppenführer*). In 1942 he was promoted again, this time to senior group leader (*Obergruppenführer*). In addition to rebuilding Dachau, he established the camps of Buchenwald, Ravensbruch, Mauthausen, and Sachsenhauser. For the new camps, Eicke trained and instructed the commandants: Rudolf Höss of Auschwitz; Paul Werner Hoppe of Stutthof and Wobbelin; Josef Kramer of Natzweiler-Struthof and Bergen-Belsen; Richard Baer of Mittelbau-Dora; and Martin Gottfried Weiss of Neuengamme and Lublin-Majdanek. Each of these commandants used torture and murder as their weapons of terror. Eicke instructed them that tolerance was a sign of weakness and should be avoided at all costs. In addition to training SS guards in the techniques of terror, he also instilled in them Nazi racial ideology, which—of course—meant a murderous hatred of all non-Aryans.

Eiche was deeply ambitious and wanted an even larger role than overseeing concentration camps. He had a new opportunity to prove himself when Germany invaded Russia on June 22, 1941. The invasion was code named Operation Barbarossa after Frederick I, the twelfth-century Holy Roman Emperor and Warrior King. Shortly before the invasion began, Hitler signed an order stating that all Soviet commissars should be shot immediately following their capture. Into the bloody maelstrom, Eicke, eager to carry out Hitler's order, led a division of the SS that murdered thousands of Red Army commissars. While enthusiastically committing murder, Eicke was wounded when he stepped on a mine. It was a minor wound, yet he returned to Germany for treatment. Having quickly recovered, he was back in Russia committing more murders. So bloodthirsty and rapacious was his division that it developed an infamous reputation not only for raping and pillaging but also for killing enemy soldiers who had surrendered and every Jewish woman and child they could find. Many of the Jewish women were gang raped before they were shot. After the war, estimates of the number of Soviet troops killed were put at more than 3 million. Of murdered Soviet Jews, the number exceeded 1 million.

For Eicke, the invasion of Russia was an adventure in mass murder. On the ground, he could see the corpses piling up, but in the air, he could get a god-like view of the immense devastation he had caused. On February 26, 1943, he took off in a Fiesler Fi 156 Storch on an inspection mission. The ground below was carpeted with death, destruction, and debris. However, Eicke failed to see the Soviet anti-aircraft battery that fired on his plane. The plane went into a dive, crashed, and burst into flames. Eicke's corpse was pulled from the burning wreckage, and he was soon given an elaborate hero's funeral at one of the cemeteries of his division near Orelka. Following the Nazi retreat, the Soviets bulldozed the cemetery, and Eicke's remains were never found. He was fortunate to have died in combat for had he lived, he would have been tried before a war crimes tribunal and sentenced to death.

These were the four men who created circles of hell on earth where desperate men were ordered to fight one another for the entertainment of guards who spent hours every day murdering those deemed to be subhumans.

# 3

# The Biggest Little Champion: Victor Perez

"Messauod Hai Victor Perez" was not a name to light up boxing arena marquees. But when shortened to "Young Perez," it meant sold-out arenas. The double-barreled name not only lit up marquees, it turned out to be an incandescent invitation to boxing fans all over France. He was a winning and charismatic athlete whose skill, stamina, and friendliness attracted a large number of fans. The attraction of Young Perez was not just for male boxing fans but for female ones as well. Women turned out in large enough numbers to see Perez fight that promoters saw them as a new customer base. They were the ticket buyers who were targeted by advertisements promoting Perez's matches. There was something about Young Perez that drew women to him. It was not his pint-size, 5'1" frame and 119 pounds of muscle. One woman said she found him adorable and sexy. He did have a handsome face; it wasn't the face of a typical boxer: mashed-in nose, cauliflower ears, thickly scarred eyebrows. Perez's face was boyishly handsome; his slicked-back, wavy black hair and large, dark, doe-like eyes were exotic. He was truly Semitic in appearance: Jewish and Arab. Or as he described himself, a towel-headed Jew. His smile was warm and eager and without guile. It was an invitation to a seduction. He projected a joie de vivre that seemed infectious. Women took pleasure in his company, and he took pleasure in theirs. He loved the company of beautiful women. Models, actresses, and dancers were his dates and bedmates.

Perez was born on October 18, 1911, in Dar-El Berdgana, the Jewish section of Tunis in French Tunisia. His parents were Khomsa Nizard and Makhlouf Rene Perez. He was one of five children but was closest to his older brother Benjamin, who began training as a boxer when he was a teenager. Benjamin encouraged Victor to join him at a boxing gym called Club Maccabi, and soon the younger Perez was an enthusiastic budding pugilist. To distinguish the brothers one from the other, the gym created sobriquets for the brothers: Victor became known as Young Perez and Benjamin as Kid Perez. They were talented regulars at Club Maccabi, each imitating the style of their boxing idol, Louis Mbarick Fall, known as Battling Siki, a French-Senegalese boxing champion. Siki, who had biceps like shiny black cannonballs, had knocked out George Carpentier and reigned briefly as the light-heavy champion. Siki had a brief, turbulent, bacchanalian life, one filled with beautiful white women, drunken orgies, fast cars, and profligate spending. The high life ended sadly: while walking drunkenly near his apartment on 42nd Street in New York City, he was shot in the back and died. He was twenty-eight years old.

Nevertheless, Siki would always remain an admired champion to the Perez brothers, who would spend hours at the gym. There they were trained by Joe Guez, who also trained the notable fighters welterweight Billy Smadja and lightweight Edmond Zerbib. Guez, who was considered the best Tunisian boxing trainer, was a clever, sharp-eyed trainer who honed the skills of the Perez brothers, believing that they had the makings of champions. He helped them eliminate their mistakes, smoothing their rough techniques and thus improving their defensive skills. He extended their endurance through long-distance runs; he taught them to block and slip punches; he taught them how not to telegraph their punches; he taught them the importance of appropriate tactics and strategies; he encouraged them as they hit the speed bags and heavy bags. Both brothers developed a fast-moving, aggressive style of nearly pushing their opponents to the ropes.

Kid Perez made a name for himself on April 2, 1928, when he became the flyweight champion of North Africa by defeating Jean Soler with a 10th-round knockout. It was the most memorable fight of the Kid's career. That same year, after three years of intense training, Young Perez, age seventeen, was impressing local boxing fans by beating most of the talent in his flyweight division. Young Perez had become a more determined and ambitious boxer than his brother. While Young's boxing career was about to take off, Kid's career stalled. Young Perez, driven by strong ambition, felt that the time was right to make his move, and that meant going to Paris. He didn't know when he headed to the City of Lights that he would be one of France's luminaries and martyrs.

By the time he arrived in Paris, he had 15 fights on his record, consisting of 13 wins and 2 draws. Following his arrival in Paris, he got one fight after another for a total of 15. From 1928 to 1930, he lost only 2 fights, 1 by knockout, the other on points. Five of those fights were declared draws. Then on February 7, 1930, following the negotiations of his manager, Leon Bellier, Perez was given a shot at France's flyweight championship. Joe Guez had told Bellier that Perez was ready to take the title and any additional fights would not enhance his skills. Bellier found the doors open to a Perez championship bout for the fighter was a crowd pleaser, a money maker who was the favorite of bettors across France. He was performing at the top of his game. Perez had developed a style all his own. He used his rapid-fire punches and high-octane energy to dominate his opponents.

While Perez was attracting an ever-increasing number of fans, he was also the target of nasty verbal darts of anti-Semitism. There were numerous organizations in France during the1920s and 1930s that promoted anti-Semitism and declaimed against immigrants from North Africa. Perez, in response to an anti-Semitic jibe, would proudly and disarmingly reply that he was not only a Jew but also a towel head. Annoyed that Perez didn't rise to combat an anti-Semitic thrust, his antagonist would turn and stride off in a state of frustrated animosity. Perez would grin and bid his defeated antagonist a sarcastic *shalom*.

For Perez, boxing was far more important than dealing with the ignorance of anti-Semites. He was doing well, defeating opponent after opponent in bouts that mostly took place at the Central Sporting Club of Paris. He was excited to have a shot at the flyweight title of France. The title was vacant, and the winner of the bout would be the new champion. His opponent was Kid Oliva, who had fought Kid Perez to a draw in 1929. In January 1930, Kid Perez had lost again in a rematch with Oliva. Now it would be the younger brother's chance to wear the crown that his brother had failed to capture. Oliva and Young Perez were evenly matched, close in height and reach. They were both eighteen years old. Oliva's record was slightly better than Young Perez's. Oliva had won 12 of his fights by knockout, whereas Perez had won 8 by knockouts. The fight would take place at the Cirque-Theatre Municipal in Limoges, Haute-Vienne, France. Young Perez trained diligently for his fight, and following his string of wins, he was confident he would defeat Oliva and be crowned the flyweight champion. But Kid Oliva proved to be a tougher opponent than Perez had anticipated. The two traded rapid-fire punches throughout the first three rounds, each attempting to drive the other into a defensive crouch against the ropes. It was a fast-paced fight and the crowd roared their approval. Though scheduled for 15 rounds, the fight suddenly ended in the 4th round when Young Perez went down for the count.

He rose from his defeat and shook off the cloudiness in his head only to wear an expression of deep disappointment. He did not accept defeat as the final chapter in his career. He was determined to take the crown if it was the last thing he did.

Eleven days later, he was back in the ring to fight Frankie Nour, whom he beat on a TKO in the 7th round of a scheduled 10-round bout. Perez thought he was on his way to another shot at the flyweight crown. He won his next 3 fights, and then fought to a draw with Britain's Johnny King at King's Hall, Belle Vue, Manchester, on March 11, 1930. He had 4 more fights, winning 2, drawing 2, before losing by a TKO to Joe Mendiola at the Central Sporting Club in Paris on January 7, 1931, but he went on to beat Mendiola on points on February 14, 1931. He had 6 subsequent fights, all of which he won, 1 by a knockout, 1 by a TKO, and 4 on points.

He now felt primed to take the flyweight title. His opponent would be Valentin "Tintin" Angelmann. It would be a 15-round fight, and the smart money was being bet on Perez. Up to that point, Perez had won 41 bouts, 12 by knockouts, and Angelmann had won 26 bouts, 6 by knockouts. To boxing fans, Perez was noted as the superior fighter. In his eighteen-year career, Angelmann did compile an impressive record consisting of 175 bouts (winning 120, 38 by knockouts; losing 39, 3 by knockouts; while 15 ended in draws). He would go on to win the International Boxing Union World Flyweight title and the National Boxing Association World Flyweight title. Though of Jewish heritage, he managed to continue boxing during the Nazi occupation of France.

The championship bout, which took place in Paris, lasted the full 15 rounds, with both fighters giving their all, each desperate to win the title. After the final round and after the fighters returned to their respective corners, Perez heard the announcement he had wanted since age fourteen. He was declared the French Flyweight champion. He received a standing ovation and loud cheers from his fans. Following a shower and a rub down, he was eager for a celebratory night on the town. He wanted to bask in the reality of his dream come true and imbibe, as if champagne, the congratulations from friends and fans.

Though elated by his win, Perez had an additional goal in mind: the World Flyweight Championship. There would be a fight to decide that title in October 1931. His opponent for the title would be the American boxer Frankie Genaro, who would be a more formidable opponent than anyone Perez had fought. Genaro had won the flyweight gold medal at the 1920 Olympic Games in Antwerp, just two days before his nineteenth birthday. While still an amateur, he had won the American National Flyweight Championship. He would end his career after fighting 134 bouts and winning 96, 19 by knockouts. He fought numerous world champions, including Fidel LaBarba, Pancho Villa, Bud Taylor, Newsboy Brown, Emile Pladner, Joey Archibald, Valentin Angelmann, Jackie Harmon, Victor Ferrand, Midget Wolgast, Frenchy Belanger, Ernie Jarvis, and—of course—Young Perez. *Ring Magazine* named Genaro the third-best flyweight boxer of all time.

Because he was determined to meet the challenge that Genaro represented, Perez trained like a demon of ambition. Just twenty-three days before his bout with Perez, Genaro had beaten Angelmann by a decision in a 15-round fight. Genaro was primed to meet Perez, who seemed in awe of such a talented pugilist. The fight would take place in the famous Palais de Sports in Paris. During the first round, Perez seemed slightly intimidated by Genaro's reputation and didn't fight well. He wasn't as aggressive as he usually was. The crowd booed his uninspired performance. On points, he would have lost that round, having suffered a profusion of rapid fire blows from Genaro. Perez was fortunate that he was still on his feet as the round ended. In his corner, his trainer yelled that he would lose unless he employed all of his skills and aggressively went after Genaro. In the 2nd round, Perez came out of his corner like an angry bull out of the chute eager to gore the torero. Genaro seemed surprised by Perez's change of tactics. It was as if he were fighting a different man. Perez was outboxing Genaro, who lacked Perez's speed. Genaro telegraphed a left hook, which Perez easily blocked, then belted Genaro's chin with a devastating right hook. In just ten seconds, Perez ended the fight by knocking out Genaro, who went down for a count of 8 then unsteadily rose to his knees but couldn't continue the fight. As Genaro returned to his corner, the referee raised Perez's right arm in victory. According to a headline in the *New York Times*, "The Throng Is Wildly Excited" by Perez's knockout of Genaro. The article went on to note that it was only Genaro's second knockout. Genaro would have 1 more fight in Europe, which he lost, and then return to the United States, where he had an additional 11 fights. Altogether he had 109 fights: 79 wins, 21 losses, 8 draws, and 1 exhibition.

Perez now held the International Boxing Union and the National Boxing Association World Flyweight title. He was the youngest French citizen to win a world championship title! He was a star, feted by Paris society as one of the hot young celebrities. He was invited to movie premiers, art show openings, and various sporting events. He barely had time to train for another fight.

In the midst of his new celebrity status, he met and began dating the French-Italian film actress Mireille Balin, herself a major celebrity.

Soon the couple were filling up paragraphs of gossip columns. Photographers followed wherever they went. Photos not only appeared in newspapers but also in news, fashion, and fan magazines. For Perez the reality of being a champ now seemed like a dream, and he could barely believe his good fortune. Yes, he had reached his goal of winning a title, but he hadn't anticipated all the social benefits that would be his. He had no experience of being so sought after for interviews and photos. He was in a glorious playland of festivities. Though many champion boxers eventually learn that a life of nightclubs, parties, and heavy drinking will deter their careers, Perez didn't consider the damage he was doing to his body. As long as the champagne flowed and the adoration continued, he was a happy man. Furthermore, his love life had become far more satisfying to him than training. He still managed to put in a few hours of training when nothing more important distracted him. He managed to rely on the value of his pugilistic skills and had sixteen fights before October 1931. Balin remained impressed by his ring performances, and the two of them would celebrate in a nightclub after each win. From a nightclub, they would go to her apartment, their little love nest, where they wouldn't arise until late the next day. Perez was deeply in love with Balin. Years later, he would say that she was the love of his life. Whether she reciprocated his love is debatable for she was known as an opportunist who would set the sails of her ambition to catch the changing winds of opportunity as she sailed into spheres of influence.

Perez was having such a good time drinking, partying, making love with Balin, and living what was a dissolute life for a boxer that he paid little attention to his career. He was still the champion and still bathed in the accolades and privileges that warmed his ego. This would soon change. On October 31, 1932, he was scheduled to fight Jackie Brown in a 15-round contest for the International Boxing Union World and the National Boxing Association Flyweight title. The bout was held in King's Hall, Belle-Vue, Manchester, England. It was apparent to all who saw the fight that Perez was not up to his previous performances. His stamina stalled early and his skills had rusted. As the fight went on, try as he did, Perez could not compete against Brown. He struggled to land punches that missed. His blocks and slips were awkward. His right crosses were easily deflected. The referee had to stop the fight (an RTD, or referee technical decision) in the 13th round when Perez could not get out of his corner. He had run out of fuel, and the engine of his stamina could not be restarted. The fight was scored as a knockout win for Brown. Those close to Perez blamed his loss on less-than-diligent training brought on by inordinate drinking and regular partying and his obsessive romance with Balin. His trainer commented that Perez had sacrificed his career for the love of a movie star. The loss came as a shock to Perez, and he briefly devoted himself to more rigorous training, winning his next 6 bouts. Thereafter he again reduced his devotion to training, winning and losing intermittently. He thought a rematch with Jackie Brown might prove his original loss an anomaly. He still didn't train rigorously for he was still addicted to the partying and bright lights of Paris. The rematch with Brown took place on March 7, 1933. Again Perez was outboxed by Brown, who won the fight on points.

Rather than staying in his weight division as a flyweight and returning to a rigorous regimen of training, Perez decided to move up to the bantamweight division and signed to fight Panama Al Brown for the International Boxing Union World Bantam title. Brown had also been trained by Joe Guez, who confided to friends that he thought Brown was a better fighter than Perez. Many thought Perez had made a mistake to move up a weight division and sign on to fight Al Brown. Perez was eight inches shorter than Brown and had a much shorter reach. It was a desperate act of redemption for Perez to have agreed to such a bout, but the crowd that showed up to see the fight in the Palais des Sports in Paris was enormous. Tickets to the match had quickly sold out.

Panama Al Brown was one of the most talented bantamweight fighters of all time. In addition to fighting in the bantamweight division, he had fought as a flyweight and a featherweight. For Perez to beat him, he would require a sledgehammer. Panama Al Brown, whose original name was Alfonso Teofilo Brown, was Latin America's first world champion and has been named the fifth-best bantamweight by www.boxrec.com. He had won the National Boxing Association and International Boxing Union bantamweight titles in 1930. When not boxing, Brown appeared as a song-and-dance man in gay nightclubs in Paris. He had a long-term relationship with writer, film director, artist, and actor Jean Cocteau. While there was some prejudice against homosexuals then, there was little against Brown, though many people found it hard to accept that a world-class boxing talent could be gay. Yet Brown was not only popular with boxing fans, he was also the toast of the town among the gay demimonde of 1930s Paris, and especially after he appeared on stage with the beautiful, sultry Josephine Baker, who regularly performed at the Folies Bergère, where she was either scantily clad or entirely naked. In America, some readers of newspapers and magazines were shocked upon learning that Baker had performed in a nightclub wearing a skirt of artificial bananas and a skimpy necklace across her otherwise bare breasts. Letters were written to editors of local newspapers decrying Baker's loose morals. Nevertheless, straight and gay audiences in Paris flocked to see Baker and Brown singing and dancing.

By 1939, Brown was residing in the safety of New York. He won several fights in the city then moved to his native Panama where he was much admired and had 7 fights, wining 4, losing 2, and ending the last with a draw. He hung up his gloves in 1942. His life after the end of World War II was neither glamorous nor fulfilling. He boxed as a sparring partner for meager sums at a boxing gym in Harlem. He drank heavily and became addicted to cocaine. What little money he had went to support his drug habit. He died penniless in 1951, age forty-eight.

But Brown was so highly regarded for his pugilistic skills in the 1930s that the boxing community bet heavily on Brown to defeat Perez. They were right to do so. Brown won his 15-round championship bout against Perez by a unanimous decision. However, Perez would not give up his ambition to defeat Brown. He trained for a rematch, and on February 19, 1934, the fight took place. It was held at the Parc du Belvedere in Perez's native city of Tunis, where he was the sentimental favorite, the neighborhood kid who had succeeded in one of the world's toughest sports. Though Perez was nine years younger than Brown, age would not be an advantage. Of Brown's 127 fights, he had won 113, lost 14, and won 47 by knockouts. Of Perez's 90 fights, he had won 76, lost 14, and won 22 by knockouts. In the 10th round, Brown raised his winning total to 114, and his knockout total to 48.

The two fighters met for their third and final bout on December 22, 1937. It was a 10-round fight held in Paris. By then Brown had won 122 bouts, lost 18, and raised his knockout total to 52. He had 11 draws. Perez had won 91 fights, lost 26, and had 28 wins by knockout. He had 15 draws. In round 5, Perez went down for the full count of ten. He finally gave up his dream of winning the bantamweight title.

While Brown's boxing career was in high gear, Perez's career slowed as he focused his attention on his affair with Balin. She attended his fights, filling him with pride whether he won or lost. He drove her around Paris in his large American convertible. They were photographed by paparazzi, and fans wanted both of their autographs. Perez could not stay away from Balin. She was his siren call, his aphrodisiac, and she would ultimately be his femme fatale.

So who was Mireille Balin? In the 1930s she was considered one of the most glamorous and beautiful stars of French cinema. She appeared in two of the most popular French movies of the 1930s: *Pépé le Moko* (1937) and *Lady Killer* (1937), both opposite Jean Gabin, who remained a popular screen star after the war. (Unlike Balin, Gabin left France during the Nazi occupation, went to Hollywood to make forgettable movies, then joined the Free French forces and fought against the Nazis in North Africa. He returned to unoccupied Paris a decorated war hero, and audiences regarded him with an affection that went beyond his being a movie star.) Balin, by contrast, was so wedded to her French celebrity status that she would remain in Paris throughout the Occupation. She enjoyed the attention of her fans, who flocked to her movies; she was flattered that women imitated her hair style and couture and that men, it was reported in gossip columns, fantasized that she was their mistress. She was well aware that she was considered not only beautiful and glamorous but also one of the best French cinema actresses of her time. Perez could hardly believe he was lucky enough to have earned the love of such a desirable and celebrated woman. His love of her seemed to supplant his love of boxing: he often gave up days at the gym just to be with her. He was drunk with his infatuation. When he saw her on the screen with Jean Gabin, he felt both privileged and jealous. When Balin would tell him that a screen romance that required one take after another was hardly a romance in progress, Perez felt reassured. He couldn't get her out of his mind. Balin's love of Perez was like a drug, and it made him feel super confident. He was so confident, in fact, that he agreed to a boxing match against Ernst Weiss in Berlin in 1938. He lost the match but felt he was welcomed by boxing fans as an athlete, not as a Jew. It was an extraordinary commitment for a Jew to fight in the heart of Nazism. Yet he came through the event with only his professional pride bruised and without a hint of being persecuted as a Jew. It would be the basis of an illusion that would prevent him from fleeing Paris following the Nazi occupation.

When the Nazis occupied Paris, the fates of Balin and Perez were headed in dramatically different directions. Balin existed in a different world than the one inhabited by Perez. Under the occupation she would be safe and secure. As a movie star, she was beloved and feted by *Wehrmacht* officers who felt honored to be in her company. Though the occupiers saw Balin as a magnetic screen star to whom they wanted to attach themselves, she saw the occupiers as her devoted protectors. Many, however, viewed her as a consummate opportunist.

For many actors to remain successful, they feel they have no choice but to be opportunists. It comes with the territory, and to be overtly principled about politics or friendships can lead to a diminishment of work. In the worst cases, it can lead to banishment, to the complete collapse of a career. It would be an irony, not an opportunity, that would exact a high price for Balin. Opportunities and the lack of opportunities during the Nazi occupation determined the course of the lives of Balin and Perez.

The Nazis, in their handsome uniforms, marched into Paris as if the Arc de Triomphe de l'Etoile had been erected in their honor. Down the Champs-Élysées they marched, the proud and arrogant conquerors. Hitler, not known for his spontaneous love of whimsy, danced a little two-step, his revenge taken for the humiliation Germany endured under the burdens of the Treaty of Versailles. For the French, the arc memorializes all those who died for the French Revolution and in the Napoleonic Wars. Beneath its vault lies the grave of the Unknown Soldier from World War I. The common soldier and generals honored by the arc must have spun in their graves. For Hitler, it was a sweet and just revenge that he had dreamt of since Germany's defeat at the end of the Great War.

For Balin, the Nazi occupation meant a change of plans and allegiances. To love a Jew was not only impractical, it was dangerous. She cast Perez aside and moved on to an affair with Tino Rossi, a popular singer and actor. They announced to the media that they were engaged to be married. Rossi's romantic ballads that had made him so popular with women were thought to have been inspired by Balin. Wherever he performed, he did so in sold-out theaters, especially in Paris. While Balin remained politically silent, not wishing to endanger herself, Rossi assisted the French Resistance during the Nazi occupation and even served three months in prison. For Balin, this was not a good move. As she became ever more popular and a darling of high society, she endeavored to ensure her safety. Her engagement to Rossi withered and then died; Balin moved on to what she claimed was the love of her life, Birl Desbok, an officer in the *Wehrmacht*.

While Balin was having the time of her life, hobnobbing with *Wehrmacht* officers, Perez was foolishly not keeping a low profile. His brother Benjamin urged him to leave Paris and return to Tunis, where he believed they would both be safe from Nazi persecution. After much urging by Benjamin, Perez finally realized the possibility of being arrested and decided to flee Paris. But then he suffered a change of mind. He was still a celebrity, a popular boxer welcomed into nightclubs and invited to many parties. His celebrity, he decided, would be his shield of protection.

The shield was illusory. On September 21, 1943, Perez was denounced as a Jew and arrested by *Milice Francaise,* a French collaborationist paramilitary force. Though no one knows for certain who denounced Perez, rumors flew that Balin told her lover of Perez's Jewish heritage and he sent word that Perez should be arrested. Perez was hunted, arrested, and shipped to Drancy along with thousands of other Jews. Drancy had become an internment camp where Jews were detained before being shipped off to concentration camps. (More than 67,000 French, Polish, and German Jews were interned at the camp, and that included more than 6,000 Jewish children.) By the time that Perez was interned the camp was no longer run by the French but by an assistant to Adolf Eichmann, SS officer Alois Brunner (who, as a war criminal, was sentenced in absentia to life in prison in 1954 and again in 2001). Brunner was known and feared for his extreme brutality and use of torture during interrogations. (After the war, he escaped to Syria where he helped the government develop techniques for torture interrogations, especially of captured Israelis.) Brunner enjoyed torturing inmates in order to extract every ounce of information about their backgrounds. He would then categorize them by their degree of subhumanity. (There is now a memorial sculpture at Drancy created by Shlomo Selinger that commemorates those tortured while imprisoned in the camp.)

On October 10, 1943, Perez was pushed into a cattle car at the point of a rifle and transported via rail to Auschwitz. He was one of one thousand prisoners on Transport 60. (He would be one of the thirty-one survivors of that transport.) Shortly after his arrival, he was sent to a subcamp, Monowitz-Buna, to work as a slave laborer for the giant industrial chemical company IG Farben. In addition to Perez, Monowitz slaves included Primo Levi (author of *If This Is a Man; The Periodic Table; The Drowned and the Saved; If Not Now, When;* and other books) and Elie Wiesel (author of *Night, After the Darkness, Dawn, Day,* and other books).

Monowitz-Buna held around twelve thousand prisoners, the great majority of whom were Jews. In addition there were non-Jewish criminals and political prisoners. Though IG Farben benefited from the slave labor of inmates, the SS (never ones to forgo an opportunity) charged Farber three Reichsmarks per day for unskilled workers, four Reichsmarks per hour for skilled workers, and one and one-half Reichsmarks for children. For those who were not sufficiently skilled or knowledgeable enough for work, the camp contained a labor education camp, but that was only for non-Jews. Jews who couldn't work were quickly gassed, their bodies then incinerated. The life expectancy of slave workers was three to four months. Those who survived longer periods were regarded as anomalies. Some were assigned to work in mines outside Monowitz. For those in the mines, life expectancy was only one month.

Perez was one of the lucky ones, for after a brief period as a slave laborer, he was recognized as the former flyweight boxing champion. The guards needed entertainment to maintain their spirits so Perez was told that he would have to fight on a regular basis. If he refused, he would be gassed. To test how well a Jew could stand up to an SS officer, Perez was forced to enter a makeshift ring with a tall, muscular example of Aryan superiority. Round after round the large muscular heavyweight pounded Perez into a bloody, battered specimen of defeated humanity. Perez looked as if he had been repeatedly run over by a locomotive. Blood poured down his face; teeth had been knocked out. After three rounds, he could barely lift his arms. Every time he attempted through typical defensive moves to forestall a beating, the SS officer knocked him to the canvas, where Perez endured painful kicks to his ribs and abdomen. The inmates, who were permitted to attend the fight had to keep their heads bowed, their eyes downcast. If they uttered encouragement, they were taken away. Here and there, an inmate would glance up and see Perez, whose face was a mask of blood; he stood in the ring being beaten, yet refusing to stay down. Every time, he was knocked down, he arose. His endurance came from years of training and pride in his ability as a boxer to withstand punishment. Not surprisingly, his endurance began to inspire the inmates who watched him endure his ongoing beating. Slowly, softly the inmates began to whisper, "Young, Young, Young." It grew to a whispered chant. Soon all the inmates were chanting together. The coterie of Nazi officers watching the fight took notice but said nothing. It was as if the chants were hypnotic. The chant "Young, Young, Young" seemed to infuse Perez like a shot of adrenalin. His eyes filled with the anger of a ferocious cornered animal. He spit out a mouthful of blood and went after the big Nazi with demonic fury. A series of rapid-fire punches landed powerfully on the Nazi's face, leaving it bloody and bruised. Welts sprang up like small mounds. Punches to the man's face were followed by punches to his midsection, then again, uppercuts, left and right hooks to the man's face. A solid punch to the point of his chin sent him to the canvas. When it was over, Perez could barely stand up. For his win, he was punished, food was withheld, and he was again forced to work as a slave laborer.

The guards and SS officers still needed entertainment, and though Perez had angered them by beating one of their own, he was brought back to fight again. Not just once, but again and again he fought, averaging two fights a week. If a scheduled opponent wasn't available, a substitute was chosen. After knocking out the SS officer, Perez had to fight a Jewish prisoner, a heavyweight named Iorry. He was a foot taller and weighed fifty pounds more than Perez. The Nazis remembered that the tall Panama Al Brown had beaten Perez, so the Nazis bet on Iorry to beat Perez. Unfortunately, they could find few other Nazis willing to take their bets. As a result, they forced a number of Jewish inmates to bet their allotment of bread on Perez to win. It was a double-or-nothing bet.

Perez was anxious about the fight because he wasn't sure he could repeat his earlier success. However, the motivation for winning was strong. He knew it would be a tough fight: he had to overcome the obstacle presented by a large, heavy man who could use his body mass to force Perez into a corner and then pummel him. Fortunately, Perez was not only a lot faster on his feet than Iorry, but his punches came faster and landed on target. Perez was able to avoid the slow-moving Iorry's punches and soon knocked him out. Again the Nazis were angrily disappointed and refused to pay off their bets: no additional bread was given to the inmates who had bet on Perez to win. From that fight on, the Nazis could not find anyone to bet against Perez. Since Perez provided such reliable entertainment, the Nazi officers arranged for him to get just enough nourishment thereafter to maintain his fighting weight and fitness. His head shaved and wearing only threadbare shoes and his striped inmate pajamas against the cold, he would do his road work running within a small, barbed-wire-enclosed, slushy, muddy circle. He would have to fight twice a week to keep himself from being starved. After each fight, he would be awarded another piece of bread and stale potato soup. His opponents, having lost their bouts with Perez, were not so fortunate: bloodied and bruised, they were dragged off to be gassed. Over a period of fifteen months, Perez scored 140 knockouts, saving himself but sadly sending most of the losers to their death.

Though American B-17 Flying Fortresses and B-24 Liberators, both heavy bombers, bombed the IG Farben factories at Monowitz four times in 1944, the factories were rebuilt and continued operating. They manufactured nearly all the explosives used by the German army as well as Zyklon-B, the deadly gas used to kill camp inmates. The cost to build the original IG Farben factories in 1942 was 700 million Reichsmarks, the equivalent of more than $2 billion in today's money.

During 1944, as Paris was about to be liberated from Nazi occupation, Balin and her lover Desbok, knowing what was in store for them, fled the city. They headed for Italy, hiding from those who might interrogate and arrest them. Their luck ran out on September 28, 1944, when they were arrested by the *Forces Françaises de l'Intérieur*, which worked with the Free French Forces once the liberation of France was underway. Balin and Desbok were arrested in Beausoleil, which is near Nice. Desbok, despised by the Resistance as an occupier, was quickly executed. As a hated collaborator, a betrayer of her country and its people, Balin was beaten numerous times. Following each beating, she was raped, then finally dragged off to a prison in Nice. Rather than being given special treatment as a famous movie star, Balin was treated more roughly than other prisoners. From the first prison she was transferred to Fresnes Prison near Paris, then released on bail on January 3, 1945. Patriots who saw her on the street either cursed her or spit at her. She was haggard and frightened. A newspaper reported that she was a broken woman who deserved to be shunned. Her aura of cinema celebrity had been shattered. For one year, the government banned her from acting in any movies. Finally in 1947, she appeared in the movie *La dernière chevauchée*. It would be her last appearance in a movie. Two years later, she had a stroke and nearly died from meningitis. Thereafter, she struggled to survive as she faded into the darkness of obscurity. Of those who remembered her, most disparaged and derogated her as a wartime collaborator. She was a shadow of herself when she died in 1968, almost entirely forgotten and poverty stricken. Throughout the war, Perez had no idea what had happened to the glamorous love of his life.

The misery of the inmates at Auschwitz and Monowitz was about to come to an end. Allied forces were well on their way to a major victory over the Third Reich. Nazis were surrendering while armed members of the Hitler Youth were conscripted into service to fight the onslaught of Russian, American, British, Canadian, Australian, and New Zealand troops who would bludgeon them into total capitulation. As the Russian army advanced, the Nazis decided to abandon Auschwitz and Monowitz in January 1945. Rather than fight against a ferocious Russian assault, the Nazis decided it was more important to kill all the imprisoned Jews who were too weak to make a trek back to Germany, where those who were able could still be used as slave laborers. To that end, SS officers began what they euphemistically called *Evakuierungs* (evacuations), but which the prisoners accurately called death marches. While suffering defeat on all fronts, the Nazis believed that the war against the Jews would be their only victory. Adolf Eichmann on his last visit to a concentration camp, commented, "I shall gladly jump into the pit knowing that in the same pit there are five million [Jewish] enemies of the state."[1]

Tens of thousands of starving, beaten, ragged inmates were marched to Germany to help sustain the defense of the fatherland. If they couldn't endure the long marches, they were shot, their bodies left in woods, along roads, or in ditches. As Martin Gilbert reported in his definitive account, *The Holocaust*, "during an air raid alert they [the Jewish prisoners] had scattered for protection in the forest, and then tried to remain there in hiding. But SS men surrounded them and opened fire, killing all but a hundred. The survivors were then marched on again, westward."[2]

Gilbert also quotes one of the men on the death march, Menachem Weinryb, who reported that

> one night we stopped near the town of Gardelegen. We lay down in a field and several Germans went to consult about what they should do. They returned with a lot of young people from the Hitler Youth and with members of the police force from the town.
>
> They chased us all into a large barn. Since we were five to six thousand people, the wall of the barn collapsed from the pressure of the mass of people, and many of us fled. The Germans poured out petrol and set the barn on fire. Several thousand people were burned alive.
>
> Those of us who managed to escape lay down in the nearby wood and heard the heart-rending screams of the victims.[3]

From concentration camps in conquered territories endlessly streaming marches went on day and night. The death marches lasted up to one month and often covered distances of hundreds of miles. In many cases the prisoners were loaded onto trains. With an average of seventy people jammed into a single freight car, they suffered from lack of oxygen, water, and food and soon perished. In January of 1945, hundreds froze in freight cars. It is estimated that in all the death marches between 250,000 and 375,000 were murdered. The brutal acts and killings frequently took place in the public streets before the eyes of German civilians. Some civilians joined in the killing sprees, angry that Jews had caused the war and betrayed Germany.

Auschwitz and its subcamps, such as Monowitz-Buna, were ordered to be evacuated on January 17, 1945. The inmates were marched to a camp named Gleiwitz. Over a period of five days, from January 17 to January 21, more than 56,000 prisoners were marched westward under the most brutal conditions. Most of the prisoners were without adequate clothing to keep themselves warm during that brutal winter;

many did not even have shoes. The bedraggled, starving remnants of the camp achingly marched on, knowing that a pause or a complaint would be resolved by a bullet to the head or into one's back. Prior to the evacuation, a small number of relatively healthy prisoners risked their lives by hiding themselves throughout the camp. They anxiously awaited the arrival of Soviet troops, who would liberate and feed them. Those in hiding were a mere handful compared to the 35,000 to 40,000 prisoners who reached Gleiwitz but not their freedom. The SS stuffed them into railroad freight cars to be transported to concentration camps in the fatherland. Of those, 9,000 to 15,000 died of exhaustion, starvation, or cold, or a combination of all three. Others were shot for not being able to keep up with fellow prisoners or for attempting to escape.

On January 18, 1945, Perez was one of the inmates on his way to the Gleiwitz concentration camp, which was near the Czech border. It was a trek of thirty-seven miles, undertaken with neither food nor water. Once in Gleiwitz, Perez was near the camp's kitchen. He spotted a stale loaf of bread, grabbed it, tore off a chunk for himself, and then attempted to hand pieces to other inmates. A guard saw what he was doing and, without a shouted order to stop, raised his rifle and quickly fired several bullets. Perez was hit multiple times and collapsed as blood flowed from his wounds. As a boxer with a powerful will to survive, he had depended on his strength and skills; as a kind and generous man, he died on January 21. He was thirty-three years old.

**4**

# The Miracle of Life
# in a Pair of Fists

Nathan Shapow was a big bear of man, two hundred pounds of solid muscle. To his family and friends, he was more like an oversized teddy bear than a wild ferocious animal. For Nazis and enemies of his family and friends, Shapow was no teddy bear: he could be as threatening and deadly as a grizzly bear in the wild. He was a complex man who wanted nothing more than to be a loving family man, a successful businessman, a patriot, and a boxer. History would throw so many combinations of punches at him that a man with less stamina and heart would have gone down for a full count and never gotten up. For Shapow, the will to survive, thrive, and fight on were the fuels that kept him going through bruising bouts with enemies who wanted to rob him and other Jews of their future. His Holocaust experiences were Job-like tests; and much to his own amazement, he passed each test, bloodied but alive.

He was born in Riga, the capital city of Latvia, on November 6, 1921, to Mordechai and Chaye Shapow. He was the firstborn; two brothers followed, Boris and Ephraim. The family lived modestly, but comfortably, in a largely Christian country where Jews were periodic victims of vicious anti-Semitic acts and at other times were merely tolerated. In families of multiple children, psychologists have theorized that either the youngest or the oldest will be the most successful. In the Shapow family that would turn out to be Nathan. In fact, from his late teenage years onward, he was known as Nathan the Strong.

But even before his teenage years, he proved to have the agility, endurance, and flexibility of a natural-born athlete. As he grew he developed large biceps and fists and thick forearms; friends told him he had the makings of a boxer, and he was drawn to the sport, which had been gaining popularity in his neighborhood. It was a sport that appealed to young Jews as a means of self-defense against anti-Semites, who might attempt to bully them. Shapow proved to be a natural. He quickly learned to jab, duck, feint, and slip punches as easily and as quickly as a duck learns to swim. When he sparred with other young boxers at the local Maccabi club, he demonstrated a flashing left hook and a rocketing knock-out right. The Maccabi was not only the site where he honed his boxing skills, it was also the place where Shapow thirstily imbibed talk of Zionism and its dreams of liberation and freedom. His trainers, who were ardent Zionists, were impressed not only by Shapow's appreciation of Zionism but also by his seemingly natural aptitude for boxing. They taught him how to hold that left hook in reserve, to feint with his right, then quickly deliver the left hook before an opponent could see it coming. It was rapidly followed by a right to the opponent's jaw. It was a perfect knockout punch. Years later, one of his opponents commented that the combination of those punches made him feel as if his head was about to be separated from his neck.

Shapow's training, toughness, skills, and even his ability to take a punch and bullishly keep coming at an opponent would be the ingredients for his survival during the bitterly oppressive days of the Soviet and Nazi occupations of Riga. Throughout his life, Shapow would never be a Jew who would obediently let himself be led to his own murder. He was neither sheep nor goat. He saw himself as an ancient Judean lion, a defender of himself as well as of his people. He knew that if faced with probable execution, he would go down with a fight, taking as many enemies with him as possible. "Better to die a brave man than be killed as a coward" would become his motto during World War II.

And it was in 1940 that Shapow began to call upon his strength as a fighter. The Soviet army occupied Riga and treated the populace, especially the Jews, as subhumans to be brutalized for the slightest infractions. In 1941, conditions worsened when the Nazis overran Latvia. The Nazis policy of exterminating Jews made the Soviets look almost beneficent by comparison. For the Nazis, the Jews were not merely subhuman, they were disease-carrying vermin who would sooner or later have to be exterminated to save the Aryan race from contamination. Under the Nazi occupation, the Shapow family considered itself lucky to eat and breathe; but they knew that each day could be their last for they lived under the implicit daily threat of being arrested, imprisoned, tortured, and sent to a concentration camp. Their future, if it existed at all, was bleak at best.

The Nazis justified their occupation because they were strong, pureblood Aryans who had the right to dominate and, if necessary, destroy lesser breeds. The Soviets had not been quite so brazen: they had pretended that their occupation was democratically approved. Their iron fist was concealed in a thick Moscow mitten, whereas the Nazis held up a starkly naked iron fist as a warning to all those who might disrespect them. Prior to the Nazi occupation, the Soviet government had ordered an election from July 14 to July 15. To ensure that the outcome reflected government goals, the Soviets informed the populace that "only the list of the Latvian Working People's Bloc must be deposited in the ballot box. The ballot must be deposited without any changes."

Of course, everyone knew the meaning of one-party rule: it was standard practice for dictatorships. However, the Soviets had such contempt for the people they governed that twelve hours before the last ballot was cast, the Soviet government in Moscow published the outcome of the election. It reported that more than 96 percent of the populace had voted and they had over welcomingly voted in favor of a Soviet government. With the rigged election serving as its justification for control of all of Latvia, the Soviets set up the apparatus necessary to govern by fear and stealth. They opened a police headquarters in Riga from which the officers could monitor the population and stamp out dissent, and which the officers did with such swift and unremitting levels of brutality that the populace lived in fear of being beaten, imprisoned, and tortured. Many friends and relatives of the Shapows were arrested, some never to be seen again. Those who were released from prison told stories of being beaten and tortured, forced to confess not only to crimes they hadn't committed but also to crimes that were never revealed to them. On one occasion nearly sixteen thousand people were rounded up and deported. The civilian population did not know what provoked the roundup.

Before the Soviets left Riga to the Nazis, Shapow had honed his survival skills. He became as slick, sly, and secretive as a cunning coyote on urban streets. He stole food for his family; he stole clothes; he bargained on the black market. His cleverness and resourcefulness made it easy for him to deal with corruptible officials. Even so, he was fortunate never to have been caught. If he had, he would have been imprisoned or, at best, sent to Russia and forced to join the Soviet army.

When the Soviets were replaced by victorious Nazi troops in 1941, more than 131,000 Jews from all the Baltic states had been deported. Some, though forced to fight for the Soviet army, were glad to turn their rifles and machine guns on the hated *Wehrmacht* and SS. Those who were not conscripted into the army were enslaved to work in factories that manufactured munitions. Very few imprisoned Latvians survived the war.

Survival became more difficult for the Shapow family under Nazi occupation. For Nathan, who stole food to feed his family, stealth and wiliness required nerves of steel, for whereas the Soviets would beat and imprison a thief, the Nazis would execute such a criminal. In Shapow's estimation, the Soviets were indeed barbaric, but the Nazis were even worse: for them, killing a Jew was as casual as blowing one's nose. To survive, Shapow became an alley cat of the night.

The SS turned the Riga Ghetto into an oversized cage in which Jewish residents were regularly terrorized by daily acts of unprovoked beatings, and arrests that led to torture, public hangings, or a gunshot to the head. Malnourished, inadequately clothed against the cold, rain, and snow, the Jews simply tried to survive. They were treated like diseased feral dogs. Nathan Shapow was determined not to succumb, not to be crushed under the Nazi jackboot.

To those SS officers in Riga who took notice of Shapow he was an affront for he did not fit the image that the Nazis promulgated of a cringing, cowardly, sniveling Jew. He was obviously strong and athletic. He had a reputation as a tough guy, a guy who could box an opponent into bloody defeat. Though he conducted himself with pride and self-confidence, he was careful not to provoke an impulsive attack by some hot-headed SS man. Yet he became the obsessional target of one officer, *Obersturmführer* Hoffman, an arrogant and sadistic man whose pleasure derived from humiliating and beating Jews. To beat up defenseless Jews was a form of daily exercise for Hoffman. As a warning to others and as means of making others fear him, he would often leave his victims prostrate, bloody, and unconscious in the street. To Hoffman, Shapow's physical attributes and pride were a challenge, one to be defeated with utter ruthlessness. Shapow's very being was worse than an impertinence. Shapow must be humiliated, brought to his knees, begging for his life. Shapow commented, "Perhaps he could not stand my attitude, for I neither looked nor felt like the Nazi's stereotype of the 'racially inferior degenerate Jew.' I was young, strong as an ox from years of football, swimming and boxing, and carried myself like an athlete. Though imprisoned in the ghetto, a slave laborer, I was not cowed."[1]

Shapow believed that years of boxing at the local Maccabi Club and on behalf of the Zionist Youth Movement, Beitar, had made him strong enough to endure whatever slave labor work the Nazis wanted him to perform. Nevertheless, Hoffman was determined not only to make Shapow's life miserable but to kill him as evidence of his own superiority and to prove to the Jews of Riga that even one of their strongest was no match for an Aryan SS man. One day, Hoffman ordered Shapow back to his small room in the ghetto. Hoffman walked behind Shapow and shouted orders at him: "*Macht schnell, macht schnell* [Faster, faster]." Once inside the small room, Hoffman pushed Shapow against a wall and called him an insect, a rodent, a dirty Jew. Just as Shapow turned around to face Hoffman, he saw that Hoffman had begun to unbutton the holster that held his Lugar. Shapow was dealt a fatal choice. He wrote that he could

> die like a coward or die as a warrior. I took a step towards him, moving slowly, almost imperceptibly, and as his hand closed around the handle of his pistol, I let my training take hold. With all my strength and skill, I threw a fast, round-arm left hook, the punch that made a legend of Joe Frazier. . . . [Hoffman] was certainly no boxer, and my left hook was enough to stun him. I followed with a classic straight right, connecting with his chin, which had veered to the side from the force of my first punch, his mouth hanging open in shock and pain. I heard the crack of bone as Hoffman's Aryan jaw broke.[2]

Not taking a chance of attracting other SS men by the sound of shooting Hoffman with the Lugar, Shapow grabbed a wooden stool and slammed it down against Hoffman's skull. He brought the stool down repeatedly, crashing it down again and again until he heard the cracking of caved-in cranium bones. Blood spattered like shrapnel onto the walls, onto Shapow's clothing; his hands were gloved in its sticky redness as Hoffman lay in a bed of his own Aryan blood. Shapow was breathing hard, his heart was pounding. He wondered how to dispose of Hoffman's body. He decided to wait until darkness descended on the ghetto, then in the quiet deadness of a moonless night, he dragged Hoffman's corpse several streets away from his room. He dumped the body in a darkened doorway, then furtively brushing against the sides of buildings like a feral cat, he made it safely back to his room. There he mopped the floor, washed the walls. Not seeing any evidence of blood, he dropped onto his bed and fell into a deep sleep.

About the same time that he awoke the next morning, Hoffman's body was discovered by outraged SS officers. They furiously declared that some Jewish scum was responsible for this cowardly act. They intended to find the Jew and make an example of him. No Jew can get away with killing an Aryan, especially a member of the SS. Jewish men were lined up and questioned. They were told to stand at attention and keep their eyes focused on the ground. They were told that if the murderer of Hoffman didn't confess, then others would have to pay with their lives for the crime. Since no one confessed and the SS didn't have a suspect, the SS commander chose two Jews at random. They were young and strong, and if given the chance, they looked as if they could have over-powered the SS commander. But with guns pointed at them, they had no chance of fighting back or escaping. The two frightened yet stoical martyrs were marched to the town square where all the Jews of the ghetto had been instructed to congregate. The two Jews had their hands tied behind their backs; each of them was instructed to stand on a low stool, then each had a noose placed around his head. The SS commander shouted an order, and the stools were kicked out beneath the feet of the two men. For a few moments their bodies jiggled like marionettes, then they went limp. They were left hanging there for all to see until their decomposing bodies were food for insects and birds. Though consumed by guilt, Shapow was relieved not to have endured the kind of retribution that he had witnessed. He had acted in self-defense. He had followed his training as a boxer: never be a victim. He knew he would carry guilt about what had happened for the rest of his life.

He wrote in his autobiography that

> a good boxer never gets caught on his heels. He ducks, he bobs, he weaves, he stays out of his opponent's reach. Those were the rules I lived by, out of the ring as well. My secret was to keep fit and strong, so that I was always looked upon as "useful" by our oppressors, while ignoring as many of the rules and regulations, especially over food and clothing, as I could without being executed. I kept out of the way of the Kapos and the SS as much as possible.[3]

Shapow proved not only to be as elusive as a jaguar in a nighttime tropical jungle, he was also a fearless and adventurous thief who not only stole food and drink for himself but also for friends and family. He concealed his treasures in a small cellar beneath his room. He was fortunate that a member of the ghetto police, Herr Rudy Harr, a former boxer, overlooked Shapow's thefts in exchange for half of what was stolen. Paying off cops has long been a tradition with unindicted thieves.

As bad as the Riga Ghetto was, it was just a way station for the Nazis. Not satisfied with dehumanizing and destroying lives in the ghetto, the Nazis constructed a concentration camp for them in Kaiserwald. There thousands of Jews were forced to be slave laborers and fed just enough to keep them constantly hungry and barely alive. Many died of disease and exhaustion. Jews had heard of mass shootings, and being a slave laborer was certainly better than being a corpse. Nevertheless, many Jews could not escape from the Nazi plan of extermination. One of the worst massacres took place in late 1941 when more than 25,000 Jews from the Riga Ghetto were transported to the Rumbula Forest not far from Riga. Over a two-day period all were murdered by the SS. It was the second-most-extensive murder of a large number of Jews. The largest massacre had occurred at Babi Yar in the Ukraine, where 33,371 Jews had been slaughtered. Once again, Shapow's luck held out: he was one of the fortunate ones for he was not rounded up for the Rumbula transport but was sent to the Kaiserwald concentration camp.

The Rumbula massacre was carried out by Einsatzgruppe A with the assistance of local Latvian collaborators such as the Arajs Kommandos of Viktors Arajs. The massacre was led by Friedrich Jeckeln, an *SS–Polizeiführer*. The other leaders of the massacre were Eduard Strauch, Hinrich Lohse, and Herberts Cukurs. Throughout the war, these men continued to carry out their murderous activities. However, after the liberation of the camps, they were tried for crimes against humanity at what was known as the Einsatzgruppen Trial, where all were found guilty. Friedrich Jeckeln was hanged. Herbert Cukurs escaped to South America, where he was tracked down and assassinated by the Mossad. Eduard Strauch was sentenced to death but died in prison before his execution could take place. Lohse was sentenced to a mere ten-year prison term. Arajs escaped and remained in hiding in West Germany, until he was arrested and sentenced to life in prison in 1979; he died in prison in 1988.

With a survivor's skill for deception, Shapow earned a place for himself in the Kaiserwald concentration camp. Prior to selecting slave laborers for the camp an SS officer had asked if any of the Riga Ghetto inhabitants had been engineers before the war. Shapow, fearing that non-engineers would be sent to extermination camps, stepped forward and said that he had performed many engineering jobs as a civilian and could do anything that required his skills. He also mentioned that, if necessary, he could perform hard labor for he was as strong as an ox. He was not surprised that rather than perform the tasks of an engineer he was put to work at hard labor. He had saved himself from likely extermination.

Though he considered himself fortunate to be sent to Kaiserwald, he quickly came to hate the camp, for it was an arena for extreme brutality and inhuman deprivations. The prisoners were forced to work 12 to 14 hours a day, every day, on a diet that was designed to ultimately lead to death. They were daily given a bowl of watery soup and a sliver of raw potato or a piece of potato skin. The prisoners were also given a few scraps of bread that were 50 percent sawdust. On such a meager diet, it is no wonder that so many of the prisoners died of starvation while others succumbed to opportunistic diseases.

However, work was not all that Shapow was required to do. Word had gotten around that Shapow had been a boxer before the war. It was decided that there should be a boxing match between Shapow and a German named Werner Samuel, who had been a professional middleweight champion. Samuel, as a former professional, was the odds-on favorite to beat Shapow. Training was minimal for Shapow, but his hard work in the ghetto and the camp had kept him strong and as fit as one could be on a near starvation diet. The bout began like a sudden storm.

> Two left jabs stopped me in my tracks and a right hook put me down on one knee. I could feel the blood gathering in my nasal passages and the roar of the crowd echoed painfully in my ears.
> The old cracked canvas beneath my knees felt rough and hard, the punches had hurt and I knew I was in danger of being outclassed. . . . His left was a tattoo on my face, followed up by stinging rights. I took the blows, and then put my chin in the way of a right hook and hit the canvas with a sickening thump.
> I shook my head to clear my fogged brain, thumbed the trickle of blood from my nose and climbed back to my feet on the count of eight.[4]

Shapow realized that if he had a chance to beat his opponent he would have to use every weapon in his arsenal. Failure could result in his death. So he resorted to the techniques of a street fighter. When one grapples in a dark alley there are no rules: winning is all that matters. Like a wild bull, Shapow head-butted his opponent, knocking him off his feet. When Samuel got up, he was met with a hard elbow to his right eye. Shapow then delivered a powerful blow to the back of Samuel's head, another to his kidneys, and a third to his already swollen ears. Shapow did everything but knee Samuel's groin. In this street fighter's brawl nothing was disallowed. With his opponent on the verge of defeat, Shapow delivered a powerful left uppercut that sent Samuel sprawling to the hard canvas. Samuel managed to raise himself, just in time for Shapow to deliver a devastating straight right to Samuel's chin. The man went down and stayed there for a full count of ten. Shapow felt he had won the bout for the Latvian Jews. His destiny would soon change again.

By August 1944, the Soviet Army was advancing toward Latvia, and so as not to interrupt plans for the continued work of Jewish slave laborers and not to hinder the goal of massive exterminations, the SS began an evacuation of Kaiserwald, transporting inmates to the Stutthof concentration camp in Poland. The camp was established in 1939 and was the first concentration camp set up outside Germany. Before the evacuation could begin, nearly all Jews under the age of eighteen and over the age of thirty were summarily executed, for the older ones were not considered capable of slave labor and the younger ones were not yet fully developed as laborers. They were useless to the Reich. Those who were regarded as too weak or too sick to survive the trip to Stutthof were also killed. The twenty-three-year-old Shapow, strong and capable of hard work for long hours, was spared and shipped off to Stutthof. Though he survived the camp, others were not so fortunate: between 63,000 and 65,000 of the 110,000 inmates died there.

The camp was notorious for having a large number of sadistic guards who enjoyed nothing so much as beating the inmates. For the guards, it was a form of recreation. And the beatings were not just administered by male guards but also a large number of female guards. There were 295 female guards at Stutthof, all of whom were infamous for their gratuitous cruelty that frequently resulted in murder. After the war, 34 of them were tried and convicted of crimes against humanity, including one who had previously been a Red Cross nurse. Several of those convicted were given death sentences and publicly hanged. Others were given moderate prison sentences. That all the guards were not tried as criminals disappointed and angered the surviving prisoners. After all, the guards were, with few exceptions, murderers.

Noted historian Martin Gilbert quotes an inmate of Stutthof:

All the Jews were assembled in the courtyard; they were ordered to run, to drop down and to stand up again. Anybody who was slow in obeying the order was beaten to death by the overseer with the butt of his rifle.

Afterwards Jews were ordered to jump right into the cesspit of the latrines, which were being built; this was full of urine. The taller Jews got out again since the level reached their chins, but the shorter ones went down. The young ones tried to help the old folk, and as a punishment the overseers ordered the latter to beat the young. When they refused to obey they were cruelly beaten themselves. Two or three died on the spot and the survivors were ordered to bury them.[5]

The SS expressed their sadism not only in deeds but also in spirited singing that cynically welcomed the Jews as they arrived in the concentration camp: "Jews, go through the Red Sea / The waves close in, / And the world is happy. / Jews are drowned."

The singing was followed by much laughter, which was followed by shouted orders to stand at attention. Though obedient to the SS commands, Shapow was filled with hatred for the guards who were as incapable of pity and empathy as serial killers. In such a threatening environment, Shapow's skills for self-preservation remained on high alert; his luck did not fail him, though to look at him one would have thought he was not long for this world. In boxing terms, he had gone from being a light heavyweight to being a straw-weight. No longer 200 pounds of muscle, he was now 105 pounds of skin and bone. He looked as if a stiff blow from the butt of Nazi rifle would kill him. Yet he maintained his usual vigilance. He was tough minded and determined not to be a casualty of the Nazis. He would hold out until the Nazis were defeated. All the prisoners had learned that the Soviets and the Americans were winning the war. It was just a matter of time until they were liberated.

They heard the SS talking about the advancing Soviet army. Though the guards spoke guardedly about it, their words were whispered among inmates. The SS also discussed among themselves stories about the Soviets not taking prisoners, of seeking revenge for Stalingrad and other atrocities. Indeed, wherever the Soviets encountered Nazi soldiers, they slaughtered them. Knowing what would happen to them if captured by the Soviets, the SS made plans to evacuate Stutthof. But the normally efficient SS took too long in planning their escape. By April 1945, the camp was nearly encircled by Soviet troops; the only means of escape was by boat. However, there was not sufficient room aboard the boats to transfer all the prisoners, regardless of how tightly they were packed onboard. Not wanting to leave witnesses behind who could testify to their atrocities, the SS marched hundreds of prisoners knee-deep into the sea and mowed them down with machine gun fire. The screams of victims could be heard throughout the day. When the slaughter was over, more than 25,000 of the 50,000 prisoners had been slaughtered. By time the Soviets arrived on May 9, 1945, the camp was nearly empty, yet a few prisoners had managed to hide from the evacuation organizers. Emerging from numerous hideouts in the camp came one hundred emaciated prisoners who greeted their liberators with tears and hugs. Some got down on their knees and kissed the hands of their liberators; others begged for a few morsels of food. The Soviet soldiers were shocked at the condition of the prisoners and several of the soldiers said they wished there had been SS available to be killed.

While those responsible for running the camp escaped from immediate execution by Soviet troops, they were not able to escape the hammer of postwar justice. There were six Stutthof trials, beginning on April 25, 1946. The first one was conducted in Gdansk (Danzig) at a Soviet-Polish court. The trial lasted until May 31. In the dock were 17 guards and kapos, including the camp commandant Johann Pauls, who stood on trial for crimes against humanity that included the murder of 85,000 prisoners. He plus 5 female guards and 5 kapos were all hanged. Only 2 kapos were found not guilty; the rest received prison terms of varying length.

One of the most notorious women to be tried for her role as overseer at Stutthof was Herta Bothe, a 6'3" guard who was known as the Sadist of Stutthof. She reportedly beat a Hungarian Jewish woman to death with a wooden block and shot two other inmates for no apparent reason. At trial, she claimed that she never killed anyone. She avoided being sentenced to death and instead was sentenced to ten years in prison. She did not serve her full sentence and was released on December 22, 1951, in an act of leniency. She died in 2000 at the age of seventy-nine, never having accepted responsibility for her acts. She merely claimed she had made a mistake by becoming a concentration camp guard rather than a hospital nurse.

A second trial was held from October 8 to October 31, 1947. There, 24 guards were found guilty of crimes against humanity. Of those, 10 were sentenced to death, and the remainder received prison terms ranging from three years to life. Five days later on November 5, a third trial commenced and after five days of hearings, an additional 19 former camp guards and officials were found guilty and sentenced to varying prison terms. One SS officer was acquitted and released. A fourth trial began on November 19, 1947, and after ten days of testimony, 26 guards and officials were found guilty and sentenced to prison for terms lasting from three months to life; 1 kapo was acquitted. At the fifth trial in 1949, Hans Jacobi, another Stutthof commandant, was found guilty and sentenced to three months in prison. *SS–Rottenführer* Emil Strehlau was found guilty and sentenced to death. The last trial took place in 1953, which concluded with a guilty verdict for Paul Bielawa, a prison guard from Third Company in Stutthof; he was sentenced to twelve years in prison.

The last trial of anyone who participated in the atrocities of Stutthof was conducted in 2019 when Bruno Dey from Hamburg was accused of contributing to the killings of 5,230 prisoners. However, he was tried in a juvenile court because he was seventeen years old at that time.

Though life for inmates at Stutthof was harrowing, Shapow emerged as one of the lucky ones. Having claimed to have been an engineer, he was transported to the Magdeburg camp, where he was told he would be assigned work that utilized his alleged engineering skills. A guard instructed him to clean oil from a pit beneath anti-aircraft guns. Shapow wondered why he would have needed engineering experience to do a janitorial job. But he performed the work reliably and never gave the SS reason to punish him. His diligence paid off, for he was soon sent to work in a munitions factory. There he worked six days a week for eighteen hours each day. On Sundays, he along with other Jewish prisoners had to clean latrines, toilets, and Nazi barracks. In addition, having cleared away dishes and utensils from the Nazi dining area, they then had to wash everything and mop the floors. On Mondays, work would resume at the munitions factory. It was a tedious routine but at least Shapow was alive, and when no one was around he stole scraps of food for himself and his fellow inmates. A clever and resourceful thief, he was never the subject of an investigation into the small quantities of missing food.

On April 16, 1945, as American artillery pounded the Magdeburg camp and as B-17 and B-24 bombers dropped their bombs in response to the commandant's refusal to surrender, Shapow wondered if his luck might be ending. Thus far, he had survived the Nazis. Would he now be blasted to smithereens by Allied bombs and artillery fire? The prisoners prayed that they would be spared.

After twenty-four hours of unremitting bombardment, it seemed as if their prayers had been answered, for the Nazis finally agreed to surrender. Before doing so however, the SS wanted to kill off all the Jews before the surrender became official. Fearing that he would be killed, Shapow climbed over a barbed-wire fence, dropped to the ground, and hid in a sewer pipe with other escapees. After twelve hours in concealment, the escapees left their hideout and came face to face with a surprised SS officer. Before the officer could react, he was quickly overcome by several men, and Shapow delivered a powerful combination of punches that left the officer bloody and unconscious. The men removed the officer's uniform, shirt, and boots. Shapow put on the officer's boots and jacket. Another man took the officer's pants, Another, the man's hat and shirt. They then scrambled to a nearby abandoned factory where they hid in the basement. While bombs rained down from British and American bombers, the men commented on the irony of hiding in a factory where they had prepared anti-aircraft shells to shoot down Allied bombers. Again, they prayed that they would not be victims of friendly fire.

The bombardment soon ended, and the escapees breathed sighs of relief. Not long afterward, American troops arrived. As they passed by each structure, they yelled for Germans to emerge with their hands in the air. If they appeared with their weapons they would be shot. No questions asked. In addition to a few German laggards, the Jewish escapees came out of the basement into the sunlight. Because Shapow was partly dressed in an SS uniform, he was taken aside and accused of being a member of the SS. An American soldier demanded to see if he had an SS tattoo. He then wanted to know how long Shapow had been a guard at the camp. Shapow insisted he was not a Nazi, but a Jew, who stole the uniform. Americans had heard many such stories from captured SS and did not believe Shapow. Nevertheless, Shapow kept telling the Americans that he was Jewish. Over and over again, he repeated himself. "I'm Jewish, and this is part of a stolen uniform." Frustrated by Shapow's insistence on being identified as a Jew, an American soldier brought over one of his Jewish infantry buddies to ascertain Shapow's genuine identity. The American Jew pulled a small prayer book from his knapsack and handed it to Shapow. "Read the first prayer in Hebrew." Shapow did so, but before he could finish it, he was instructed to recite the balance of the prayer from memory. He did so in fluent Hebrew. The American soldier retrieved his prayer book and embraced Shapow. Shapow breathed the air as a free man for the first time in six years. He and the men with him were given new clothes and small quantities of food to fill their shrunken stomachs. Those who ate too much or too quickly experienced spasms of pain and vomited. Yet they were excited finally to have nourishing food that their bodies had craved.

Karl Rahm and Siegfried Seidle, the commandants who brutally controlled the Magdeburg camp, were eventually captured and tried for crimes against humanity. They were found guilty and executed. The men who had escaped the commandants' wrath and sadism would have preferred the opportunity deliver their own personal justice but were appreciative that the two SS men were executed.

Following his release from Magdeburg, Shapow, a committed Zionist since his youth, made his way to what was then Palestine. There he was reunited with his father, who had left Riga before the war. One day while walking on the streets of Tel Aviv, Shapow collided with the man who had robbed him, his brother, and their mother of the money they had needed to escape from Riga prior to the Nazi invasion. This man had promised to deliver exit papers as well as train and boat tickets that would guarantee the Shapows' safe escape from Riga. He had asked for a large sum of cash, all the money that Shapow's mother had. She paid it. However, when she arrived at the point of departure, she was told that all of her documents were forgeries. Bereft, anxious, and fearful, she returned to her home and lived with debilitating stress. It was too much for her, and she died of a heart attack. Shapow immediately recognized the con man, grabbed him by his shirt collar, and slammed him against a wall. He then beat him into unconsciousness. It was an act of unsatisfactory revenge, for he could not bring his brothers and mother back to life. Shapow had wanted to kill the man but refrained from doing so. What good would it do? The man suffered a terrible beating for what he had done and that would have to be sufficient justice.

Shapow found a more satisfying outlet for his need to settle scores and win a more important battle for the Jews than beating up one con artist. Shapow wanted to destroy those who proposed driving the Jews into the sea; it would be his means of spitting in the face of the Nazis. He joined the Irgun and fought for Israeli independence. He was a brave soldier who killed a number of Arab soldiers and later was honored for his heroism and commitment to Jewish independence. One day, on leave from the army, Shapow met a beautiful petite woman named Hela. Shapow and Hela soon fell in love and married. Following Israel's declaration of independence and recognition by President Truman, Shapow and Hela moved to the United States, first living in Chicago, then in Los Angeles. Shapow began a successful trucking business, and he and Hela raised their two children, Michael and Adina.

I asked Mike his impressions of his father (and he said his sister, Adina, agrees). He told me that his father's

> WW II experiences were life altering horrid events full of suffering and constantly looking death in the eye. Losing his family and friends in Riga ghetto affected him terribly and changed his whole life. Often having terrible nightmares and crying out in his sleep it was definitely PTSD. He was able to manage it so very well by having a zest for life and family. Boxing gave him an edge for survival in the camps and allowed him to steal food; the SS would look the other way because he was a great athlete and a great boxer; he became so popular in the camps that he was called "Nachman *der Stärkere*" (Nate the strong one). He always shared his loot with his mates which made it somewhat easier for them to survive. When dad walked into a room he had presence and when he spoke everyone would listen with admiration and respect. He was my hero, a humble gentle giant; adversity never scared him, for he always overcame it. He was our family's security and an example to humanity. After all he went through and not allowing it to affect his day to day management of life is beyond me.[6]

# 5

# 200 to 1

A young man of twenty, Salamo Arouch arrived at Auschwitz in 1943 along with fifty thousand other Greek Jews. The railway boxcar journey to the camp had been harrowing; by the time the train arrived in Auschwitz, the air in the boxcar was permeated with the stink of urine and feces. A few had vomited. Some had wrapped articles of clothing around their faces to filter out the nauseating odor. When the prisoners detrained, they were hungry and dehydrated. Arouch had no idea what to expect, but he knew it would be bad. He didn't yet know of the gas chambers and crematoriums, but he knew—from looking around—that he was now in a prison where the inmates looked as if they had been starved and beaten: they were skeletal and bruised; their eyes and cheeks were sunken. Their skin was as pale gray as that of corpses. They were the walking dead. A sleek black Mercedes was driven up to the waiting inmates. A low-ranked soldier-driver opened his own door then opened the door for the rear-seated passenger. The commandant emerged like the master of a plantation. There he stood: his head capped with a peaked visor sporting the Nazi eagle, a swastika emblem, and a death's head skull, his feet encased in shiny black boots, and his torso draped in an elegant black-leather coat decorated with two rows of silver buttons and a red-and-black swastika armband. The commandant surveyed with surly superiority the desperate faces before him. He barked that the newcomers should stand at attention, then looking them over, he asked if there were any boxers present. Arouch dutifully raised his hand and was directed to step forward. "You're a boxer?" "Yes." "You're too short and skinny to be a boxer." "I am, and I can prove it."

With a stick, the commandant drew a large circle in the dirt. He directed Arouch to enter the circle then instructed another inmate to join Arouch. The two men were each given worn-out pairs of old boxing gloves to put on their fists. They put on the gloves then looked at the commandant for instruction. Their expressions radiated fear and anxiety. The commandant asked their names. Arouch's opponent was a frightened young man named Chaim who had some experience as a boxer. "Now fight!" ordered the commandant. In a matter of minutes, Arouch had flattened his opponent with a left to the temple and a right to the jaw. The commandant was impressed but still skeptical; he wanted additional evidence that Arouch was a boxer. He directed a 6-foot, 200-pound Czech to enter the ring with the 135-pound, 5-foot 6-inch Arouch. Like many short boxers engaged in taking on a taller man, Arouch knew the importance of attacking the midsection of an opponent and how to get under his arms and punch up to the jaw and the side of his head. He would have to land his punches rapidly then move out of the range of the taller man's fists. He did not want to get his head pummeled. It was a technique made famous years later in America by heavyweight champion Rocky Marciano, who used his short arms to get under the longer arms of his opponents. Arouch aimed his jabs at the Czech's jaw and head, then he would move away, coming back to attack the Czech's midsection and kidneys. A couple of punches may have landed on the man's genitals. Arouch's punches were rapid-fire rights and lefts. As quickly as he moved, Arouch could not avoid receiving several blows to the top of his head. Yet he had managed to soften up his target who seemed confused about where Arouch's next blows would land. Sensing his advantage, Arouch delivered a solid right to the Czech's solar plexus then another to his liver. The big Czech folded like a half-cut tree, and Arouch delivered a devastating right upper-cut to his opponent's jaw that caused the man to topple to the ground.

No wonder Arouch won the bout. His father had taught him the elements of the sweet science when Arouch was fourteen years old. He learned a classic style of boxing that was based on throwing a series of left jabs followed by right crosses. The technique served him well. By age seventeen, he had won the middleweight championship of Greece and the Balkans, and by 1939 his record stood at 24 wins, 0 losses. He was chosen to be a member of the Greek Olympic Boxing Team but never got to participate. Instead he was drafted into the Greek army, becoming a member of the army's boxing team, and he proceeded to have three successful bouts that ended when he knocked out each of his opponents. Because of his clever and fast foot movements in the ring, he was known as "the ballet dancer" and to some as "the ballerina."

His hometown of Salonica (Thessalonica), where he was born in 1923, celebrated Arouch's achievements in the ring. He was also the pride of the local Jewish population, and Salonica had a long-established history of Jewish life going back two thousand years. The city came to be known as the "Mother of Israel." It had the largest Jewish population of any city in Greece. Jewish life in Greece was settled and traditional. There were synagogues that dated to the second century BCE. And even Aristotle wrote of his friendship with a Jewish philosopher from Syria who he said not only spoke fluent Greek but had the soul of a Greek. While Jews had enjoyed friendly relations with their non-Jewish neighbors for centuries, the climate of friendship turned cloudy in some quarters after the Italian fascist army invaded the country on October 28, 1940. The Italians invaded because the Greek dictator Ioannis Metaxas had refused to capitulate to an ultimatum issued by Mussolini. In response to the invasion, 12,898 Greek Jews joined the Greek army. They thought of themselves as being as Greek as anyone else, and they patriotically fought against the invasion of their homeland by Italian fascists in Albania and Macedonia. According to Martin Gilbert, "613 Jews from Salonica were killed in action, and 1,412 became total invalids. Among the Jews who fought was the Greek national hero Mordechai Fraggi, who was killed in action."[1]

The Greek army succeeded in driving the fascists out of their county, but then in 1941 there was a powerful *Werhmacht* invasion of Greece. Again the Jewish soldiers fought alongside their fellow Greeks against the *Werhmacht* onslaught. The Jews were celebrated as dedicated fighters. There were so many Jewish soldiers in the 50th Brigade of the Greek army that it was commonly known as the Cohen Battalion. It didn't matter, for the Greeks were overwhelmed by the enormity of the Nazi forces, which occupied Salonica and Macedonia on April 9, 1941.

Soldiers of the Greek army had put up a valiant fight against the Nazis, but they had been outnumbered and outgunned. The Greeks had been no match for the enormously powerful Nazi war machine. Once the Nazi jackboot pressed down on the necks of their Greek victims, there was little the Greeks could do to protect their Jewish countrymen. Yet here and there a few heroic endeavors helped save the lives of Jews. In Athens, for example, more than 1,200 Jews were saved from Nazi liquidation by the issuance of false identity cards supplied by Archbishop Damaskinos and Police Chief Angelos Ebert.

However, such acts of decency could not prevent a slow, steady, and inexorable tide of anti-Jewish laws from being enacted and enforced as in other conquered lands. Max Merten, a German citizen, was put in charge by the Nazis for overseeing the enforcement of anti-Jewish rules in Salonica. He quickly banned all Jewish newspapers and welcomed the distribution of two pro-Nazi newspapers: *Nea Evropi* (New Europe) and *Apogevmatini* (Evening Press). Jewish homes and community centers were given to the Nazi occupiers. All radios that were owned by Jews had to be turned over to the occupiers, and Jews were banned from all restaurants and cafes. Denied access to food, particularly as a result of a brutal famine, sixty Jews a day died from starvation from 1941 through 1942. On July 11, 1942, many Jews felt their lives as Greek citizens were about to end. The day became known as the Black Shabbat, for on that day Max Merten ordered that all men age 18 to 45 of the city of Salonica were to be rounded up like cattle and corralled in Eleftherias Square (Freedom Square). While in the square the Jews were forced to spend hours performing calisthenics while guns were pointed at them. The Jews were told that anyone who did not perform would be regarded as a traitor and shot. Four thousand of the strongest-looking men were selected to construct a road linking Salonica to Keterini and Larissa, where there was an epidemic of malaria. After ten weeks of hard work and little food, 480 of those originally chosen died from either exhaustion or starvation or malaria. Those who were not chosen for hard labor were transported to Auschwitz.[2]

While the Jews labored under barbaric conditions, there were Greeks, both Jews and non-Jews, who wanted the release of the Jewish slave laborers. To effect the release, Merten and the Nazis demanded a payment of 3.5 billion drachmas. The community was able to come up with 2 billion. The other 1.5 billion could not be raised no matter how hard and desperate were the efforts to do so. In exchange for the lower amount of drachmas, the residents of Salonica would have to give up ownership of the Jewish cemetery, which contained from 300,000 to 500,000 graves. Once the cemetery was in German hands, its destruction commenced. However, the destruction proceeded too slowly for the Germans who were in charge of overseeing the removal of all the gravestones, so they ordered local government officials to hire five hundred additional workers to speedily destroy the cemetery. When the destruction was complete, the cemetery was turned into a massive quarry where broken gravestones were turned into building materials. (Today the cemetery is the site of the Aristotle University of Thessaloniki.)

While the destruction continued, Jews found life in Salonica so re-strictive that five thousand of them departed for the safety of the Ital-ian zone.[3] Unfortunately, that safe haven did not weather the storm of occupation and vicious anti-Semitism. Of those who did not leave for the Italian zone, there were 250 angry and determined Jews who joined the Greek People's Liberation Army and the National Liberation Front and fought guerilla battles against the occupiers. They not only fought against the occupiers, they also fought against the thousands of traitor-ous Greeks who served the Nazis. Historians now estimate that more than twenty thousand Greek citizens collaborated with the Nazis.

By 1943, the plight of the Jews of Salonica had become even more ominous. To deal with the "Jewish Question," the Nazis sent two of their more vicious anti-Semitic SS ideologues to Salonica on February 6, 1943. They were Alois Brunner and Dieter Wisliceny. Brunner, as Adolf Eichmann's assistant, was responsible for sending more than 100,000 Jews to concentration camps. He was also the commandant of the Drancy internment camp outside Paris, and from there he sent 24,000 Jews to concentration camps. Following the end of the war, he escaped capture and trial as a war criminal by going to Syria, where he joined the Ba'ath Party and became a salaried employee of the government, giving advice on how to administer torture techniques while interrogating prisoners. Wisliceny made sure that all the Jews of Salonica were confined to a ghetto. He then determined when they should be sent to a death camp and killed. He was known as an expert on efficient means of liquidating the Reich's enemies. Unlike Brunner, he was not able to escape after the war, and in 1948, he was extradited to Czechoslovakia, tried for war crimes, and met his fate dangling at the end of a hangman's rope.

Shortly after their arrival, Brunner and Wisliceny eagerly set about their mission. First they ordered that all Jews display a yellow Star of David on their garments. Those who failed to do so would be shot without explanation. After Brunner and Wisliceny had confined the Jews to several ghettos, they further circumscribed their freedom: Jews were restricted to specific neighborhoods and could go about only dur-ing a few prescribed hours each day. Violators would be shot on the spot. By the end of February 1943, the anti-Semitic laws had resulted in all Jews being confined to three ghettos: Kalamaria, Singrou, and Vardar/Agia Paraskevi. From there it became easy for the SS to transfer the inhabitants to the Baron Hirsch Transit Camp, which was adjacent to a railroad station. There Salamo Arouch and thousands of other Greek Jews were forced into boxcars to take them to the death camps. Unfortunately for the Jewish captives, the SS were able to employ the services of a Jewish police force headed by Vital Hasson. He was not only head of the police that drove the Jews to their death, he was also a bounty hunter for the Nazis. He would cross borders to search for Jews who had escaped Nazi roundups and bring them to the SS. In addition, he stole jewels from Jewish women, often raping them and pimping them to the Nazis. He was so cold-blooded and callous that he did nothing to save his parents from a trip to a death camp. It was not until 1946 that the allies caught up with Hasson, who had been on the run, and turned him over to Greek authorities. He was tried, sentenced to death, and executed.

The death trains to which Hasson delivered his fellow Jews began departing Greece on March 15, 1943. He was able to cram 1,000 to 4,000 Jews onto a train, which went either to Auschwitz or to Treblinka. The deportations ended on August 7, 1943, after all the Jews of Salonica had been sent to concentration camps. Upon their arrival, nearly 90 percent of the Jews were immediately sent to gas chambers and then cremated. The Arouch family, five in all, were among those carted off like cattle to their fate in Auschwitz. Oddly, more than three hundred Jews who claimed Spanish ancestry were sent to Barcelona and Morocco.

Arouch, his father, his mother, three younger sisters, and his brother Avram arrived at Auschwitz on March 15, 1943. It was about 6 p.m., and the prisoners were in a state of confusion, panic, and desperation. A distraught Arouch spotted a friend from Salonica. He asked where all the others whom he had known from the ghetto were now housed. He was told that they had all been gassed and incinerated. Arouch thought his friend was delusional, driven mad by desperation. However, he soon came to realize that his friend was not delusional, for shortly thereafter Arouch's mother and sisters were gassed and incinerated. Still later, he learned that his father, who had grown too weak for slave labor, had also been gassed. Then his brother was shot for refusing to remove the gold fillings from the teeth of gassed Jews.

Arouch may have been destined for the same fate as the rest of his family. Before he could demonstrate the pugilistic skills that would save his life, he was taken away by SS guards, stripped of his clothing, and hosed down and disinfected like a farm animal. His head was then shaved and his arm tattooed with a serial number, 136954. Branded, he was treated like a beast awaiting slaughter. Poked with sticks, whipped, and driven to the center of the camp with the other new arrivals, he had to stand at attention as the commandant addressed the prisoners. It was at that time that Arouch got to prove himself a proficient boxer, a role he would have to perform sometimes two or three times a week for nearly two years. It would keep him alive as long as he kept winning his bouts.

Upon observing Arouch's winning skills, the commandant exclaimed, "Look what we have here! A real Yid fighter." From then on Arouch was spared from performing hard labor. He was assigned to be a clerk and given sufficiently minimum nourishment so that he could continue as a camp boxer. He said that the fights were like cockfights where the guards cheered, cursed, and bet on the winners. And Arouch was always a winner, fighting desperately not to be sent to the gas chambers.

His most difficult fight was against a German-Jewish boxer named Klaus Silber. The German had an even more impressive pre-camp record than Arouch, for he had won 44 bouts and lost none. He was a favorite of the commandant and the guards, for even at Auschwitz he had never lost a bout. Silber was favored to win and very few of the guards were willing to bet on Arouch. By the time Silber and Arouch were matched to fight, Silber had won 100 fights in the camp. His record placed him at the pinnacle of the camp's boxers. The match-up of Arouch and Silber generated the kind of excitement that one would expect from a world-class fight between two internationally celebrated athletes. Even the commandant expressed his good fortune in having two superb athletes ready to kill one another for the pleasure of the SS.

As the two boxers approached the ring, the excitement of the crowd was palpable. The guards shouted encouragement to Silber, their favored boxer, and abuse at Arouch whom they all expected to see dragged off to the gas chambers following his loss. The two men came at each other like blood-thirsty pit bull terriers, each knowing that the loser would likely be killed. From the opening bell, their fists flew with the intensity of bullets. Each landed as many punches as possible while attempting to block and slip punches that could result in a knockout. Their energy seemed to come from multiple shots of adrenalin. Desperation and grim determination shone in their eyes. Their rapid-fire fists kept the audience enthralled, some of whom enthusiastically pantomimed upper cuts and hooks. Though bruised and bloodied, neither man gave evidence of experiencing pain. The blood flowed and dribbled, red welts grew around their eyes, but neither boxer gave an inch. Their intensity was propelled by the possibility of defeat. Their arms grew tired, they breathed heavily, they staggered about the ring, but no man was going to show a hint of weakness.

Then Silber found an opening and delivered a short, hard right that Arouch was unable to block. The punch seemed to have come out of nowhere. That right landed on the point of Arouch's chin, causing his head to snap backward, then flop forward. Arouch went down like a suddenly tranquilized animal. Arouch lay on the canvas for no more than three or four seconds then shook his dazed head, dispersing clouds of confusion from his mind. He scrambled to his feet, fists flying at Silber, who looked surprised that Arouch had been able to recover so quickly and commence a wild onslaught. At first Arouch certainly looked as if he had been knocked unconscious and should have been out for a full count, if not longer. But Arouch was fighting for his life and he was not about to surrender his life to men who wouldn't think twice about executing him. He must fight on, no matter how hard it was to continue. He went after Silber with the ferocity of an angry wounded animal. And he certainly looked wounded: the skin around is eyes was swollen and discolored, his lower lip was torn and bleeding. Blood poured out of his nose. Yet he was unstoppable. He delivered a devastating combination of blows, causing Silber to reel backward. Then Arouch delivered two rapid-fire jackhammer rights to Silber's jaw. Silber collapsed like a marionette with cut strings. He lay unconscious, blood dribbling from his gums where a tooth had been dislodged. More blood flowed from his broken nose. As his arms lay limp at his sides, he was dragged away by his ankles like a dead bull that had died from the matador's final thrust. Silber was never to be seen again. For the SS it was great entertainment having two Jews attempt to kill each other though a few complained that they had bet on the wrong boxer. For Arouch, his win meant that he had another day to live in hell. And in the hell of the boxing bouts in the camp, Arouch knew he had been forced to be the instrument of Silber's deadly end, but he also knew that he was the solitary instrument of his own survival.

And so it went for Arouch. He went on to double Silber's winning record, winning during the course of his imprisonment two hundred fights. Two of his fights ended in draws because Arouch was suffering from dysentery, but draws, fortunately, were not death sentences, and so Arouch remained a betting favorite for the SS and it was hard to find anyone willing to bet on his opponents. Arouch's performances in the ring were widely popular and he never disappointed those who cheered him on. It is ironic that those who cheered for him to win were also the same men who would have delivered him to the gas chambers had he lost.

In addition to allowing Arouch to live, winning resulted in an extra portion of bread (sometimes even a full loaf) and soup and an occasional piece of rotted meat. For the losers who were not immediately taken out and shot or gassed, losing resulted in significantly reduced food allotments or no food for several days. The malnourishment and weakness that would follow meant that the loser would be too weak for slave labor and would be killed, a useless commodity. Arouch hated it all. He hated the guards, he hated what happened to his opponents, he hated the world that would permit such bestiality to continue. But his choices were starkly existential: fight or die.

The choice at one point became more agonizing than usual. There was a boxer at Auschwitz named Jacko Razon. He had been a boyhood friend of Arouch from Salonica. Their friendship had developed because, as teenagers, they had both fallen in love with boxing and often trained together. By 1944, Razon was proving to be one of the few unbeatable boxers at the camp. He was another Silber: he had won 120 fights at the camp, and the SS was eager to watch a match between Razon and Arouch. They speculated on who would survive such a match. Having trained together in Salonica, each man knew the style, the strengths, and weaknesses of the other. It wasn't only as journeymen boxers that they knew each other. They had also been members of the Greek army boxing team. Following the army's defeat and surrender to the conquering Nazis, Razon was taken into captivity and sent to Auschwitz.

Each man trained for the fight, perhaps wishing that a deus ex machina would prevent the fight from taking place. However, it was no artificial rescue that prevented the fight. Instead, it was the advance of Allied forces that resulted in the camp's liberation. The two men felt a profound sense of relief. Fate, however, plays tricks on those who think that fortunes have been made and misfortunes painted over.

When the movie *Triumph of the Spirit*, about Arouch's time as a concentration camp boxer, was released, Razon was incensed. The story, he claimed, was about him, not Arouch. He sued the producers of the movie, and an out-of-court settlement was reached. How many men forced to box for the pleasure of murderous Nazi guards would also have felt that Arouch's story was theirs? There were other superb Jewish boxers at the camp including Victor (Young) Perez (see chapter 3), Kid Francis, and Leone Efrati. Arouch did not get to fight those three, all of whom were murdered by the Nazis. Whether Arouch would have beaten those boxers is a game for pundits of pugilism to play. Efrati had been ranked the tenth-best featherweight in 1939 by the National Boxing Association. He lost a chance to win the NBA featherweight title in a bout against Leo Rodak at the Coliseum in Chicago. The decision awarding the win to Rodak was hotly disputed by Efrati and his manager, and it has been speculated that if the Italian-born fighter and resident of Chicago had won, he would not have been deported to

Italy and sent to Auschwitz by the Nazis, where he was murdered in 1944. He was inducted into the Jewish Sports Hall of Fame in 2000. Kid Francis, whose birth name was Francesco Buonaugurio, was born in Naples in 1907. He appeared on the cover of *Ring Magazine* in 1931 and was known for his appreciation of classical literature, especially the writings of Ovid. At a slim but muscular 5'4" and having fought well in 135 bouts, he was a dominant figure in the bantamweight division. When the Nazis conquered France, the Kid, who was living in Marseilles at the time, was captured and sent to Auschwitz, where he was murdered in 1943.

Those who survived and were strong enough for hard manual labor were woken each day at 4 a.m. They were given a watery breakfast, marched outside, and told to get to work. Those who did not work fast enough received a few lashes of a whip or strikes from a wooden cane or pounding from a rubber hose. As long as Arouch kept winning, he had the privileged position of a clerk. He could see the other prisoners suffering during the day and marched back to their barracks at nightfall. If Arouch was assigned to kitchen duty, he would smuggle morsels of bread for those who slept near him. They gratefully gobbled whatever crumbs Arouch was able to give them. Those slave laborers, during the bitter coldness of winter, wearing nothing but pajamas or rags, often developed frostbite on their fingers and toes and so became candidates for death. Even some of the older boxers were sent to the gas chambers to make room for younger boxers who had recently arrived at the camp. The turnover from the death of overworked inmates and the arrival of new inmates meant a continuing high level of productivity, and the Nazis were, if nothing else, devotees of high levels of productivity. The moving assembly line for maximizing the production of cars has been attributed to Henry Ford (a hero of the Nazis and the only American celebrated in *Mein Kampf*), but the assembly line for maximizing the use and disposal of human lives was purely a Nazi phenomenon.

Life was so grim and desolation so widespread that for many of the inmates death was preferable to days of torturous existence. For still others, there was the desperate hope of escape. One night Arouch was invited to join a team of ten inmates who were planning to escape. The ten inmates, some of whom were boxers, decided they would rather attempt an escape than end up killed like unproductive and useless farm animals. Arouch thought it over and decided he had a better chance of survival as long as he could continue winning his boxing matches. He declined to go but wished his fellow inmates success. The ten managed to breach the gates and escape into nearby surroundings. The SS were soon aware of the escape, alarms were sounded, searchlights were directed along the perimeter of the camp, and guards with trained German shepherds were sent out to search for the escapees. The dogs barked as their handlers ran toward where the escaped men were hiding or running. The escapees knew what awaited them if they were captured. They split up, each man taking a different route. It was useless. They failed to elude their captors, and they were brought back to the camp at the points of rifles and bayonets. Once on the grounds of the camp, they were beaten and stomped on. Their bloodied bodies, still alive, were given over to hangmen who lynched them for all the inmates to see. Their bodies were left dangling until their flesh rotted and was food for insects and birds.

For still others, revolt against the guards was their only option. A number of Jews, upon arriving at Auschwitz-Birkenau, had been forced into the *Sonderkommandos* (Special Commandos—a word euphemistically used to disguise the actual work of the disposal units). The job of the *Sonderkommandos* was to dispose of the bodies of those who had been gassed and incinerated. The members of the *Sonderkommandos* were forced to do as they were ordered on pain of death. On October 7, 1944, they revolted and attacked Nazi concentration camp guards.

> It was an enterprise of supreme hazard, and of supreme courage. . . . More than three hundred Greek Jews were among the Sonderkommando preparing for revolt, among them Errera de Larissa, a former lieutenant in the Greek Army. . . . Some of the Sonderkommando at Crematorium IV attacked the SS so viciously with axes, picks, and crowbars that several SS men sought cover behind the barbed-wire fence, shooting at the prisoners with their pistols. . . . The arrival of SS reinforcements on motorcycles, from the SS barracks inside Birkenau, brought the revolt at Crematorium IV to an end. All those who had taken up weapons, and all who had set fire to the crematorium roof were machine gunned.[4]

Though all the inmates who revolted were killed, they managed to take twenty guards with them to their graves. The Jews had also succeeded in blowing up the crematorium, a accomplishment for which they were honored after the war.

Bob Young, director of *Triumph of the Spirit*, told me that he spent three months at Auschwitz during the filming. While he was able to imagine the desolation and cruelty endured by the inmates, it was nothing compared to what the inmates actually had to endure. "It can only be imagined," he said.[5]

Liberation from the hellish camp could not have come too soon. While Auschwitz was liberated on January 24, 1945, by Soviet Union soldiers of the First Army of the Ukrainian Front commanded by Marshall Koniev, Arouch was not among those liberated, for he had been transferred to Bergen-Belsen on January 17. He had to wait until April 15, 1945, to be liberated by British troops. Arouch was lucky to still be alive: more than fifty thousand inmates had died at the camp. Because Arouch's life as an inmate had consisted of boxing to stay alive, it was not a habit easily broken. Arouch asked British officers if they knew of any boxers who might like to fight in an exhibition for the entertainment of the liberating troops. Two boxers were found, and in quick succession Arouch knocked out each one.

The allies were appalled by what the SS had engineered at Bergen-Belsen, and those in charge were put on trial. In the autumn of 1945, the British military established a tribunal in Luneburg, where 48 guards—37 of whom were members of the SS, and 11 others—were charged with war crimes. The camp commander, Josef Kramer, and 11 others were found guilty and sentenced to death. The executions were carried out on December 12, 1945. Of the other defendants, 19 were sentenced to prison and 14 were acquitted.

Arouch had had enough of Europe. While many had resisted the Nazis, many more turned a blind eye to their atrocities or were conveniently complicit in their activities. Many camp inmates, after being confined to displaced person camps, washed their hands of Europe and sailed to either the United States or to Palestine, where they desperately fought to have a Jewish homeland that would protect them from future holocausts.

In Israel, Arouch met and married another Bergen-Belsen camp survivor, seventeen-year-old Marta Yechiel, who had also been a citizen of Salonica. The couple had four children. Settled in Tel Aviv in the soon to be recognized state of Israel, Arouch enlisted in the Israeli Defense Forces and ferociously fought to establish a homeland for himself, his family, and all those who had survived the Holocaust. He fought as hard as he had for his survival at Auschwitz. He was determined that he and his family would prosper. He fought again in the Six-Day War. As a civilian, he managed a shipping and moving company and agreed to one last boxing match. On June 8, 1955, he entered the ring in Tel Aviv to fight Italy's Amleto Falcinelli. Arouch was knocked out in the 4th round. The need to punch his way out of a death sentence had left him years earlier. He was now a free man, no longer fighting just to survive. His long and heroic life ended at age eighty-six on April 26, 2009, following a stroke.

# 6

# Sinto into the Ring

He came into the ring, his hair dyed blond, his body covered with white powder. Who was this outrageous boxer? Was he trying to mock the world of boxing? Was he mocking the Aryan ideal of a blond warrior? The Nazis in the audience jeered and laughed. Was this man supposed to be a worthy contender for a title? He was a clown, better suited to the circus than to the boxing ring. That's what the Nazi sports establishment thought. Later they simply regarded him as a mongrel, worthy of no more than sterilization or extermination.

He was Johann Trollmann, a young boxer who would be derogatorily known as the "Gypsy in the Ring." His family called him Rukeli, but schoolmasters gave him the name Johann for it was a Germanic name, and if the boy wanted to attend school with German youth he would have to assimilate into German culture. Nevertheless, he was derided as a *Zigeuner* (Gypsy). *Zigeuner* derives from Greek and means untouchable. Gypsies were considered untouchable due to their alleged criminality, lack of national loyalty, unhygienic way of living, and non-adherence to civilized standards of morality.

Trollmann was born in a bar on December 27, 1907, near Hannover, Germany. He was one of nine children in a Sinti family, all of whom lived in an apartment without running water and plagued by mice and insects. The family shared outhouses with numerous other families. Each outhouse toilet had a hole in the ground bordered by wooden planks. All of the family's food was cooked in one large ceramic pot. To support themselves, the Trollmann family did manual work on farms: harvesting crops, planting seeds, caring for animals, shoveling manure out of barn stalls, doing minor carpentry repairs, and so forth. They moved from farm to farm, often in caravans.

As a member of a class stereotyped as deracinated, untrustworthy Gypsies, the Trollmanns were thought to be prone to low-level crimes and minor cons. In folk tales, Gypsies were often presented as kidnappers who would either demand money for the release of captive children, sell the children to circuses or farm owners, or put them to work as slave laborers. While many people use the word "Gypsy" to refer to vagabonds or other unsettled groups of people, the word is considered pejorative by those to whom it is applied. The more accurate term would be either "Sinti" or "Roma." The Sinti migrated to Germany from India in the late fifteenth century and spoke a language that was part German and part Romani. They settled in Germany, Austria, and Switzerland. There were offshoots in France and northern Italy. From the times of their various arrivals, restrictions were imposed on them. In many cases, governments encouraged them to leave. Nobody wanted them. The Sinti were the largest of the so-called Gypsy groups in Germany. As a male Sinti, Trollmann was known as a Sinto. In Austria, the largest Gypsy group was the Roma.

Author Sybil Milton writes,

> Although the Sinti and Roma minority in Germany and Austria represented less than one percent of the general population—a maximum of 35,000 in Germany and a maximum of 11,000 in Austria, they were stigmatized by the Nazi government and majority society as nomadic, socially marginal, economically unproductive, sexually licentious, criminally "inclined," and racially inferior. . . . [The Nazis] defined Sinti and Roma as social outsiders, thereby facilitating their persecution by health, welfare, and police bureaucracies, and finally, providing the rationale for their exclusion, concentration, and annihilation.[1]

As a member of this marginalized and distrusted minority, Johann Rukeli Trollmann was treated as an alien, a non-citizen who should not be permitted in Germanic society. He looked different than the other kids in his class. He was swarthy and had long, dark, curly hair. Children can be cruel to those who are different from their own perceived view of normality. And far as Trollmann's classmates were concerned, he deserved to be ostracized, bullied, and held in contempt. He was not a submissive boy and so would not tolerate being the target of abuse. His illiterate father decided that Rukeli should learn the manly art of self-defense. At the age of eight, he was sent, along with a friend who was already taking boxing lessons, to the Schaufelder Street Sports Center to learn how to box.

Jud Nirenberg writes in his biography of Trollmann,

Rukeli was eight years old when he visited a boxing hall for the first time. A friend brought him to look around the local school's sports hall, where the friend had been training for a few weeks. Boxing was illegal, partly because many saw it as a foreign import, something English. And England, so few years after the Great War, was no friend. The few who boxed in Germany were the well traveled; sailors, traders, soldiers who had picked it up as prisoners of war. For a boy like Rukeli, there was something glamorous in it. It was illegal and associated with rough types but here it was, this enticing, forbidden fruit and a chance to prove who was toughest.[2]

After minimal training, Trollmann entered the ring to box an older boy who had been training at the gym long before Trollmann entered it. Trollmann, as expected, lost his first fight against that older boy and suffered a bloody nose. While many boys would have called it quits at that point, Trollmann was smitten. He loved boxing. It made him feel as if he could be in control of his life. And he soon began displaying some of his natural talent: his fists would fly with a rapidity and accuracy that impressed all those he faced. In addition, he was able to use his fast footwork to evade the punches of his opponents, then quickly darting in close to deliver a series of devastating combinations of blows. By the time he was nine, he had won three fights. The other boys at the gym, none of whom were Sinti, initially smirked at the skinny little swarthy kid who thought he could box. Now, whenever he walloped an opponent, they cheered him on, patting him on the back as he left the ring. No longer did Trollmann feel like an outcast.

By 1925 he had acquired a trainer named Karl Leyendecker, a fighter pilot in World War I who had been wounded and who had the gravitas and mien of a proud warrior. The boys in the gym idolized him and faithfully enacted his every instruction. His hours-long training sessions were rigorous but his students never complained. The few who considered the training too onerous just quietly left the gym. Not Trollmann.

Nirenberg writes that Leyendecker

> noticed Johann Trollmann right away and kept a careful eye on him during sparring. When Rukeli had a fight, the trainer liked to go along to stay in his corner, and to carry his spit bucket. He chastised Rukeli at times, especially for not keeping his fists up where they could best protect his face yet there was no missing the student's discipline, his willingness to do as instructed or his raw talent.[3]

Leyendecker, who was not a by-the-book pedagogue, never stood in the way of Trollmann developing his own style, and it was a unique one. It was a style of bobbing and weaving, of fast footwork, of darting in and darting out that would distinguish such later pugilists as Sugar Ray Robinson and Muhammad Ali. In Germany during the Nazi era, boxers were supposed to stand their ground as if glued in place and trade punches with their opponent. They were like pugilistic automatons though they did not have to goose-step into the ring.

By age eighteen, Trollmann had become a local district champ and was earning more money than his father. Soon thereafter, Trollmann joined the boxing section of the Hannover Workers Sports Club that was run by socialists and communists, who had no prejudice against Jewish and Sinti boxers. They were such ardent anti-nationalists that they refused to sing the German national anthem and disdained the awarding and wearing of medals that indicated superiority in a sport. They believed that sports were for everyone to enjoy. While there, Trollmann proved himself to be one of the most clever and adept amateur boxers in Germany.

He decided that his amateur days should be put behind him. He could earn a lot more money and fame if he turned professional. In 1929 he signed a contract to be managed by Ernst Zirzow of Berlin, a clever ring promoter and savvy negotiator. In addition, Trollmann agreed to be trained by the finest boxer in Germany, Erich Seelig, a Jew, who at various times was the middleweight and light heavyweight champion and who later was forced to leave Germany with the barrel of a Gestapo Luger pressed against his forehead. Zirzow signed Trollmann up for one fight after another, often as frequently as one a month. From 1929 through 1932, fans could watch Trollmann take on and defeat the best regional boxers in Germany.

In 1928 he thought he was good enough to participate in the Amsterdam Summer Olympics, but as a Sinti who danced around the ring, he was not seen as a real German who boxed in a traditional German style. Trollmann was deeply disappointed by his country's rejection of him but thought he could make up for the snub by defeating any boxer willing to enter the ring and face him. He would prove himself to all of Germany just as he had proven himself as a young boy in the boxing gym. Though the German Olympic Committee never spoke of its mistake in not permitting Trollmann to represent Germany, members of the committee often came to watch him fight. They watched as he won bout after bout, and Trollmann made a point of beating those who had represented his country at the Olympics. It wasn't only the usual boxing fans who came to watch the new star of the ring box: His dark good looks, long curly black hair, muscular athletic physique, and dancer-like movements in the ring made him popular with women too. Trollmann, a romantic opportunist, dated and bedded a number of his female fans. They turned out in droves for his fights the way later generations would flock to attend the concerts of their favorite rock musicians.

In 1933 a new and dangerous opportunity arrived for Trollmann. It was the year that Hitler came to power, and anti-Jewish rules were changing German society, especially in boxing. Seelig was the reigning middleweight champion and light heavyweight champ. On November 12, 1931, he had won the German middleweight title by defeating Hans Seifried. Then on February 26, 1933, he went on to win the German light-heavyweight title by defeating Helmut Hartkopp. Yet he could not remain in Germany to enjoy the benefits that accrued to champions. The Nazi-controlled German Athletic Commission warned Seelig that if he tried to defend his titles, he would be killed. The commission then stripped him of his titles. At the point of a gun, he and his parents left Germany for France, where Seelig had several fights before leaving for America via Cuba. In Paris in 1934, he had lost an opportunity to win the European middleweight title in a bout with Gustave Roth. Once in America, he proceeded to have one fight after another, defeating former champion Mickey Walker and going on to fight the talented Billy Conn. By the end of his career in 1940, Seelig had compiled a record of 40 victories, 7 draws, and 10 losses. His German titles were never restored.

Into this vacuum stepped Trollmann, eager to win the title and thumb his nose at the Olympic authorities who had denied him the opportunity to represent his country. His opponent would be Adolf Witt (aka, Vit), who was a favorite of the Nazis, who regarded him as a perfect Aryan specimen. The fight, however, turned out not to be what the Nazis had expected: Trollmann, ever fleet of foot, danced around his frustrated opponent, who delivered uppercuts and hooks to the air. Trollmann laughed at the swish-swish of Witt's gloves passing before his face. Trollmann, with his fists as fast and fleeting as stinging wasps on an attack, dropped Witt six times, knocking him about the ring as if he were a child's plastic blowup dummy. One could have said of him as boxing fans said of Muhammad Ali that he "floated like a butterfly and stung like a bee."

Those not consumed by prejudice cheered Trollmann's skill and whooped their approval whenever he landed a lightning combination of punches. Another contingent in the audience was not at all happy; they let their anger erupt in loud boos. They were Nazis who regarded Trollmann's demonstration of pugilistic pyrotechnics as not in the German tradition of flat-footed, stand-your-ground boxing.

Their anger was apparent in the faces of the Nazi ring judges; they attempted to end the fight after the 6th round. The destruction of the Aryan Witt was a symbolic disaster, something that the Nazis could not permit.[4] The Nazis attempted to end the fight without declaring a winner. They wanted the fight immediately cancelled, erased from the history books as if it had never taken place. There was outrage among Trollmann's fans as well as among those who regarded the cancellation of the bout as a denial of reality. The crowd forced the judges to rescind their decision and award the light-heavyweight title to Trollmann, who bowed his head and wept after the judges handed him his championship belt. The Nazis went home fuming; they could not permit a "Gypsy" to beat an Aryan, just as they could not let the expelled Jew, Erich Seelig, remain a champion. The undoing of Johann Trollmann's title began a week after his fight. The German Pugilism Association, chaired by a viciously racist Nazi named Georg Radamm, told the German public that Trollmann had demonstrated an un-German style of boxing that was an insult to Germanic tradition. Therefore Radamm stripped Trollmann of his light-heavyweight title, letting the fighter know that he wasn't entitled to be called a German pugilist.

Less than two months passed, and Trollmann was permitted to fight again. He lost weight so that he could enter the bout as a welterweight. To ensure that Trollmann did not win, he was also told that he had to fight in the German style: no fancy footwork, no bobbing and weaving, no darting in and darting out. Just stand in place and trade punches with his opponent. To further guarantee the outcome, Trollmann was told that his loss would spare his life. His opponent would be a notoriously effective brawler named Gustav Eder (aka, Iron Gustav). On July 27 1933, the two fighters would meet at the Bock *Brauerei* (Brewery) in Berlin. The two men were both 25 years old. Eder had won 32 of 49 bouts, 13 by knockouts. Trollmann had won 30 of 53 bouts, 11 by knockouts. The fight was scheduled for ten rounds. Eder was slightly shorter and lighter than Trollmann, and some thought Trollmann had an advantage for those reasons. Even without the racial laws that favored Eder, he would have been a tough opponent for Trollmann. Eder had been celebrated as the welterweight champion of Germany for all but a few months during a career that spanned twenty-one years. He lost his first attempt at the European welterweight title to Belgian Gustav Roth in 1931 then won the German welterweight title against Jupp Besselmann in 1933. He successfully defended the German title numerous times. He went on to win the European welterweight title in 1934 when he knocked out Nestor

Charlier. He then lost the title to another Belgian fighter, Felix Wout-ers, in 1938 but won the German welterweight title against Alex Hus-ditsch in 1939. He lost the German title to Dietrich Hucks in 1947, then won it back four months later in a bout with Alois Ulderich. By the end of his career, he was considered one of the top ten German fighters of the twentieth century.

Trollmann, with the mind of a nose-thumbing satirist, decided to enter the ring as a parody of an Aryan warrior. He dyed his hair a pale blond and covered his body in white powder. The crowd, even the Nazis among them, howled with laughter. And to demonstrate that he was not fearful of fighting by standard Nazi rules of comportment, Trollmann stood still and traded punches with his opponent. Unable to evade the stinging blows directed at him, Trollmann suffered a bloody, broken nose and puffed swollen eyes. Blood mixed with the white powder to create a gooey, sanguinary ointment that oozed over his face and dripped onto his chest and shoulders. Yet Eder also suf-fered from Trollmann's powerful blows and his face was as bloody as a slab of raw beef. Though Trollmann delivered numerous powerful blows, he was not able to put Eder away. The two continued trading punches. Trollmann was sent to the canvas twice, but sprung up with the tenacity of a terrier. He was finally knocked out in the 5th round by a pair of rapid shots to his head.

Though he had made a satiric physical statement on Nazi racial policies, he was never again able to obtain a title fight in any weight division, for the boxing commission informed him that a "Gypsy" would never again be allowed to fight for a championship. The spirit of a rebellious warrior had been blown away by a hurricane of racial politics. Yet Trollmann continued to box in sanctioned and unsanc-tioned bouts, primarily for the money. The sanctioned matches were small regional ones that drew little or no media attention. Trollmann boxed because it was his profession. He had no other skills for earning a living.

He displayed his usual pyrotechnical skills in nine professional fights. The small crowds cheered him on, but he fought like one who knew his glory days were well behind him. Whenever the boxing au-thorities learned of one of his upcoming matches, they forced him to be a human punching bag. He collected his money then went into the night like a stray dog that had been kicked out of one warm shelter after another. Finally the boxing commission revoked his license to box, flinging him onto the garbage heap of failed dreams. Every time he attempted to arrange to get back in the ring, he was threatened with death. He did manage to fight at a few regional country fairs, but the money he earned was meager. It wasn't enough to live on. Fed up and disgusted by the restrictions placed on him, he threw away his boxing gloves. It was two years into the life of the Third Reich, and Trollmann knew that he would never again get a shot at wearing a championship belt. He became an itinerant farm worker, and it provided his only source of income.

The racial vilification that he and other Sinti experienced poisoned their existence. There was no escape from it. Trollmann existed in a dreary dystopia. Though his ambition to be a championship boxer had been suffocated, Trollmann found alternative happiness when he fell in love with eighteen-year-old Olga Bilda, a German girl who tried to look like a typical Aryan by dyeing her hair blonde. However, once again Nazi law would put its jackboot on the neck of Trollmann's happiness: six months after the wedding, Nazi law declared that "Gypsies" could not marry Germans. Trollmann attempted to bypass the law by evading its enforcers. He and his wife moved from address to address, never leaving a forwarding address. In March 1935, Olga gave birth to a baby girl that the couple named Rita Edith. The daughter, as a half Sinti, was vulnerable to being a victim of the Nuremberg racial laws. With a baby to care for, it was difficult to move from address to address. So to protect his wife and daughter from being sent to a concentration camp, Trollmann divorced Olga in 1938. Trollmann hoped that without his daughter's Sinti father in the family picture, Rita would be safe. However, when he subsequently learned that the Nazis regarded mixed race Sintis as more of a threat to their ideas of racial purity than pureblooded Sintis, he grew increasingly anxious about Rita's safety. Perhaps Olga could hide the fact that Rita's father was a Sinti.

Unfortunately, Trollmann was still well known. Try as he did, he could not successfully hide in the shadows of anonymity. People recognized him. They would ask for his autograph. His popularity did not go unnoticed by the Gestapo, and he was soon arrested and sent to a labor camp. Then he was unexpectedly released. Feeling lonely and defeated, feeling as if his freedom was hanging by a withering string, he settled for an anonymous living as a factory worker and an occasional bartender. However, bar patrons would occasionally recognize him. Those who were drunk and feeling mean and inspired would challenge him to a fight. It unnerved Trollmann that he was still being recognized. He had thought that his fame had faded and that boxing fans were focused on the new stars of the ring. When recognized, he would deny his identity, but sometimes he would be drawn into a fight by the opportunity to earn a small sum of money. In every case, he left his challengers on a dirty, beer-stained floor or on the dirt of a darkened alley, their face bruised and swollen from his rapid-fire blows. Such fights never lasted more than a few minutes. When rubbing his knuckles after a fight, Trollmann would look around, half expecting to see a pair of Gestapo agents ready to arrest him. Then he would move on to another bar and hide in a friend's home until he felt safe. His actions were like those of a criminal hobo never venturing into the light of day. Yet he knew that his opportunities to remain free were shrinking, and he figured that sooner or later the Gestapo would clamp a pair of cuffs on his wrists and haul him off to prison.

Being a Sinti, Trollmann was living in a cage that got smaller day by day. Restrictions increased and in 1938, the "Gypsy Office" in Hannover told the Sinti they had a choice: either be sterilized or be interned in a concentration camp. About 10 percent of the Sinti population, including Trollmann, opted for sterilization, while others hoped that they could evade detainment in the camps. Nevertheless, many were rounded up and sent to a camp at Altwarmbuchener Moor. The SS decreed that each pure Sinti had to carry a brown identity card at all times, while each mixed-race Sinti had to carry a blue ID card.

On October 17, 1939, Reinhard Heydrich issued an order (*Festsetzungserlab*) prohibiting all mixed-race "Gypsies" and pure "Gypsies" from moving from their residences; in addition, their addresses had to be registered with the Gestapo. This was an essential form of census for maintaining the addresses of all Sinti so that they could be quickly identified and deported to concentration camps. While Sinti were being prepared for deportation, the German military saw no reason not to use Sinti and Roma as cannon fodder. In 1939, no longer able to maintain his anonymity and evade conscription, Trollmann was drafted into a *Wehrmacht* rifle company and sent to fight first in Poland, then Belgium and France, and finally on the Eastern Front, where he was wounded. He was permitted to go home for a brief furlough and recuperate from his wounds. Yet while he was fighting and nearly dying for the Third Reich, other Sinti were regularly being sent off to concentration camps in Germany and Austria. Others were being murdered in the infamous Chelmno extermination camp. No matter how bravely Sinti and Roma soldiers fought for the Reich, they were all dishonorably discharged from the military in 1942. Trollmann awaited his fate with deep foreboding.

Oddly, the military did not officially discharge Trollmann because he was a Sinti; rather, they pronounced him dishonorably discharged because he had been wounded. It was as if they were saying because you were wounded you did not fight bravely enough and are no longer of use to us. Soon thereafter he was arrested by the Gestapo and sent to the Neuengamme concentration camp. There he again attempted to hide his identity, but the commandant, a former boxing referee, recognized him. He assigned Trollmann the job of training the guards to box. Trollmann had to undertake the training sessions at night after working twelve hours a day in one of the 150 SS–owned factories or in the camp's farm fields where vegetables were grown. If he were seen stealing vegetables, he would have been quickly shot, no questions asked. At the end of his twelve-hour shifts, he was exhausted and hungry, for the slave laborers were given far fewer calories than they burned during the day. Some soup and rotten potatoes did not make for a healthful diet.

At night, while training the guards to box, Trollmann was like a worn-out, heavy bag, not moving, just standing there and absorbing punch after punch. By the time he returned to his barrack, he was bruised over much of his body. His only rewards were a few additional scraps of food and a slice of bread. He managed to share his meager allotment with several other starving slave laborers. Though he was given more food than his fellow inmates, it was not enough to maintain his weight and health. He was emaciated, and his condition rapidly deteriorated, yet he continued to endure the punishing blows of the sadistic guards. His friends were worried about his worsening appearance, the bruises and cuts on his torso and face that never had a chance to heal. Trollmann's friends in the barrack decided that Trollmann would not live much longer if he continued to be pummeled night after night. Led by a communist resistance leader named André Mandryxcs, the inmates agreed to fake Trollmann's death and arrange for him to be sent to another labor camp. They exchanged his uniform with that of a dead inmate and alerted the camp doctor that Trollmann had died. He was listed as dead on February 9, 1944. The body of the dead inmate was quickly cremated and buried, and it was fortunate for Trollmann that the commandant never asked to see it. Typical of the SS's scrupulous need to balance its books and maintain its usual parsimony, it billed the Trollmann family for the cost of the cremation and funeral.

Meanwhile, Mandryxcs managed to provide Trollmann with a new identity and mysteriously had him transferred to the nearby camp of Wittenberge. Relieved, Trollmann arrived at the camp believing that his ersatz identity would keep him from having to train more guards how to box. He was not to be so lucky. Before he could adjust to the new rules and brutal conditions of the camp, he was recognized by a notoriously vicious kapo and hardened professional criminal named

Emil Cornelius. Trollmann had lost sixty pounds since his incarceration. He looked like a skeleton wrapped in a sheath of sickly pale skin marked by bruises and cuts. His expression was that of a desperate and frightened feral dog, one that has been repeatedly kicked and beaten. That Cornelius recognized him surprised Trollmann; he was hardly the fit boxing star who had dazzled fans just a few years earlier. To the Nazis, Trollmann was just another slave laborer, a commodity, whose only ID was his prison number, 9841. For Cornelius, however, Trollmann represented an opportunity to pick on someone who was once thought invincible and was now a defeated wreck of a man. Cornelius took sadistic pleasure in hitting Trollmann with a club or a section of rubber hose. Each blow proved to Cornelius his own strength and Trollmann's weakness and submission to a stronger man.

When the inmates learned of Trollmann's identity and saw Cornelius's mistreatment of him, they managed to talk the kapo into having a boxing match with Trollmann. They organized a match that would be widely attended for everyone wanted to see the former star of the ring. Was he still the old "Gypsy in the Ring?" The camp's guards attended, and when they got a look at Trollmann, they bet on Cornelius to win. The inmates had no money to bet, but they wanted to see Trollmann beat the hated kapo. Though tired and in obviously bad shape, Trollmann called upon his old ring skills, and with a sense of vengeance for the beatings that Cornelius had administered, Trollmann managed to land hard punches on the kapo's face and skull. Trollmann continuously danced around the confused kapo, darting in, landing punch after punch, then darting away as Cornelius swung wildly at a phantom. Cornelius did not land a single blow. The inmates cheered Trollmann's ring technique and marveled at his ability to dash out of the range of Cornelius. That a man so beaten down and emaciated could put up such a remarkable fight won him the plaudits of his fellow inmates. The guards, meanwhile, screamed and cursed at Cornelius. In a final display of skill, Trollmann knocked out the humiliated kapo, who flopped to the ground like a dying fish out of water. He lay there for several minutes then raised himself from his supine position and with one hand wiped blood from his mouth and nose. His eyes raged with vengeance.

His humiliation would not go unanswered. For the next few days, Cornelius proceeded to assign Trollmann to back-breaking work and denied him food. When Trollmann didn't move fast enough, Cornelius whacked him with a club. Then in a fit of rage, he rushed at Trollmann from behind and hit him on the head with a club. Again and again, he brought the club down on Trollmann's bleeding skull. Trollmann collapsed. He was no longer breathing. It was obvious that he was dead. Cornelius reported the death as an accident and threatened a witness with death if he revealed what had happened to the SS. But the SS did not care. Trollmann was just another dead Sinti. He would soon be replaced by another slave laborer. After all, each slave laborer eventually succumbed to malnutrition or disease and was replaced by a relatively healthy specimen who would also deteriorate, die, and be replaced.

Trollmann was thirty-six years old when he died. As a younger man, he thought he would be the most celebrated boxer in Germany, perhaps in all of Europe. At some point, he dreamed of even being a world champion who would beat challengers not only in Europe, but also in North and South America.

In 2003, seventy years after he had become a German champion and then was stripped of the light-heavyweight title, he was officially recognized by the German Boxing Federation as the 1933 Light Heavyweight Champion. His surviving relatives received his championship belt. In 2010, a temporary monument was erected in Berlin's Viktoria Park to commemorate Trollmann's achievement as a boxer and mourn his death, though there were very few who remembered him or had seen his fleeting victories. The monument was an exact replica in concrete of a boxing ring. Like Trollmann's title, it was soon removed. Trollmann had fought heroically, both as a free man and as an inmate of a concentration camp. He had an innate dignity that the Nazis were not able to quell even when he satirically appeared in the ring as an ersatz Aryan. To the end, he was another Holocaust hero. In 2016, the Nobel Prize–winning author Dario Fo published *Razza di zingaro*, a novel based on the life of Trollmann.

## 7

# Harry Haft: Contender

Before his grueling time as a concentration camp boxer, the young Harry Haft was tortured by a sadistic Nazi. The Nazi grabbed one of Haft's hands, placed it on the jamb of a doorway, then slammed the door against the young man's hand. All five fingers broke like pretzels. He screamed in pain and stared at his hand gloved in blood. His knuckles and fingers never healed correctly. And then, years later, for $200 he was given a chance to fight the future undefeated world heavyweight champion Rocky Marciano. Had he won, it would have been a stunning victory, placing him on the road to being a big name in boxing, a possible contender for a shot at the heavyweight or light heavyweight title. But according to a bitter and traumatized Harry Haft, he was ordered to take a dive. If he didn't he would be killed. And so the young man who had survived the concentration camps where he had been forced to fight other Jews saw his boxing career end in defeat. The SS had not been able to defeat him, but the Mafia did.

Harry Haft was born on July 28, 1925, in Belchatow, Poland. He was fourteen years old when the Nazis invaded his country. Because he was a Jew, his days of freedom were limited. Yet he made the most of his life. He was as clever as a hunted urban coyote, avoiding the clutches of the Gestapo while managing to feed himself and his fatherless family (his father had died when Harry was three years old). He became a successful smuggler, a dealer in contraband. He stole what was not nailed down and then traded or sold it for food and clothing. He was a Jewish Artful Dodger with a double price on his head: one for being a Jew and the other for being a thief. His career as a minor criminal came to an end when he was finally arrested in 1942.

Rather than being tossed in a jail cell, Haft was compelled to work in a cement factory that was part of Auschwitz. He was one of many Jews forced into slave labor, beaten, cursed, and given starvation rations of barely edible food. Yet he had a strong will to survive; he would not let the Nazis destroy him. He used his smuggling skills to stay alive, bribing his way to better treatment with stolen commodities. In his biography of his father, Alan Scott Haft writes,

> Harry made his way easily to the middle of a large freight train and crouched underneath a sealed boxcar. He picked up a piece of scrap metal and used it to pry open the lock. Then he slid open the door just enough to see what good fortune lay inside. The boxcar was full of tobacco products. He quickly chose to take a case of cigars rather than cigarettes. He pulled the door shut, secured the lock, and concealed the case as he walked back to the construction site.[1]

Haft turned his treasure of cigars into currency that was used to bribe a guard named Naparella, who was the foreman of the construction crew to which Haft had been assigned. The guard had Haft place the box of cigars in the trunk of his car and drove both of them to the town of Poznan, where the guard had three girlfriends, each of whom helped to stash all that Haft was able to steal. Prior to the theft, Naparella had been minimally friendly to Haft. Now he became become Haft's protector, a fellow thief and a fence.

For weeks Haft continued to enjoy privileges denied to others, but his privileged position would not last long. As a Jew he was designated for extermination. So he was packed into an overcrowded bus and shipped from the cement factory to Auschwitz, where his arm was tattooed with the number 144739. There Haft was thrown together with an old friend named Schlemek. They were assigned to take the bodies of Jews who had been gassed and heave them like garbage into ovens to be incinerated. Alan Scott Haft writes,

> Harry tried not to look at the faces of the dead, but he could not help it. It took two men to toss an adult into the fire, but Harry was expected to handle the bodies of children on his own.
>
>   Harry and Schlemek were directed by the guards to throw [a fellow worker's] body into the fire. Harry grabbed the legs and Schlemek the shoulders, and just before they heaved forward, Harry caught sight of the man's face. His eyes were open; he was not dead. Next, they reached for the man's wife and threw her in beside him.[2]

The SS guards took note of Haft's muscular physique. They thought he could be of more profitable use and so relocated him from the crematoriums to the coal mines, where he encountered a former thief and smuggler, now an SS guard, named Schneider. They had previously stolen diamonds, and Schneider decided that they should forge a new and mutually advantageous relationship. Schneider, thinking of what might be in store for him if Germany lost the war, decided that Haft could serve as a postwar witness to testify that Schneider had not been a war criminal. In return for his future testimony, Haft would receive sausages, chocolate, and whiskey. But the relationship had another dimension, which was presented to Haft a few days after it had begun: "You are going to entertain my friends the other officers and soldiers. You are going to be a boxer, and on Sundays you will fight. Next Sunday, we will hold boxing matches in the street in front of the officers' quarters."[3]

Haft would have to engage in bare-knuckle brawls with other prisoners. The winner would receive extra rations. The bouts would end when one fighter could no longer continue fighting. A makeshift ring of four posts connected by ropes was set up in front of the officers' quarters. There were three rows of seats surrounding the ring. A band of Jewish prisoner-musicians with string instruments would provide the musical accompaniment for the pounding of fists and the flow of blood. The SS assembled amidst much joking, laughter, and imbibing of whiskey. Haft's first opponent was a skeletal, half-starved creature who had been yanked from his barrack to be beaten for the entertainment of the officers. The man's eyes were large with fear. His large bony hands trembled. He looked as if a single punch might kill him. Haft felt sorry for the man and initially tried to spare him the effects of a beating. He delivered less than killer punches. But that wasn't what the audience bellowed for: "Kill the little Jew bastard, kill him." They shouted for the men to fight like tigers, not pussycats. They howled for blood. They hurled anti-Semitic tropes like grenades. Haft was finally told by Schneider to finish off his opponent or suffer the consequences. The consequences were enumerated: kill or be killed. Haft quickly knocked out his opponent, who was carried from the ring. Haft beat five other men that night, knowing that the more brutal his attacks, the louder the guards' cheers. If he didn't satisfy their thirst for blood, they would demand his blood, Schneider continued to warn him. Fight to the death if you want to live. The SS rewarded Haft's brutality by nicknaming him "the Jew Animal."

The Jew Animal's reputation spread beyond the camp, and generals and other high-ranking officers wanted to see the renowned Jewish gladiator pummel Jewish opponents into bloody unconscious submission or be killed trying. This was sport not seen since the days of the

Roman Coliseum, and the SS officers loved it. They then decided to heighten the excitement: rather than watch Haft fight skeletal opponents, the Nazis arranged for a more evenly matched bout during which even more blood than usual might flow. Haft at 5'9" would tangle with a 6'3" unbeaten Jewish-French fighter, a favorite of the Nazi generals. The generals brought their man to the camp in a limousine. The fight would consist of three-minute rounds and would go on until one man could no longer fight.

Haft was not a trained pugilist. He had seen the typical German boxer, stand in the ring and trade punches, toe to toe, with an opponent. Haft imitated what he saw. The Frenchman, however, was a trained boxer. He could dance around the ring, darting in to land a punch then darting out to avoid being hit. Haft stood in the center of the ring and yelled at his opponent to meet him in a face-to-face fight. The Frenchman did not oblige. He darted in, pounded Haft's nose and eyes with a series of powerful jabs and combinations, then darted out of the range of Haft's fists. The skin around Haft's eyes was bruised and swollen, the lids nearly closed. Cuts were soon opened around Haft's eyes and on his lower lip; blood veiled his cheeks and chin. Realizing that he was losing the fight and perhaps his life, Haft set a trap: retreating into a corner of the ring, he all but seemed to ask the Frenchman to finish him off. The Frenchman came at Haft, delivering powerful jabs and right crosses; it looked like the end for Haft. Then with the desperate ferocity of a cornered animal, Haft threw a series of uppercuts and hooks that landed on the Frenchman's chin and head. The blows were driven with the angry force of sledgehammers. The Frenchman's head rocked from side to side, snapped backward as if on a spring. He wobbled, his eyeballs rolled up into his head like a pair of unlucky numbers in a slot machine. He thudded to the ground like a large uprooted tree. The generals cursed their fighter because they'd just lost thousands of marks to the camp's SS guards. The defeated boxer was dragged by his legs from the ring. Dirt and blood were smeared on his unconscious face. A few minutes later, several shots from a Luger pistol were heard, but that did not break the merriment and laughter of the guards.

As if his gladiatorial combat and work in a crematorium had not sufficiently traumatized Haft, he witnessed acts of such base depravity that he not only lost faith in God but also in the possibility that humanity could maintain even a sliver of decency in the face of organized genocide. In the barracks late one night, he witnessed a group of Russian prisoners approach an inmate who had fallen into a deep sleep on his bunk. One of the Russians took a cord that held up his pants, wrapped it around the neck of the startled prisoner and began to choke him. Fully awake, the prisoner grabbed for the cord as his legs thrashed about like the tail of a beached fish. He screamed for help, but soon he had no breath. He lay on his bunk dead, the cord still tightly wrapped around his neck. Now the group of Russian prisoners took out crude knives and cut slices off the dead man's buttocks. They devoured the bloody flesh with the rapaciousness of hungry wolves. Once satiated, they fell asleep with their victim's drying blood on their own faces.

The camp was hell on earth, worse than anything in Dante's *Inferno*. Haft desperately needed to escape. How could one go on living amidst such misery and sadism? He and his friend Peretz decided that they would find a way to escape at the first opportunity. That opportunity occurred as the Americans and Soviet troops were closing in on Poland and Germany. The prisoners were to be evacuated via what became known as a death march: Laggards and those too weak to trudge the long distance were shot on the spot.

As the long line of skeletal marchers in their prison rags proceeded, yelled at and periodically whipped by their SS guards, Allied bombs exploded nearby, providing a distraction and cover for an escape. As the guards and inmates scattered to avoid being blown to bits, Haft and Peretz took off running. As they approached a ditch, they were hit by flying debris from a nearby explosion; gunshots followed. The two men fell into the ditch, Peretz, a bloody mess, flopping on top of Haft. He was dead. Two SS guards approached, searching for escaped prisoners. When they saw the two bloody bodies in the ditch, one of the guards was about to fire his gun to make sure the escapees were dead but the other guard told him not to waste his ammunition on a pair of corpses. Covered by Peretz's blood, Haft breathed in the smell of death; though scared, he was glad to still be alive.

Haft lived in the forest for several days. He fed himself with roots, berries, leaves. As he wandered, he was drawn to the sound of a man singing in German. Haft spied the man bathing in a nearby river, his clothes and rifle and holstered pistol lay on the nearby shore. Haft picked up the SS soldier's rifle, pointed it at the bather, and fired. The bullet missed the astonished victim, who ran out of the river toward Haft.

Harry reached for the handgun and emptied the contents of the chamber into his target. The soldier was probably dead, but Harry was blind with rage. He battered the man's skull with the butt of the rifle until it was a bloody, pulpy stump.

The SS man had rations of food and water near the clothing, and Harry sat under the tree and nourished himself. He removed his bloody clothing and washed himself in the river. He dressed himself in the soldier's uniform, baggy on his 110-pound frame. He pulled an eye patch out of the shirt pocket and placed it on his left eye to complete the disguise. He gathered the soldier's remaining personal belongings and continued on his way.[4]

Haft made his way to a farm house, where an old couple took him in, provided food, and offered him shelter for the night. After a satisfying dinner, the couple began to interrogate Haft. His German was not that of a native. His answers to their questions were unconvincing. When the farm woman saw him getting ready for bed, she noticed that he had removed the patch from his left eye and there was no wound visible. The couple accused him of being an impersonator. Haft pulled out the pistol and shot first the farmer and then his wife. He gathered up as much food as he could carry and cautiously, but quickly, left the farmhouse.

Haft wandered for days in the forest. Finally, he came across a platoon of American soldiers. Seeing his uniform, the soldiers demanded that Haft drop his rifle and pistol. Haft, not being able to understand English, dropped his rifle and pistol, then raised his hands above his head. As the American soldiers drew near, Haft dropped to his knees and with one finger traced a Jewish star in the dirt. His eyes pleaded for understanding. Then he rolled up the sleeve of one arm and revealed the numbers that the SS had tattooed on him. Again he looked up at the faces of the soldiers and could see sympathy in their eyes. One of the American soldiers was able to converse with Haft in Yiddish. Haft could not contain himself. The hair-raising story of life in the camps, of having had to fight to survive, of his fortunate escape from the death march all poured out of Haft like rivers from a burst dam. For the first time in years, he felt safe.

It was not long afterward that Haft was placed in a displaced persons camp in Deggendorf along with thousands of other Jewish survivors of the camps. He spent much of his time thinking about what his future would be. Europe was a bloody land of murderous anti-Semites, their helpers, and those who remained silent. What Jew would want to remain there?

Haft was not trained for any profession. His only skill was that of a boxer. Might he try for a career in boxing? His question was answered when he heard of a Jewish boxing championship to be held in Munich in January 1946. Haft decided to enter the competition. He figured that he had developed sufficient pugilistic skills while in captivity. Still he knew he would have to prepare himself for bouts against men who would be spending hours each day training themselves. So he threw himself into a rigorous training regimen. At 160 pounds, he decided to fight in the light-heavyweight division but he also thought he might test himself as a heavyweight.

There were dozens of elimination bouts, and Haft proved himself a winner in all that he entered. His reputation as a fearless and fearsome pugilist spread among the American soldiers. They said that Haft had the makings of being a real champion back in the States. They were further impressed when in a period of two hours Haft knocked out both a heavyweight contender and a light-heavyweight contender. Then when it came to a final bout, Haft was told he had to chose between fighting as a light-heavyweight or a heavyweight. The heavy-weights were the more popular fighters so Haft opted to enter the ring as a heavyweight.

Haft was like a recently caged and hungry tiger released to attack and kill its prey. He trotted into the ring almost unable to wait for the first round to begin. As soon as the bell sounded, he rushed at his op-ponent, landing lefts and rights, uppercuts and hooks, again and again. Slowly but surely his opponent caved, finally collapsing in the ring. He had barely countered any of Haft's blows. In less than one minute of that first round, Haft emerged as a dynamic pugilistic force. He was voted the outstanding boxer of the tournament and received a medal from General Lucius Clay. The crowd cheered and whooped their ap-preciation.

Haft now knew he would go to the United States and become a professional boxer. A few months later, he boarded a troopship, the *Marine Marlin*, sailing from Bremerhaven, Germany, and bound for New York City. It was a city that had welcomed millions of Eastern European Jews. Through an uneventful crossing, Haft could barely wait to see his new land. On finally disembarking he reflected that neither the Gestapo nor the SS would ever again throw him into a concentration camp. He was surprised that his reputation as a boxer had preceded him, for shortly after taking up residence at a relative's home, he was the subject of a local newspaper story that informed readers that Harry Haft, a former inmate of Nazi concentration camps who had successfully fought in seventy-five boxing matches as a pris-oner and then won a postwar heavyweight championship, was now settled in the United States.

However, before Haft could embark upon his career as a profes-sional boxer, he had to unlearn the German style of toe-to-toe boxing. His career would be stillborn if he boxed flat-footed, attempting to trade punches with an opponent. Haft hired a manager, a man named Harry Mandell, who was little help in getting Haft the kind of training he needed for they didn't have the money to hire a sophisticated trainer. A few of the well-known trainers who were fixtures at Stillman's Gym in Manhattan thought Haft had potential, but none of them embraced Haft as a client. Yet they gave Haft pointers and he was able to spar in the ring with a few notable boxers. From them Haft was able to add to his skills, but he still remained a crude ring performer. Nevertheless, Mandell was able to arrange for Haft to have several fights, and he won all of them. The money he earned for the fights was just barely enough to keep a roof over his head and food on his table. He did, however, benefit from the freebies that many boxers are given.

> Mandell stopped off at the Everlast factory in the Bronx. Harry was treated to all the courtesies given to professional boxers. He was given all of his boxing equipment, headgear, shorts, gloves, robes, cups and shoes for free by Everlast for promotional purposes. The clerk asked about Harry's accent and when he heard Harry's story he had a white Star of David stitched on his purple fight trunks. The Jewish emblem on his trunks was very important to Harry, who wanted to be known as a Jewish fighter.[5]

One of the professional fighters who befriended Haft was Harold Green, a powerful welterweight and middleweight who had defeated Rocky Graziano in two fights and then was paid to lose in their third encounter. Haft was surprised to learn of the fix, and this would prove portentous for his fight with another Rocky, the bruising heavyweight slugger Rocky Marciano. Green warned Haft to be wary of the mob. As his career advanced they would attempt to get their hooks into him. Yet without the mob, Green himself had compiled an impressive record of 71 wins, 23 by knockouts, 14 losses, and 2 draws. Green's daughter, Allyce Schwartzbart told the *Las Vegas Sun*, "My father fought in an era where you did what you were told to do. He never had the management that could get him a shot at a title. But my father was never bitter."[6] After all, he beat two future title holders, not only Rocky Graziano, but also Joey Giardello.

Beginning in 1948, Haft had a series of fights that would elevate and spread his reputation, leading to a possible shot at the light-heavy-weight title. He knocked out Jim Letty in the 2nd round of their bout, earning $70. For his next fight, a week later, he knocked out Gilbert Cardione, also in the 2nd round. Rather than enjoying an increase in earnings however, Haft was paid $60 for the fight. Following his fight with Cardione, Haft had 5 more fights in 1948, winning each one, 4 by decisions, 1 by a knockout.

However, the following year would not be one of multiple wins for Haft: he lost a series of fights, the first one to Pat O'Conner, then one to Dom Bernardo, and then one to Toby Reid followed by loses to Henry Chemel and Danny Ruggerio. Managers and fight fans no longer viewed Haft as an up and coming fighter, someone who could pack an arena. He had to prove himself, or his fight career would stall. On May 30, 1949, a determined Harry Haft, professional boxer, proved invincible in his fight with Johnny Pretzie. Haft fought as if his life depended on the outcome; certainly his future as a boxer did. So brutal was his devastating attack on Pretzie that the referee had to stop the fight in the 4th round.

His next fight would be against the talented and undefeated boxer Roland La Starza, a fighter who came close to defeating Rocky Marciano. In a career that included 57 wins and 9 losses, from July 1947 to August 1961, La Starza fought some of the most talented heavyweights of the era, including Rocky Marciano in 1950 and 1953. On March 4, 1950, La Starza came as close as any opponent had to beating Marciano. The scoring for that fight was 5–4, 4–5, and 5–5, which should have amounted to a draw; however, New York and Massachusetts had a supplemental scoring system that permitted Marciano to be declared the winner. Up to that bout, La Starza had been undefeated with a record of 37–0. Feeling that he was a victim of a manipulated scoring system, he told the sports reporter for the *New York Herald Tribune*, "The fact is [Marciano's] manager Al Weill was matchmaker for the Garden. I would say that had a lot to do with the decision." La Starza never backed down from his belief. On February 13, 1953, La Starza defeated Rex Layne at Madison Square Garden in New York City. That set up a rematch with Marciano for the heavyweight title on September 24, 1953, in the Polo Grounds (the hometown stadium for the New York Giants). While Marciano was a 4 to 1 favorite, La Starza hoped to prove that his previous loss could be overcome. The fight did not turn out as La Starza had hoped.

*Life* magazine reported:

Trying to knock the challenger out with one punch, the 29-year-old Marciano was over-eager and awkward. He lunged, butted, hit below the belt, on the break and after the bell. Once, he swung so wildly that he missed and slipped clumsily to the canvas. Outboxing the champion and avoiding his blows, La Starza managed to win four of the first six rounds. In the seventh, Marciano changed his tactics, started aiming at La Starza's body as well as his head in an attempt to wear the challenger down. He succeeded.

The Associated Press reported:

Sliced around both eyes and bleeding from a cut on the bridge of his nose, the well-battered La Starza took a tremendous beating in the last five rounds before Referee Ruby Goldstein wisely stopped the slaughter.[7]

La Starza commented after the fight that Marciano is "a great fighter. He's definitely a better fighter than when I fought him before—5,000 percent better."

Haft was just itching to have a shot at the hard-hitting La Starza. A win could put him in position to be a title contender. Haft didn't believe that their weight and height differences would have an effect on his ability to either outpoint or even knock out La Starza. Haft weighed 175 pounds to La Starza's 185. Haft was 5'9" to La Starza's 6'0". Haft had sparred with La Starza at Stillman's Gym in New York and had never been hurt by the hard-hitting heavyweight from the Bronx. On June 27, 1949, at the Coney Island Velodrome in Brooklyn, the bout took place. Haft, full of confidence and eager to prove that he was a winner, was the fired up aggressor, chasing La Starza around the ring, challenging him to fight toe to toe. But La Starza was as quick and untouchable as the wind. He would occasionally pause and Haft would land a few hard combinations, but Haft was unable to stop La Starza. In the 4th round, La Starza had had enough of the dance and landed a series of hard rights to Haft's jaw. Haft either went down from the rights or he slipped on the wet canvas, as he later claimed. He did not take the 8 count on one knee as he was supposed to but stood up with his right hand gripping the rope and his left hand down at his side as he was taught to do in Europe. In such a position, he would not have been able to defend himself. Referee Teddy Martin stopped the fight and awarded a TKO victory to La Starza. Haft and his manager, Mandell, bitterly complained about the decision. But the ruling was chiseled in cement, and nothing they could do would turn it to dust. Commentators said that Haft, having had numerous bouts in the United States, should have known how to take an 8 count. They said he screwed himself. Then on July 18, 1949, with less than a month to barely recover from his defeat, Haft got a second chance to prove himself to fans and promoters: he was scheduled to get a shot at Marciano in the Rhode Island Auditorium in Providence. It would be the fight that changed Haft's life.

Mandell and his new partner, Saul Chernoff, who had bought a piece of Haft, took their fighter to train at Greenwood Lake in upstate New York. They stayed at the famous Brown's Hotel (where Jerry

Lewis allegedly got his start as a young comedian and waiter). Haft ran three miles every morning and worked out on the heavy bag and speed bag in the afternoons. He also skipped rope, shadowboxed, and sparred. One day he bumped into Charley Goldman, Marciano's trainer. Goldman, a derby-wearing character out of a Damon Runyon story, had trained five world champions. As a young bantamweight fighter, the diminutive 5'1" Goldman had 137 recorded fights but his career as a boxer ended because he repeatedly broke the brittle bones in his hands in the ring. Now his fingers and knuckles were as gnarled as old tree branches. Haft had originally met Goldman at Stillman's Gym. The two had established an immediate bond when they discovered that many of their Polish relatives had been murdered in SS–run concentration camps. Though he was Marciano's trainer, Goldman gave Haft a number of tips on how to fight Marciano: stay away from him so he can't pound your midsection. With short arms, he's an inside fighter. Punch and get away from him. In addition to this advice, Goldman arranged for Haft to spar with another heavyweight whose style of fighting was similar to Marciano's.

While Mandell was pleased with Haft's progress and rigorous training, he wanted to make sure that his fighter was psychologically prepared for the fight with Marciano so he arranged for Haft to have a session with a hypnotist, hoping that the session would reduce Haft's vulnerability to feeling the pain of Marciano's notoriously hard punches. Following the session, the hypnotist told Haft he was ready for the fight.

On the evening of July 18, 1949, Haft entered his dressing room at the Rhode Island Auditorium. He was getting advice from Mandell when Charley Goldman burst into the room. Red-faced Goldman was furious, indignant, a hornet about to sting. He accused Haft of hurting his reputation, for Haft had told former light-heavyweight champ Maxie Rosenbloom that Goldman had given him tips on how to fight Marciano and said he might even have a chance to defeat Marciano. Word had gotten back to Al Weill, Marciano's manager, who screamed at Goldman, denouncing him as a traitor. Goldman demanded to know if Haft had been so indiscreet as to blab to Rosenbloom. Haft apologized and was able to cool Goldman's red-hot anger. It didn't matter because Weill had banned Goldman from Marciano's corner, an indignity for any trainer but especially for one as admired and proud as Goldman. Haft again apologized and Goldman departed, repeating a few words of advice about staying away from Marciano and saying he would watch the fight from a seat near the ring.

Haft put on his trunks with the Star of David stitched on one side. It was reminiscent of the yellow star that all of Hitler's Jews had to wear, though the one on Haft's trunks was worn with pride. A few minutes later three tough-looking mobsters entered the room. They told Haft that if he didn't take a dive in round 1, he would be killed. Haft was nonplussed. He couldn't believe that such a thing could happen in America, but the threat entered his consciousness and grew, a counterweight to the session with the hypnotist. By the time he entered the ring he was fearful of even attempting to win. But he didn't take that dive in the first round. Something of his survival instincts came to the fore and drove him to fight on. This was no Nazi concentration camp fight, but like those fights, his life depended on the outcome. In the first round, Haft landed a hard right to Marciano's gut but it had little effect. In round 2, Marciano poured on a series of powerful blows, and just before the bell sounded ending the round, Marciano delivered a hard right to Haft's jaw and then delivered a pair of lefts to Haft's head. Haft was damaged and not ready for the fight to resume in round 3. Alan Haft quotes John Hanlon from the *Providence Journal* on the fight's final round:

> Two hard punches to Haft's head—a left and a right—were Marciano's openers in the third. At the halfway mark, Haft rallied briefly. But it was too late. After several damaging blows to Haft's head, Rocky delivered the crushers. The first was a left coming up to the midsection. Then, as Haft doubled up from the force of the wallop, Marciano shot a short right—down and across to put Haft out of the action.
>
> Haft received a fine reception as he left the ring, for the spectators realized that he had made a game attempt against forbidding odds. Not once did he back away from Marciano's punishing right hand and on several occasions stood toe to toe and slugged it out with his heavier opponent.[8]

Though his career ended in frustration that night, Haft soon married and had three children. He operated a fruit and vegetable store in Brooklyn. His experiences in the camps had traumatized him, leaving him angry and bitter. His hair-trigger temper could be explosive, and his wife and children were often frightened by his outbursts. Boxing writer Robert Mladinich told me that when he interviewed Haft, he met a broken man.

Alan Scott Haft sent me the following letter that he'd written to his father.

Dear Popsie,

You've been gone nearly 12 years, and I miss not having a father. Growing up, you beat me, for my childish misbehavior. The rage you had inside, you often took out on me. I feared your very presence. You broke furniture and punched out windows—abused mom to no end. Despite the abuse, mom always protected you—excused your behavior because of your "background." I could not excuse you, until I learned what that background was. I was ashamed of you. You could not read or write. You spoke broken English with a thick accent—and had those green numbers on your arm.

I wish I knew then, what I know now. You suffered terribly at the hands of the Nazis. You saw horror, and were forced to participate in it. After you told me all about your ordeal, what you had to do just to live another day, it helped me understand why you were who you were and are who you are. I now see how sorry you are for the abuse—

How can anyone judge you? They call you a Holocaust survivor— but does anyone really survive. It has been said that the Nazi's murdered your soul.

Popsie, I have spent my later years trying to make the world better for you. Your story was published by Syracuse University, you were inducted into the Jewish Sports Hall of fame, there is a major motion picture about your life; I know that you would have been happy that I made you famous.

Despite the physical and psychological abuse—I would want you to know I forgive you. Mom died this summer. She was the angel sent by God to care for you.

Now it's your turn to take care of her.

Love,

Alan[9]

Victor "Young" Perez. *Cyber Boxing Zone*

A young Harry Haft. *Alan Haft*

Harry Haft, heavyweight boxer. *Alan Haft*

Nathan Shapow and his wife, Hela. *Dr. Morris Shapow and Adina Shapow*

Witold Pilecki, Polish anti-Nazi resister. *Polish National Digital Archives*

Abba Kovner, leader of the Avengers, testifying at Eichmann trial. *Israel Government Press Office*

Heinrich Himmler and Reinhard Heydrich. *Anonymous*

U.S. Supreme Court Justice Robert Jackson, Nuremberg prosecutor. *Maurice Consant, U.S. government photographer*

Senator Thomas J. Dodd, Nuremberg prosecutor.
*U.S. Senate Historical Office*

German boxing champion Max Schmeling. *U.S. Library of Congress*

# 8

# Run for Your Life

Though two of the concentration camp boxers in this book successfully escaped from confinement, the vast majority of inmates either
perished in gas chambers or attempted to tough out their confinement
until liberated by either the Soviets or the Americans.

The 144 inmates who succeeded in escaping were unyielding
risk-takers who wanted to seize their freedom. They knew that if
they were caught they would wind up with the 900 others who had
failed in their attempts and were subsequently tortured then executed.
Though burdened by doubts, fears, and anxieties, those attempting to
escape focused, like lasers, their thoughts and plans on getting beyond
the electrified wires and the range of machine gun bullets. They were
willing to risk brutal death in exchange for the rare possibility of freely
living without fear and animalistic degradation. Once beyond the net
of the Gestapo, escapees were nearly drunk with excitement; they felt
as if they had been born anew.

One of the most audacious escapes was devised by Eugeniusz
Bendera and largely carried out by a former Polish Boy Scout named
Kazimierz Piechowski. (The latter was imprisoned because the Nazis considered the Polish Boy Scouts a criminal organization, for
its members had committed acts of sabotage, including blowing up
military transports). Working as car mechanics at Auschwitz, Bendera
and Piechowski carefully devised a plan that few would have dared
to execute. Their plan was given urgency when Bendera learned that
he was scheduled for execution. So on the morning of June 20, 1942,
the two men, along with Stanisław Gustaw Jaster and Józef Lempart,
a Catholic priest, pushed a cart filled with garbage into a storage unit.
The guards thought it nothing unusual. Once inside the unit, the men

broke into a nearby room that contained military uniforms. There they changed into the uniforms of *SS–Totenkopfverbände* guards; next, they armed themselves with four machine guns and eight hand grenades.

Parked outside the storage unit was a Steyr 220 staff car that Bendera had often repaired and driven through the camp when returning it to SS commandant Paul Kreuzmann. Guards tended to ignore Bendera, thinking that he was merely chauffeuring Kreuzmann. They would even salute the passing vehicle. The four men got into the car, acting with nonchalance, even laughing. Bendera drove the car and his ersatz SS passengers to the main Auschwitz entrance, known as the *Arbeit Macht Frei* (Work Sets You Free) gate. Piechowski, who was the most fluent and articulate in German, opened a window and shouted for the guards to open the gate. The guards saluted the commandant's car and promptly opened the gate. Nervously smiling, worried that they would be followed, yet delighted by the ease of their escape, Bendera and his passengers proceeded for thirty-seven miles.

Deeply ensconced in a densely wooded forest, they abandoned and hid their getaway car. The escapees decided that they would have a better chance at evading capture if they split up. In case one of them was captured, he would not know where the others had gone. He might be tortured, but he would be unable to provide information that would lead to the others also being captured. Piechowski made his way to Ukraine then back to Poland, where he joined the Polish Home Army and fought against the Nazi occupiers. In retaliation for his escape, the Nazis arrested his parents and sent them to Auschwitz, where they were tortured and murdered. After the war Piechowski earned a degree in engineering but was arrested and sentenced to ten years in prison for being a member of the anti-communist Polish Home Army. He was released after seven years and died in 2017.

Bendera followed a different route to the Polish Home Army, where he served, fighting Nazis until the end of the war. In postwar Poland, he had an uneventful postwar life and died in 1970.

Józef Lempart walked for nearly ninety-six miles. Near total exhaustion, he arrived at a monastery in Stary Sącz. Though the Nazis were unable to find him, they did find his mother, whom they arrested and sent to Auschwitz. The SS said her arrest was in reprisal for her son's escape. Not surprisingly she was murdered. After the war, Lempart left the priesthood, married, and had a daughter. While crossing a busy street in Wadowice in 1971, he was crushed by a speeding bus and died soon afterward.

Stanisław Gustaw Jaster, the youngest of the escapees, joined a secret anti-Nazi underground military organization. From there he joined the Polish Home Army High Command in Warsaw and became a personal assistant to Witold Pilecki (one of the most daring Holocaust heroes to have escaped from Auschwitz). Jaster's parents were also arrested in reprisal for their son's escape. While in Auschwitz they were tortured by the SS who wanted to know the whereabouts of their son. Unable to provide that information, they were gassed and incinerated. None of the escapees' parents, no matter how brutally they were tortured, were able or willing to provide information about their sons' whereabouts. Jaster, angry and frustrated that he could not save his parents from imprisonment and doom, devoted himself to defeating those who ran the SS and Gestapo. As a member of the Home Army, he led numerous attacks against the Nazis who were responsible for transporting prisoners to Auschwitz. On one mission, he and his comrades killed all the Nazis involved in charge of a transport train; they then freed all forty-nine of the prisoners, who escaped through the countryside, some of them joining resistance groups.

Jaster could not have had a more remarkable and significant boss in the Home Army than Witold Pilecki, who was a man of unusual courage and determination. Prior to the war, Pilecki's appearance was that of a strikingly handsome Aryan. His slick blond hair and sharp facial features made him the ideal image of an SS officer. After the war, following years of imprisonment and torture, his face had become sallow and aged, his hair darkened and drab, his features no longer sharply chiseled. Yet his proud countenance was still that of a man of courage and firm beliefs. He would stoically accept his communist-imposed death sentence knowing that he had always acted as a Polish patriot. During his truncated life of forty-seven years, he had been a Polish cavalry officer, a spy, a hunted resistance leader, and a voluntary prisoner of Auschwitz.

Pilecki and an army officer named Włodarkiewicz founded the Secret Polish Army, in which Pilecki served as a cavalry captain. The two men were dedicated to their vision of Poland as a state that would no longer have to cower under an occupation of Nazi cruelty. Pilecki was the more adventurous and daring of the two. As a leader of the underground resistance fighting the Nazis, he disguised himself as a proper businessman, a manager of a cosmetics company, and spied on the occupiers. Had he been caught, he would have been tortured for information and then executed. Yet he seemed as invisible as the air though capable of fierce winds of resistance. He fought courageously in many battles against Nazi troops, invariably leading his comrades to a series of victories. He was like one of those dashing figures from fiction, the Scarlet Pimpernel or Zorro, men who could achieve one victory after another but whose identity would remain a mystery.

Unlike his comrade Włodarkiewicz, Pilecki was a non-sectarian liberal and internationalist. Włodarkiewicz, by contrast, was an extreme right-wing nationalist who wanted Poland to be populated exclusively by Christians. He thought that if there were any Jews left in Poland after the war, they should be expelled. In support of such a program, Włodarkiewicz espoused classic anti-Semitic canards about Jews taking over the world through either a secret capitalist or communist cabal, never considering that communists and capitalists detested one another. From there he developed an inchoate plan to form a fascist puppet government that would make peace with the Nazis but not be controlled by Nazis. He apparently wasn't sure who would win the war. This was too much for Pilecki. He thought Włodarkiewicz was not only unreasonable but also dangerous, for one could never come to terms with the barbarian Nazis. In addition, Pilecki had no prejudice against Jews. The Jews had long lived in Poland and, he believed, had made significant contributions to Polish culture. Włodarkiewicz seemed unable to accept that the Nazis regarded all Poles as subhuman, a race to be exploited and perhaps ultimately exterminated.

Unable to bridge the gulf that separated their opposing views, the two had a nasty falling out, and Włodarkiewicz would find it difficult to forgive Pilecki. However, faced with the continual onslaught of Nazi atrocities, Włodarkiewicz finally realized the impracticality of his plans and agreed that the Home Army should present a united front against the invaders of their country. Nevertheless, he continued to regard Pilecki as a naive idealist at best, a danger to Polish society at worst. To others, he would attempt to undermine Pilecki's reputation, expressing his scorn and contempt for Pilecki's worldview. Intraparty grudges for Pilecki were a waste of valuable time. One was either in favor of the Nazis or against them. And if against them, then one had an ethical and patriotic obligation to combat them. The Nazis were Poland's enemy, said Pilecki, and the mission of the Home Army must be to sabotage their dehumanizing institutions and destroy its agents whenever possible.

To that end, Pilecki made one of the war's most memorable contributions to Holocaust history. The resistance was asking for a member to volunteer to be taken prisoner and sent to Auschwitz so that a full report could be made available to the Allies about the nature and extent of atrocities committed at the concentration camp. As a deeply faithful Catholic layperson and Polish patriot, Pilecki believed he had a Christian duty to volunteer, for it could mean that the lives of prisoners could be saved or at least improved. Włodarkiewicz was happy to see him go, no doubt wondering if Pilecki would ever return. Pilecki's superiors were apprehensive but nevertheless approved the plan and provided Pilecki with a false identity card in the name of Tomasz Serafiński.

On September 19, 1940, Pilecki deliberately went out onto a Warsaw street and stood in the midst of a roundup by the Gestapo. He and two thousand others were scooped up in the Nazi dragnet. He was taken to a barracks where he was questioned and beaten with rubber truncheons for two days. His interrogators never learned of his secret military missions against the Nazis. Not satisfied with Pilecki's claims of ignorance and of being nothing but an apolitical businessman, the Gestapo agents sent him to Auschwitz, where he was tattooed with the number 4859. Never one to pay obeisance to unlawful authority and being a fighter for liberty, Pilecki organized hundreds of Auschwitz prisoners into a secret resistance movement. They secretly disseminated information to the Polish government in exile in London, which made the information available to British and American officials. In addition to smuggled written messages, Pilecki used a radio transmitter that had been secretly built by members of the resistance. It took them seven months to build the transmitter using stolen parts. Pilecki broadcast messages to the Polish Home Army and to the Polish government in exile until the autumn of 1942, when the SS grew suspicious after hearing rumors of the transmitter's existence. The guards searched the camp, questioning prisoners about the existence of a radio transmitter, but Pilecki had disassembled it and unobtrusively disposed of its parts. Nothing was ever discovered, and the SS soon believed that it had never existed.

Pilecki hoped that the hundreds of inmates whom he had organized would rise up and topple the SS who ran the camp. In his messages smuggled to the Polish government, he urged them to drop a brigade of Polish soldiers into the camp while simultaneously having the Polish Home Army launch a massive attack on the camp. By 1943, the Gestapo, through its policy of torturing possible resistance fighters, ascertained that there might be an attack on Auschwitz. Under the direction of *SS–Untersturmführer* Maximilian Grabner, the guards hunted down, arrested, tortured, and ultimately killed many resistance members within the camp. That put an end to Pilecki's plans. He now believed that any rebellion, even if one could be instigated, would fail and result in unnecessary deaths.[1]

He decided that he would be more valuable in the fight against the Nazis if he were no longer in the camp. How to escape and bring his eyewitness accounts to the Home Army? So many who had attempted to escape were not only captured but murdered, their debased bodies made into grotesque exhibitions of threat.

Pilecki's opportunity to escape suddenly was made possible, however, when he was assigned to the night shift at a camp bakery, which was just outside the electrified fence that surrounded the camp. He and two fellow inmates carefully planned an escape that would be simple and violent. During the night of April 26, 1943, they brutally attacked and overpowered a guard, beating him into bloody unconsciousness. They decided not to kill their victim but were careful that he should not be able to alert other guards when he recovered. They used rope from the bakery to tie his wrists behind his back, turned him on his stomach, then pulled up his legs behind him, tying his ankles to his wrists. They stuffed a wet, flour-laden kitchen towel in his mouth. They then cut the phone line. It was dark and the darkness would conceal their flight. Before they dashed into the night, they took with them dozens of secret Nazi documents that detailed orders to commit atrocities and evidence of those atrocities. They believed that once those documents were in anti-Nazi hands there would be action taken to destroy the camp and liberate its inmates.

The three men walked for hours, trudging through a forest, managing not to get lost. They finally arrived at the village of Alwernia where a sympathetic priest hid and fed them. He cautioned them to be circumspect, for SS informers were in the village. He gave them clothes that would be worn by locals. The following morning, they continued on their way, looking over their shoulders to make sure they weren't being followed. They managed to get to Tyniec, where local members of the resistance provided them with more food, additional clothing, and boots.

They were still not safe for by now the beaten SS guard had been discovered and the SS and Gestapo were searching for the escapees. Travelling by night, they continued on to Bochnia, where members of the resistance hid them in a safe house that was owned by the man whose name, Tomasz Serafiński, Pilecki had used as a nom de guerre during his internment.

Pilecki showed the commanders of the Home Army the smuggled Nazi documents and told them stories of the terror and atrocities experienced by the inmates of Auschwitz. He quickly became frustrated by the Home Army's decision not to attack the camp. He could barely contain his anger at what he viewed as the indifference or fear that kept the army from a commitment to launch an attack. The army brass claimed that his report of the atrocities at the camp contained many exaggerations, all created to generate an attack of the camp. They could not believe, for example, that there were gas chambers for killing massive numbers of men, women, and children; they could not believe that bodies were incinerated and that sterilization was a common practice. It seemed grotesque and impossible that the camp should contain even one crematorium let alone three and that eight thousand people could be daily pitched into the ovens. The willful blindness of those in charge of the army was unconscionable to Pilecki. Yet he would not cease in his revelations.[2]

From Bochnia an angry Pilecki set out for Warsaw, and after several days on the run, he arrived on August 25, 1943. There he joined the intelligence and counter-intelligence division of the Home Army. Though he again tried to convince the leaders of the Home Army to attack Auschwitz, he was overruled because it was ascertained that the army did not have a sufficient number of soldiers and even if they did, they did not have a powerful enough armory of weapons to overwhelm the camp's defenders. An attack, it was decided, could only be successful if the British and American allies were to join in. They would not. Even the Soviet army, which could easily have launched an attack against the camp, chose not to do so. And appallingly, Pilecki's estimate that by March 1943 there would have been 1.5 million people gassed and incinerated in the camp did not affect their decision. Pilecki's estimate did not include those who died of starvation and disease.[3]

After the war Pilecki, though grateful that the Soviets had liberated Auschwitz, participated in the formation of a secret anti-communist unit within the Home Army. And when Poland became a satellite of the USSR, Pilecki's anti-communism became known to the Ministry of Public Security. In 1947, Pilecki was arrested and tortured: his accusers wanted to know the names of his fellow anti-communists. Pilecki's collarbones and arms were broken. Pliers were used to yank out several of his fingernails. The pain was excruciating. During the grueling hours of screaming torture, Pilecki revealed not one name. Drifting in and out of consciousness, his broken body in pain and bleeding, he lay in his darkened cell. He was about to become a dead man but until then he would be as uncommunicative as a statue.

Though his physical torture had ceased, Pilecki was about to undergo psychological torture, betrayal, and humiliation. On March 3, 1948, Auschwitz survivor and the future puppet prime minister of Poland Józef Cyrankiewicz, did as he was ordered to do: he obediently testified against Pilecki. Charges against Pilecki included crossing the border illegally, using forged documents, carrying illegal arms, spying for the government-in-exile, and planning to assassinate officials of the Ministry of Public Security. Pilecki denied the assassination attempt as well as the espionage charges; however, he admitted that he had passed information to the Second Polish Corps, which Pilecki said was entirely legal since he was an officer of the corps. It didn't matter to the court, for Pilecki's fate had been pre-determined. He was sentenced to death on May 15 and was soon executed by a single pistol shot to the back of his head. The execution took place in Mokotów Prison in Warsaw on May 25, 1948. Pilecki died as a martyr to patriotism, never betraying himself by denouncing his devotion to a democratic Poland, never betraying his comrades. Upon his death, however, he became a non-person. It was not until the tight yoke of communist oppression was removed that Pilecki's reputation as a Polish hero, patriot, and martyr was firmly established. Today he is a Holocaust hero, and the "Witold Report" is regarded as an essential document on the atrocities of the Holocaust.[4]

Another extraordinary and courageous Auschwitz escapee who wrote a report on the atrocities in the camp was Rudolf (Rudi) Vrba. He had been born Walter Rosenberg in 1924 in Slovakia. Photos of him as a young man show a handsome face topped with thick black hair. A pleasant smile enhances his features. His prominent cheekbones, strong jaw, and Roman nose give him the appearance of a Mediterranean movie actor. In addition to his good looks, he had a brilliant scientific mind, and his ambition was to be a biochemist. His plans, however, were interrupted when he was among 800 of 58,000 Slovakian Jews who were arrested and sent to jail in a financial arrangement with the Nazis. The Slovakians paid the Nazis to cart off their despised and unwanted Jews. In exchange, the Nazis permitted the Slovakians to confiscate Jewish property and resell it to their countrymen for bargain-basement prices. Vrba refused to be a victim of the government, the Nazis, and neighborhood Slovakians. He regarded the Slovakians who participated in the sell-out of the Jews as nothing but mendacious traitors. He cursed them all and set out to escape to Hungary. He later wrote that he would not be "deported like a calf in a wagon" and decided to join the Czechoslovak Army in exile in England and set off in a taxi for the border. He made his way to Budapest but then decided to leave the country. However, shortly after he arrived at the border, he was identified as a Slovakian Jew and quickly arrested.[5]

He was first sent to jail and then to Majdanek concentration camp, which had been constructed as a slave labor camp but was then converted to an extermination camp. It operated on the outskirts of Lublin and had seven gas chambers. From Majdanek, Vrba was transported in a windowless rail car with other Jews, all herded together like cattle for the slaughter, to Auschwitz. He planned to escape from the freight train, but when the SS warned their captives that they would kill ten Jews for each one who escaped or attempted to escape, Vrba changed his mind. Once in Auschwitz, he found another rebellious young man named Alfred Wetzler, an Orthodox Jewish editor with a warm, knowing smile and sparkling eyes that concealed a red-hot anger for the Nazis. They soon became friends and knew that one day they would escape from the hellhole in which they had been flung like remnants of garbage.

Vrba and Wetzler, like all inmates, suffered the humiliation of having their bodies and heads shaved, then forced to wear pajama-like uniforms and crude wooden shoes. Once shaved and deloused, each inmate suffered the indignity of having a number tattooed on his forearm, being branded like a cow. Vrba's number was 44070. All the prisoners were similarly attired, and their rags implied that they were subhuman mongrels, not worthy of decent clothes or decent treatment. SS officers, by contrast, were models of power and elegance: they wore tailored black uniforms designed by Hugo Boss that not only implied power but also authoritarian menace. The camp guards, however, generally wore gray uniforms with a skull on the tip of the right collar. The skull was an emblem of menace: look at the faceless skull and see an image of your destiny either in the gas chambers or in the ovens.

As degraded as his humanity was, Vrba maintained a fierce will to be free. He wanted to be assigned to a work detail outside the camp gates, for it was in the open where he believed he would have a better chance of escaping than if he were assigned to work at one of the camp buildings or crematoria. He volunteered for farm work, not knowing that the farm was part of the Auschwitz camp.

Working on the farm did not last long, for an older man, a kapo named Frank, purchased Vrba for a single lemon (citrus fruits were a rare commodity and much desired to fight off colds and scurvy). Vrba was an attractive commodity, for he was young, strong, and smart. Frank put the young man to work in an SS grocery store. Vrba worked diligently and had access to basic food supplies and soap and water. As a result, he stayed clean, healthy, and fit. Frank appreciated Vrba's hard work and treated him with kindness. When the SS passed by or were standing by a window or by the door to the store, Frank would often pretend to beat Vrba with a broomstick or short club or just his fists. His blows, which could not be fully seen by the SS, fell as harshly as those delivered by stuntmen in Hollywood movies. When Vrba resumed working, he exhibited neither cuts nor bruises.

Other camp inmates were not so fortunate. Beatings with rubber hoses, wooden truncheons, metal pipes, and rifle butts were commonplace. On July 17, 1942, the notorious Heinrich Himmler arrived at the camp to make an inspection. He observed the gassing of inmates and smilingly uttered his approval. He moved on to observe an inmate being beaten to death for the crime of missing a button on his tunic. Again he smiled and nodded his approval. He told his SS men that he was proud of their discipline and lack of sympathy for subhumans.

As if assessing the value of a farm animal, the SS decided that Vrba's strength could be better used as a slave laborer, a cog in the machinery of extermination, than in the light work of a grocery store clerk. He was abruptly ordered from the grocery and sent to join a clean-up crew that would unload dead Jews from incoming freight cars and sort out their property, often contained in battered suitcases. Those who appeared to be healthy and strong were selected for slave labor; all others were herded into gas chambers.

> Our first job was to get into the wagons, get out the dead bodies—or the dying—and transport them in *laufschritt*, as the Germans liked to say. This means "running." *Laufschritt*, yeah, never walking—everything had to be done in *laufschritt, immer laufen. . . .* There was not much medical counting to see who is dead and who feigns to be dead. . . . So they were put on the trucks; and once this was finished, this was the first truck to move off, and it went straight to the crematorium.
>
> The whole murder machinery could work on one principle: that the people came to Auschwitz and didn't know where they were going and for what purpose. The new arrivals were supposed to be kept orderly and without panic marching into the gas chambers. Especially the panic was dangerous from women with small children. So it was important for the Nazis that none of us give some sort of message which could cause a panic. . . . And anybody who tried to get into touch with newcomers was either clubbed to death or taken behind the wagon and shot.[6]

The guards perceived Vrba to be a diligent worker who didn't cause trouble. He was obedient and trustworthy. He was a safe choice for promotion and so was elevated to being an assistant registrar and then promoted again to registrar of block 10. He had his own bed and room and no longer had to wear the prison pajamas, an unusual arrangement for a Jew at Auschwitz. Guards were overheard saying that

Vrba could be trusted and was nearly as efficient as a regular Aryan. Unbeknownst to the guards, Vbra secretly took extensive notes about his work and wrote detailed information about the inmates he was able to question. He hid his writings knowing that if he could manage to escape he would be able to present a horrifying picture of life in Auschwitz.

It took years, but Vrba finally saw that he would have an opportunity to escape. A kapo named Yup told him that on January 15, 1944, Vrba would be one of a group of inmates who had been chosen to help build new railway tracks that would deliver prisoners to the edge of the crematoria. He was told that the tracks were being built so that 1 million Hungarians could be transported to the camp then quickly and efficiently gassed and incinerated.

Vrba drew up escape plans with Charles Unglick, an imprisoned French army captain. They planned to make their move on January 26, 1944. As the day of their planned escape drew near, Vrba began to have doubts about the likely success of the plan. He thought that there were better than even chances that they would be caught. It was too risky, and if they were caught Vrba's report on conditions in Auschwitz would go up in smoke along with the bodies of the escapees. He told Unglick he wanted to postpone their escape until he saw a good chance of success. Unglick, however, was ready to go. He had been imprisoned long enough and did not know when another opportunity would arise. He was insistent and Vrba wished him good luck. Unglick hoped to see his friend on the outside. They briefly embraced, and Unglick departed.

Just as Vrba had suspected, Unglick was spotted by guards and they blasted his body full of holes with machine gun bullets. His bloody corpse was dragged by its heels to the center of the camp and propped up on a chair. It was left there for two days as a warning and threat of what awaited anyone who intended to escape. The SS guards were proud of their capture and execution of Unglick and would point an index finger at the prisoners, imitate the *ratatat ratatat* sound of machine gun fire, and then laugh. Unglick's gruesome end was not the only one the prisoners had witnessed. When an earlier group of inmates attempted to escape, they too were gunned down by machine gun fire. Their bodies were also dragged to the center of the camp and dumped like a pile of garbage. Their mangled bodies were drenched in blood, some lying face down in the mud, others with their blood-caked faces turned to the sun. The guards propped up most of the corpses in sitting positions, one body leaning against another for support. As the flies invaded the dead, the guards placed a large sign, like a welcoming banner, across the bodies. In large, bold letters, it proclaimed, "We're back!"[7]

Cautiously weighing the opportunities to escape, Vrba was not dissuaded by the threats of the SS, nor by the deaths of others who had failed to escape. His escape would be successful. He and fellow inmate Alfred Wetzler, prisoner number 29162, would succeed where others had failed. Wetzler, who was working in the camp's mortuary, developed a plan that impressed Vrba.

In his book *Escape from Hell* (1963), Wetzler describes how they managed to escape. The camp's underground resistance organization helped to plan the escape. A locksmith named Otta made a key that would open the door to a small shed that contained clothes for the escapees to wear instead of their pajama-like uniforms. Their new clothes consisted of leather shoes, socks, underpants, shirts, and even suits that had been tailored in Amsterdam. The underground also arranged for them to have vitamins, glucose, and margarine, all of which had been manufactured in Auschwitz. Once they had reached freedom, they would be able to transmit valuable information to the anti-Nazi forces. The information consisted not only of Vrba's meticulous notes but information compiled by the underground resistance that included diagrams of the crematoria, the number of transports to the camp, the number of people daily gassed, and the names of the SS guards, all of which would be useful information for the Allied forces and postwar tribunals.

Vrba and Wetzler, like impatient caged wild animals, were finally ready to make their getaway to freedom. On Friday, April 7, 1944 (Passover eve), wearing civilian suits, overcoats, and boots, the men crouched and ran to a large woodpile. Around the woodpile, they hurriedly sprinkled Russian tobacco that had been soaked in gasoline. Its presence would prevent dogs from sniffing out their whereabouts. Then through an opening in the woodpile, they crawled inside and hid themselves in a hollow space that the underground had carved out for them.

Though their disappearance was soon discovered, their hideout was not. That same day, *SS–Sturmbannführer* and camp commander Fritz Hartjenstein was informed that two Jews were missing from the camp. The two escapees, who were scrunched together like moles in an underground bunker, continued to hide in the woodpile. They remained there for three nights and four days. Constant rain poured through spaces in the woodpile, soaking their clothes and both men developed sore throats. To keep from coughing, they tightly tied strips of flannel across their mouths. Finally on the night of April 9, one of the members of the underground named Adamek urinated on the woodpile while whistling a Polish song. It was the all-clear signal. The two men crawled out of the woodpile and unfolded their stiff and aching bodies and stretched their limbs. They had been so scrunched up in their hideout that they had developed muscle spasms. They were weak and undernourished yet determined to succeed in their journey. Their eyes took several seconds to focus clearly, and the men then studied their map. It outlined a route along the Sola River that they could follow to Slovakia, eighty-one miles from the camp. They would have to live off the land, finding nourishment wherever they could.

To avoid capture, they traveled by night, their boots slogging along the muddy banks of the river. They had some bread that the underground had given to them. They drank water from the river and used the same water to wash their faces. On April 13 they came to a farmhouse where a Polish woman offered them food and shelter. As the men ate fresh bread and slurped down spoonfuls of thick potato soup, the farm woman explained that if the Gestapo found out that she had helped Jewish escaped prisoners, she risked immediate death. Nevertheless, she did not turn from the task of helping the two men. They thanked her.

The next night, they again thanked her and departed the farmhouse and continued on their journey. A few miles on, April 16, they were spotted by the Gestapo. They took off running into a densely wooded area where they crouched behind thick bushes. The Gestapo, not having tracking dogs, lost sight of the men. They searched a small area then gave up their hunt. Vrba and Wetzler cautiously continued on their journey. Whenever they heard the distant voices of soldiers or police or the rumble of jeeps and trucks, they concealed themselves behind trees and waited for the noises to fade into the distance.

They were getting closer and closer to the Slovakian border, and just before they reached it on April 21, the two men were again helped by a pair of sympathetic anti-Nazi Poles who gave them food and shelter. Vrba had been trudging along in ill-fitting boots since the onset of the journey. Now his feet were so swollen that the wet leather painfully pressed against his toes and insteps, creating blisters and abrasions. His toenails, sharp as razors, were cutting into surrounding flesh. He could not pull off the shrunken wet boots. One of the Polish men gave him a knife, and Vrba cut away sections of the boots until he was finally able to free his feet. The Pole then gave Vrba a pair of bedroom slippers that were made of a soft cloth and did not scrunch his toes together. Vrba and Wetzler thanked their hosts and continued toward their destination. They were grateful to the Polish peasants who helped them and didn't turn them over to the police. The two finally made their way into Slovakia where they were put in touch with a Jewish doctor who said he would help them reach the Slovak Jewish Council. He escorted them to a local railroad station and handed them tickets to Zilina, in northwestern Slovakia. Soon after their train pulled into the station in Zilina, and they were met on the station platform by Erwin Steiner, then driven to the Jewish Old People's Home where the council had its offices.

Vrba was given a small office where he began to sketch the layout of Auschwitz I and II, including the position of the railroad tracks upon which prisoners were transported to the camp. He had many notes on scraps of paper and set about writing a report of all that he knew about Auschwitz. Over a period of three days he wrote and rewrote the report. He worked closely with Wetzler, and the two men were tireless, often working throughout the night until their room was illuminated by sunrise. Wetzler wrote the first part of the report, together they wrote the second part, and Vrba wrote the third part. Upon discovering that they had failed to include some vital information, they rewrote the entire report. It took six rewrites for them to feel satisfied that they had included all the necessary and pertinent information. As the report was being written, they handed off pages to Oskar Krasniansky, who translated it from Slovak into German. Though the original report in Slovak was lost, the German translation was completed and ready for perusal on April 27, 1944, twenty days after Vrba and Wetzel had crawled into the woodpile.

What happened to the original report written in Slovak remains a mystery. The men had hidden it behind a painting of the Virgin Mary that hung in their apartment in the Jewish Council. They had given a copy of the report to a man named Josef Weiss, who worked at the Bratislava Office for the Prevention of Venereal Disease. He, in turn, provided copies to Jews in Slovakia who had friends and relatives in Hungary. They translated the report into Hungarian, hoping to make it more readily available to large numbers of Jews. They hoped that the warnings implicit in the report might fire up a resistance movement. What resistance there was by Jews was limited. A Romanian Jew named George Mantello, first secretary of the El Salvador mission in Switzerland, publicized the Vrba-Wetzler Report. A German translation of the report was finally published in Geneva in May 1944 by the World Jewish Congress. It received generous coverage in Swiss newspapers, generating furious outrage among the high command of the SS and the Gestapo. To members of the Nazi high command who realized the war was lost, the report could be used as evidence of war crimes. The report, they believed, would result in vicious reprisals and judicial retribution. The effort to keep the Nazi's crimes hidden from the Allies had failed. According to British historian and professor Michael Fleming, at least 383 articles about Auschwitz appeared in the Swiss press between June 23 and July 11, 1944, all as a result of the Vrba-Wetzler Report. Fleming added that this figure "exceeds the number of articles published about the Holocaust during the entire war in the *Times*, the *Daily Telegraph*, the *Manchester Guardian* and the whole of the British popular press."[8]

The report unfortunately had no effect on the lives of the more than 100,000 Hungarian Jews who shortly after their arrival in Auschwitz were gassed and incinerated from May 15 to May 27. Others however, such as the famed handbag designer Judith Leiber, managed to outwit the Nazi roundup of Jews, though more than 12,000 Jews from Budapest were arrested, shipped to Auschwitz, and killed. Not enough Jews were aware of the report and so were not convinced that Auschwitz meant death. They believed their captors who told them that they would be resettled in a forced labor camp, comfortably housed, and decently fed.

The Allies were infuriated by what they learned of the atrocities being committed at Auschwitz. President Roosevelt and King Gustave V of Sweden wrote to the Hungarian head of state Miklos Horty that the deportations of Jews should cease immediately. Roosevelt backed up his words with a threat: if the deportations did not cease, military action would be taken. It was not long afterward that British and American bombers dropped tons of bombs on Nazi offices and barracks in Budapest, killing more than five hundred people. Horty finally used his influence to stop the deportations, much to the anger of Eichmann and Himmler.

On January 27, 1945, the Sixtieth Army of the Ukrainian Front (a division of the Soviet Red Army) liberated Auschwitz. The soldiers of the Sixtieth Army were hardened by brutal combat and many battlefield atrocities, but what they saw at Auschwitz disgusted them. They had never seen the results of such grotesque cruelty. In the main camp, they found 1,200 starving skeletal prisoners who were barely alive. They were figures out of a nightmare. In Birkenau, the soldiers came upon 5,800 more prisoners. They had all been too weak to make the death march trek out of the camp, but the SS departed so quickly that they failed to kill the living evidence of their crimes, though they burned papers that could have been used as evidence of their gruesome crimes. The gas chambers and crematoria remained. The angry Ukrainian soldiers encouraged the inmates to batter their former tormentors, and those who had the strength attacked the few remaining guards. They did so like a pride of ravenous lions, not only beating the guards with their fists but also with clubs and the rifle butts that the soldiers offered as weapons. The soldiers shot a few of the guards left alive by the inmates. Organized vigilante vengeance would follow the unconditional surrender of the Reich (see chapter 9).

Vrba, not being a vigilante, had other means of seeking justice. After the war his commitment to the prosecution of Nazis led him to testify, via affidavit, against *SS–Obersturmbannführer* Adolf Eichmann, one of the major organizers of the Holocaust, and *SS–Obersturmführer* Robert Mulka, who was second in command to *SS–Obersturmbannführer* Rudolf Höss, the Auschwitz camp commandant. Eichmann, following a trial in Israel for war crimes, genocide, and crimes against humanity, was executed in 1962. His body was cremated and his ashes were taken by an Israeli naval patrol boat and scattered just outside Israeli territorial waters. Mulka went on trial in Germany and was found guilty of executing 750 inmates of Auschwitz; he was sentenced to fourteen years in prison. In 1968 he was given a compassionate release from prison due to illness and died the following year. In 1985, Vrba testified against Holocaust denier Ernst Zundel.

Like many Jews displaced by war, Vrba settled in Israel. He was hired as a biochemist at the renowned Weizmann Institute in Rehovot. However he didn't stay in Israel for long. He was angry that a number of Hungarian Jews who had read the Vrba-Wetzler Report and had failed to warn their compatriots of what awaited them at Auschwitz had now achieved high-ranking positions in the Israeli government. Finding their presence unbearable, he left the country. He next settled in England, where he worked for two years in a neuropsychiatric research unit then spent seven years at the Medical Research Council. From 1973 to 1975 he was a research fellow at Harvard Medical School, where he met his second wife, Robin Vrba. In August 1966, he became a naturalized British citizen. Vrba died of cancer, age eighty-one, on March 27, 2006, in a hospital in Vancouver.

Vrba's close friend and fellow escapee, Wetzler, died in February 1988 in Solvakia, where he had written his version of the escape from Auschwitz: *Čo Dante nevidel* (1963), later published in English as *Escape from Hell: The True Story of the Auschwitz Protocol* (2007).

Wetzler and Vrba were honored for writing the first detailed report on Auschwitz to reach the West that the Allies regarded as credible. Martin Gilbert wrote, "The report . . . telling for the first time the truth about the camp as a place of mass murder, led directly to saving the lives of thousands of Jews—the Jews of Budapest who were about to be deported to their deaths. No other single act in the Second World War saved so many Jews from the fate that Hitler had determined for them."[9]

# 9

# Vengeance Is Mine

Though Johann Trollmann said that he would have liked to get even with the Nazis who destroyed his life and career, he did not survive his torturous existence in Auschwitz. Many of those who did survive were so angry at the Nazis that nothing short of murder could satisfy their desire to get even. But how could anyone possibly even the score for 6 million dead Jews who had been mercilessly slaughtered? Killing 6 million Nazis was unrealistic. Then how to exact revenge? At least one could make examples of some of those who would not be tried in international courts. Thousands of vicious SS guards could be hunted and executed.

Though hundreds of avengers were preparing to exact revenge, most Jewish survivors of the camps were intent on rebuilding their lives and starting new families; for them, living and producing children was revenge enough against a murderous Nazi regime that had aimed to destroy them. They believed that rebuilding for the future was the best means for responding to the vast calamity that had befallen the Jews. For those who wanted revenge, however, such an attitude seemed to diminish the tragedy of the past. Only physical retribution would satisfy their sense of right and wrong. They did not regard their mission as quixotic; rather, it was necessary. The world should know that from now on no Jew would get on his knees and be shot in the head. Jews would fight their enemies to the death. Vengeance would be a warning to the world to never attempt genocide again.

For those who deemed themselves avengers, the burning impetus for revenge as a message to the world would require them not just to kill members of the SS and Gestapo but also German citizens who were complicit in the crimes of the Nazis. The avengers believed that just because ordinary German citizens had looked away and not participated in the crimes, that did not make them innocent. Daniel Jonah Goldhagen in his book *Hitler's Willing Executioners* notes the Holocaust was carried out not just by the SS but also by tens of thousands of non–SS Germans who took pride that others were killing and torturing Jews.

As early as 1942 there was a Jewish call to arms. Not only must the slaughter of Jews be stopped, but those who committed acts of genocide should pay with their lives. Jewish newspapers in Mandate Palestine daily ran editorials demanding that there be retribution for the murder of Jews. Wherever Jews were being murdered, the murderers should suffer the same fate as their victims. Yitzhak Zuckerman, one of the leaders of the Warsaw Ghetto Uprising, claimed that all the Jews he knew were obsessed with revenge. There was a rage to destroy the destroyers.

Dina Porat, a highly esteemed Israeli historian and biographer, estimated that between 200 and 250 Holocaust survivors exacted revenge against the Nazis. They did so with guns, knives, garrotes, poisons, and explosives. And to make sure that Nazis could not become enemies of the new state of Israel, Mossad, Israel's equivalent of the CIA and considered the world's most efficient killing machine, hunted and executed an estimated 1,500 Nazis. The details of their missions remain a government secret.

In the world of Jewish revenge, the most celebrated group to exact retribution was Nakam (Revenge). The group was led by a charismatic poet and eloquent guerrilla fighter named Abba Kovner who believed in proportional revenge. Large-scale revenge was not only impractical but also impossible. To use a more recent military term, Kovner wanted to embark on a mission that would "shock and awe" the Germans. He told his followers that "the Germans should know that after Auschwitz there can be no return to normality."[1] His words had a hypnotic effect on members of Nakam.

"Members of the group believed that the laws of the time were unable to adequately punish such an extreme event as the Holocaust and that the complete moral bankruptcy of the world could only be cured by catastrophic retributive violence."[2]

The group decided that it would poison a large number of Germans. It developed interlocking networks of underground cells, each member prepared to carry out specific tasks. Before they could put their plans into action, they had to raise large sums of money not only to cover their own considerable expenses but also to bribe those who could secretly open doors and provide classified information. Once the money had been raised, they began acquiring poison and infiltrating various parts of the German infrastructure. The Jewish Brigade, which had been formed in 1944 by recruiting Jews from Mandate Palestine and was commanded by British Jewish officers, helped to fund Nakam. They provided Nakam members with forged British currency and weapons. Their role was crucial to the success of Nakam's activities.

Shortly after the end of World War II, after the Jewish Brigade had valiantly fought alongside the British in Italy, it formed a group known as *Tilhas Tizig Gesheften* (Kiss My Ass), often referred to by its initials *TTG*. TTG went after the Nazis like lions after gazelles. They assassinated members of the SS and *Wehrmacht* wherever they could find them. They would kidnap members of the SS, then torture them into providing information on the whereabouts of those who had committed atrocities against Jews. Once the brigade had extracted the information, it would dispose of its kidnapped victim, leaving a corpse where other SS men could see it. Other times, dressed as British soldiers, two or three of them would knock on the door of an SS officer's home and tell him he was wanted for questioning. The SS officer would reluctantly accompany the TTG men, getting into a car with a British army insignia. But instead of being driven to a British army office, the SS man would be driven to a darkly wooded area, dragged from the car as he loudly protested, dumped deep in the woods, forced to kneel and beg for his life, then shot in the head. His body would be left in the woods. When the brigade disbanded in the summer of 1946, many of its members joined Nakam. They brought with them British army uniforms and credentials, but best of all they kept their military weapons and so were well armed for the task of assassination. According to historians of Israel's secret wars, the members of Nakam were reputed to have killed about 1,500 Nazi war criminals. Members of Nakam later said that while there were war crime trials of top Nazi leaders, many SS officers who had carried out the gruesome murders of Jews freely returned home. While the majority of SS officers did not garner much media attention, the Reich's leaders such as Goring, Hess, Donitz, Frank, Keitel, Speer, and Rosenberg were vilified in the international press as they were tried at Nuremberg. Those men were not the targets of Nakam, for they would be imprisoned or executed. Nakam was out to get those who seemed to believe they would not be held accountable for their crimes.

While 6 million Germans could not be executed, Kovner nevertheless espoused the need for proportional retribution. He thought that poisoning a large number of German civilians would come close to being symmetrical justice. So a group of former camp inmates and members of the Jewish Brigade led by Joseph Harmatz and Kovner decided on two plans. One was to poison a large number of residents in several German cities; the other was to poison all of the Nazi POWs who were being held in an American camp near Nuremberg, the city of Hitler's most dramatic rallies.

Rich Cohen writes,

> The soldiers of the Avengers would scatter, traveling to a handful of cities near concentration camps or else of symbolic value to Nazi Germany. Munich, Berlin, Weimar, Nuremberg, Hamburg. Using forged papers, they would take jobs in the city waterworks, learning the sewers of each town. At the given moment, the Jews would shut off the valves to those neighborhoods where foreigners lived, then fill the pipes with poison. Death would flow from the faucets, killing without discrimination, young and old, healthy and sick, five cities in an instant. An eye for an eye. Plan A.
>
> Plan B was the fallback. Captured Nazis, just the highest ranking officers, were being held in the former concentration camps, awaiting trial for war crimes. Plan B was to poison the bread these men ate with each meal. Both plans, A and B, relied on the chaos of Liberated Europe, a babble of languages, a stream of refugees, confusion on the roads, a land with no one in charge, where a saboteur could vanish in a column of DPs [displaced persons].[3]

Abba Kovner was well suited to such a task for he had been a courageous guerrilla fighter against the Nazis who occupied his home city of Vilna. There he had organized what came to be known as the Vilna Ghetto Uprising, a vehement struggle that had failed to succeed yet had the effect of mobilizing numerous Jews against the Nazi invaders. While in Vilna Kovner also issued a 1942 manifesto titled "Let Us Not Go Like Lambs to the Slaughter." It is considered the first writing by a Jew warning that Hitler intended to exterminate all the Jews of Europe. He added that many of the Jewish residents of Vilna had already been slaughtered in the Ponary Massacre and the fate of the rest of the Jews would be the same.[4] In his manifesto Kovner used the phrase "like sheep to the slaughter." But when many Jewish residents read it, they found it to be an unbelievable accusation; they thought it was—at best—a wild exaggeration, something designed to stir them up, to enlist them in a rebellion that would be doomed to failure. The few who believed it joined Kovner's underground military organization and pledged to do all in their power to fight the Nazis and prevent them from killing more Jews. As fierce and determined as Kovner and his comrades were, the Vilna Ghetto uprising, as many Jews had suspected, failed to achieve its military goals. Failure, however, did not deter the underground from fighting on. They were more fiercely determined to fight against the Nazis than they had been. They escaped into Rudniki Forest where they joined Soviet partisans who were known for their vicious and remorseless treatment of captured Nazis, who were often beaten to death for they were not worth the price of bullets. Together the Jews and the Russian partisans ambushed and killed Nazi soldiers and sabotaged convoys of trucks and tanks, killing those who survived the attacks. From dead Nazis the groups grabbed guns, ammunition, and grenades.[5]

Because Kovner was an inspiring and intuitive leader of the Jews who had escaped from Vilna and organized the resistance to the Nazi occupation, he was looked upon as a natural leader, someone who commanded respect and admiration. Historian Dina Porat says, "His was a personality you could not ignore. Whose vision and thoughts about Jewish history were of the highest level. . . . He gave them goals and they followed him for those goals."[6]

Based upon Kovner's record, Nakam members trusted his decisions and were inspired by his courage and commitment. Two of his most trusted and devoted lieutenants were a pair of courageous women named Vitka Kempner and Ruska Korczak. As members of Nakam, the two women said of themselves that they were as much avengers as the men. Kempner, a young woman of only nineteen during the Vilna Ghetto uprising, had risked her life smuggling weapons through the city's sewers. She became renowned among guerrilla fighters after blowing up a Nazi train with a homemade bomb. She and Kovner became lovers; in 1946, they married. Korczak, also a young woman of extraordinary courage, helped to smuggle weapons to those fighting the Nazis in Vilna. In addition, she helped to smuggle Jews out of the city and to safety. She and Korczak remained close friends though she was rumored to be another of Kovner's lovers. Supposedly no jealousy over the affections of Kovner dampened the relationship of the two women.

Joseph Harmatz, a close friend of Kovner, was also a member of the Avengers and a vital member of the Vilna resistance. At age sixteen, as an idealistic communist, he had joined the underground and smuggled partisans through the city's sewers to safety in the nearby forests. There they were trained and armed so that they could join the fight against the Nazis. When it came to carrying out the planned poisoning of Germans, Harmatz, posing as a Polish displaced person named Maim Mendele, was charged with infiltrating the municipal water-supply company as well as finding rooms in which the conspirators could conceal themselves in Nuremberg. There was a shortage of rooms because much of the city had been destroyed by American and British bombs. Nevertheless, Harmatz was resourceful and determined to carry out Nakam's plans. Using real and forged British currency, he bribed a number of landlords to make rooms available for his comrades. In addition, he bribed foremen and managers at the water company. As a result, he managed to get Willek Schwerzreich (Wilek Shinar), an engineer from Kraków who spoke fluent German, employed by the municipal water company. Schwarzreich stole a copy of a diagram that contained the plan of the water system. The diagram identified the main water valve into which poison could be poured. He reported his findings to Kempner and also to David Ben-Gurion, Israel's future prime minister, who said he was more interested in creating a Jewish state than in exacting revenge, though he did not dissuade the Avengers from going forward with their plan. In an interview many years after the war, Harmatz confirmed Plan A to kill Germans.

> "So the group set out with a simple mission. Kill Germans," Harmatz said flatly.
>
> How many?
>
> "As many as possible," he quickly replied.[7]

In July 1945, Kovner, disguising himself as a Jewish Brigade soldier on leave, left for Milan. There he boarded a ship for Mandate Palestine. Though he wanted to move as quickly and as quietly as possible after disembarking, he was arrested by Mossad, confined to a small apartment, and interrogated for three days by Mossad's chief, Shaul Meirov. After being released from his temporary confinement, Kovner met with numerous Jews hoping to get poison for his mission in Germany. Years later he claimed that he met with Chaim Weizmann, the visionary Zionist leader, a brilliantly inventive biochemist, and first president of Israel. Kovner said that Weizmann approved Plan B, which seemed far more practical and less likely to raise anger against the Jews than Plan A. He supposedly put Kovner in touch with the Katzir brothers, who were sympathetic to Kovner's revenge plot and convinced the head of chemical storage at Hebrew University to give Kovner poison. Kovner was given the poison and planned on returning to Germany. Still posing as a member of the Jewish Brigade on leave, Kovner traveled to Alexandria in Egypt where he boarded a British destroyer bound for France. In his rucksack he carried several documents, all of which were fake. The documents identified him with a false name as a soldier in the Jewish Brigade. His rucksack also contained two canisters of deadly poison. As the boat approached the coast of Toulon, France, the captain announced through the public address system that a member of the Jewish Brigade should come to the bridge. The captain, in calling for the soldier, used the fictitious name on Kovner's identity papers. Kovner was startled that the captain would know the fictitious name, for only a few people in Mandate Palestine had been made privy to it. Kovner, fearing that he would be searched, quickly withdrew one of the canisters of poison from his rucksack and poured the contents into the sea. He then handed the other canister to a friend, Yitzik Rosenkranz, and told him to bring it to Kempner in Paris. He also handed Rosenkranz a note to be delivered to Kempner. He instructed him to go ahead with Plan B. After this, he walked to the captain's quarters, where he was arrested by the British police. The police questioned him for hours, which produced no information because Kovner could not speak English. It was a perfect defense. Frustrated, the police called in an interpreter who was no more successful in gaining answers to police questions, for Kovner maintained his ignorance of any plot. He would shrug his shoulders and state that he had no knowledge of any plot. Unsatisfied with the interrogation, the police had the interpreter tell Kovner that because he was uncooperative he would be returned to Alexandria and locked up until the government decided to release him. When Kovner asked what crimes he was being accused of, he was handcuffed. After disembarking in Alexandria, he was taken to a bleak, bug-infested jail in Cairo, pushed into a cell, and left there for two months. Rich Cohen writes,

> Years later, a Haganah veteran talked of the case saying Abba's arrest had been engineered at the highest level, perhaps by Ben-Gurion himself. When the Jewish leaders realized that Abba had left the country with the poison, they tipped off the British. They did not want Abba punished—just detained. His plan might greatly damage their cause.[8]

In Paris, Kempner got together with Pasha Reichmann, a resourceful fighter who had distinguished himself in various military encounters against Nazi troops. As a young man he had been a member of the Polish Communist Youth Organization in Lodz. After the outbreak of war, he impressed his comrades by his fierce hit-and-run attacks on Nazi soldiers. He and his wife organized a group of underground fighters. They stole the parts used to manufacture rifles then assembled their own. In short order, they had a sufficient number of weapons so that all twenty-one members of their group were well armed. Once armed, they connected with Ukrainian partisans and Soviet paratroopers. They merged to form a partisan battalion that engaged in successful acts of sabotage. From hidden places in forests, they picked off

*Wehrmacht* soldiers, stole the dead soldiers' weapons, then quickly retreated into the density of thickly wooded forests before anyone could launch a counterattack. In one of the encounters, Reichmann was badly wounded, soon recovered, and again participated in the fight against Nazis. In 1944 he met Kovner in Lublin, who was so impressed by Reichmann's intelligence, tenacity, and commitment that he asked him to serve as his second in command. While Kovner was imprisoned by the nascent government of what would become Israel, Reichmann served as head of Nakam.

Though Nakam had to discard Plan A, Reichmann and Kempner organized the means for effecting Plan B. A number of Nakam members were brought aboard to help carry out the plan.

Finally by April 1946, all the elements of Plan B were in place and the operation was a go. A friend of Reichmann named Yitzhak Ratner set up a laboratory in Paris where he tested various formulations so that he could create a tasteless and odorless formulation of arsenic. After much experimentation, he created a mixture of arsenic, glue, and water that could be applied with a paint brush onto loaves of bread. He tested his mixture on several cats that died. Satisfied that he had created a perfectly odorless, tasteless formula, he contacted friends in the tanning industry, which used arsenic as a leather preservative. They arranged for him to receive forty pounds of arsenic, far more than anything Kovner could have delivered. The next step was to have a special formulation of arsenic, glue, and water smuggled into Germany. Jewish Brigade members, still in British army uniforms, concealed the poison compound in water bottles. If stopped by civilian or military police, the soldiers could show false papers identifying them as part of a medical team who were delivering hot water bottles to a hospital in Germany. The bottles were finally delivered to the *Konsum-Genossenschaftsbäckerei* (Consumer Cooperative Bakery) near Nuremberg. This bakery had the contract to prepare all the bread consumed by SS prisoners in Stalag 13-D (Langwasser Internment Camp).

SS prisoners of war in Stalag 13-D were not the only prisoners of war targeted by Nakam. Plans to poison prisoners at a prison camp near Dachau were also underway. There a survivor of the Warsaw Ghetto Uprising, Simha Rotem, was using a nearby bakery to prepare poison bread. Rotem was clever and perspicuous as a well-trained spy. He successfully befriended the manager of the bakery, took him out drinking, told him ribald stories, and got him so drunk that he passed out. Rotem then proceeded to lift the manager's keys and make copies of the particular ones necessary to open the bakery. While the manager was still out cold, Rotem returned the keys to one of the manager's trouser pockets. He and two Nakam members were now ready to sneak into the bakery late at night and paint loaves of bread with arsenic and glue. However, just days before the sabotage was to take place, Reichmann received word from one of his operatives, a Jewish officer in the American army, that the two Nakam operatives were wanted by the military police. If caught, they could be forced to reveal information about the planned poisoning of prisoners at Stalag 13-D. Not wishing to endanger the success of that operation, Reichmann called off the Dachau attack on April 11, 1946.

To proceed with the poisoning of the prisoners at Stalage 13-D, two Nakam operatives managed to be hired by the Allied command. One of the men, Leipke Distel, a concentration camp survivor, posed as a Polish displaced person who was awaiting necessary papers so that he could go to Canada and work at his uncle's bakery. He explained his situation to the manager of the Consumer Cooperative Bakery and offered to work for nothing. He was taken on and he secured entrance to the bakery's storeroom after bribing the manager with alcohol and cigarettes. The Nakam plotters secretly met each night in a rented room near the bakery. One question in particular concerned the plotters: How do we poison the SS prisoners while not harming their American guards? To solve the problem, Harmatz was able to get several of his co-conspirators clerical positions in Stalag 13-D. They learned that on Sundays American guards were issued white bread and the SS were given only black bread. Problem solved.

Nakam now had six operatives at the Consumer Cooperative Bakery in Nuremberg. Each of the Nakam members was able to smuggle in several water bottles full of arsenic, glue, and water under their raincoats. Once inside, they took up several floorboards, hid the water bottles below floor level, then covered the bottles with the previously removed floorboards. It took several days to hide all of the water bottles. Then the operatives were ready to start painting the poison onto loaves of black bread. On Saturday, April 13, Nakam members were pleased that the bakery workers had gone out on strike. Though that meant the bakery would be free of many workers, it also meant that two Nakam members who were bakery workers also had to strike in solidarity with their fellow workers. Only three members of Nakam stealthily entered the bakery and proceeded to paint three thousand loaves of black bread with a mixture of arsenic, glue, and water. Shortly after they finished, they left the bakery as quietly and as quickly as stealthy cats. They then prepared for their escape.

The following morning, the bread was delivered Stalag 13-D to feed more than two thousand SS prisoners of war. As the prisoners bit into the bread some questioned the odd taste, yet they ate it. Though the poison was tasteless, the glue wasn't. In addition, the presence of the poison could alter the taste of the bread. Most of them became severely ill. Panic erupted among captives and captors who suspected that the prisoners were victims of sabotage. The American military, not wanting to be responsible for two thousand dead SS officers, supplied dozens of ambulances that rushed the prisoners to several nearby hospitals. Each of the prisoners had his stomach pumped clean. None of them died. Why the prisoners survived was the question that confounded the perpetrators. They speculated that the poison had been spread too thinly to kill anyone; or perhaps the prisoners did not consume a lethal quantity of arsenic. Regardless of the reason, the Nakam plotters were disheartened that their scheme to exact revenge had failed.

> According to previously classified files from the U.S. military's Counter Intelligence Corps, which investigated the 1946 incident and which the Nuremberg prosecutors did not have access to, the amount of arsenic used should have been enough to cause a massive number of deaths. The files were obtained by the AP through a Freedom of Information Act request to the National Archives.
>
> In one memo from 1947 stamped "confidential," investigators write that at the bakery they found "three empty hot water bottles and a burlap bag containing four full hot water bottles." An analysis of the contents "revealed that they contained enough arsenic mixed with glue and water to kill approximately 60,000 persons."
>
> Another confidential report said a chemist called in to help in the investigation had determined "10 kilo of pure arsenic was present, mixed with water and glue for adhesive purposes."
>
> Laboratory investigators found arsenic on the bottom, top and sides of the bread, and reported that doctors said the SS men exhibited symptoms "similar to cholera and included vomiting, diarrhea and skin rashes" The report added that the most amount of arsenic found on a loaf was 0.2 grams—which fell well within the range of 0.1–0.3 grams that would be in most cases lethal.
>
> To this day, it remains a mystery as to why the poison failed to kill Nazis. The prevailing theory is that the plotters in their haste spread the poison too thinly. Another is that the Nazi prisoners immediately sensed something was off with the bread and therefore no one ingested enough of it to die.[9]

Although the American military attempted to keep the story of the poisoning under wraps, it was soon uncovered by unidentified sources and handed over to reporters. On April 24, newspapers in Europe and America published the story that nearly 2,300 Nazi victims had been hospitalized possibly as a result of poisoning. The *New York Times*, for one, reported on April 23, 1946, that 2,283 German prisoners of war had fallen ill from poisoning, with 207 hospitalized and seriously ill. Though not stated, the implication was clear: victims of the Holocaust had attempted to take revenge on the men who had killed millions of Jews. Years later, the German government revealed that it had evidence against those who attempted to poison the prisoners but had decided not to prosecute the perpetrators, considering what they had suffered at the hands the Nazis. The survivors of the camps had sufficient reasons for their attempt to kill the SS, but prosecuting them would have been a double punishment.

Interviewed by an Associated Press reporter seventy years after the failed plot, Joseph Harmatz gave his account of what had happened.

> There were deep reservations even among the Avengers that [Plan A] would kill innocent Germans and undermine international support for the establishment of Israel. Either way, when Kovner sailed for Europe with the poison, he drew suspicion from British authorities and was forced to toss it overboard before he was arrested. Following that setback, attention shifted toward Plan B, a more limited operation that specifically targeted the worst Nazi perpetrators. Undercover members of the group found work at a bakery that supplied the Stalag 13 POW camp at Langwasser, near Nuremberg, and waited for their chance to strike the thousands of SS men the Americans held there. It came on Apr. 13, 1946. Using poison procured from one of Kovner's associates, three members spent two hours coating some 3,000 loaves of bread with arsenic, divided into four portions. The goal was to kill 12,000 SS personnel.[10]

"While the mass death count of the first plan would have been disastrous for the Jewish people, the second's more direct route was easier to accept, since its targets were the worst of the worst," said Dina Porat, the chief historian at Israel's Yad Vashem Memorial. "The terrible tragedy was about to be forgotten, and if you don't punish for one crime, you will get another," she explained. "This is what was driving them, not only justice but a warning, a warning to the world that you cannot hurt Jews in such a manner and get away with it."

"Even if they were ultimately unsuccessful," she said, "the Avengers' act was steeped with symbolism for a burgeoning state of Israel fighting for its survival in a hostile region.

"What is Zionism? Zionism is the Jews taking their fate in their own hands and not letting the others dictate our fate," she said. "This is what they wanted to show. You cannot get away with such a terrible deed."[11]

After the attack, Harmatz and others had to flee quickly. They were helped by sympathizers. At the border of Czechoslovakia, an Auschwitz survivor named Yehuda Maimon met them and helped lead them to safety, often bribing officials who pretended that they were unaware of who the plotters were. There had been stories in the newspapers about unidentified plotters, and border guards were instructed to demand identifying documents from all those who attempted to cross borders. After taking them through forests and over mountains, Maimon managed to get them into Italy. From there he smuggled them into the south of France. In the postwar chaos, it was easy for the Nakam plotters, using false papers, to board a ship and sail safely to Mandate Palestine. About thirty former Nakam operatives arrived by the end of July, following a brief detention by the British, who exercised control of Mandate Palestine and were limiting the number of immigrating Jewish refugees. The British government was fearful of an Arab uprising caused by too many Jews entering the country. So as not to antagonize the Arabs, the British strictly limited the number of Jewish immigrants. Nakam members who did make it into the country were warmly received as heroic freedom fighters at Kovner's kibbutz, Ein HaHoresh. In addition to that welcoming party, the Nakam members were received as returning heroes by Haganah and the Israeli Labor Party. As military heroes, they traveled throughout the land as guests of whomever they visited.

While most of the Nakam members decided to stay put and help develop the land of Israel and build a state for Jews, a few of the militants decided that their mission of revenge was not over. They were led by a man named Bolek Ben-Ya'akov, for whom revenge was a principle doctrine worth pursuing. They were also assisted by a Labor Party politician named Abba Hushi, who served as mayor of Haifa from 1951 to 1969. He was an important advocate for workers and carried out numerous municipal improvements that helped modernize Israel.

During an interview in the 1980s, Ben-Ya'akov said he could not have looked at himself in a mirror if he had not attempted to seek revenge for all the Jews that the Nazis had killed. Another Nakam member who took pride in his attempts to seek revenge was Maimon.

From the retirement home outside Tel Aviv where his grandchildren frequently visit him, the 92-year-old Yehuda Maimon, who goes by the nickname Poldek, fixes a steely gaze with his piercing blue eyes. He looks back with satisfaction at carrying out his "duty" for revenge before starting anew in Israel:

"It was imperative to form this group. If I am proud of something, it is that I belonged to this group," he said. "Heaven forbid if after the war we had just gone back to the routine without thinking about paying those bastards back. It would have been awful not to respond to those animals."[12]

Nakam's worldview, according to two Israel terrorism experts, Ehud Sprinzak and Idith Zertal, was similar to that of groups that believe the world is so evil it deserves large-scale catastrophe. Unlike most terrorist groups that say they commit their acts to create a new and better world, Nakam was prepared to kill indiscriminately. The Nakam operatives came from "heavily brutalized communities," which sometimes consider catastrophic violence.[13]

Of course Nakam would disagree with such an assessment for they believed that the Nazis deserved death. If anyone had offered to forgive Nakam for acts of revenge, Nakam members would have rejected the offer as stupid. If anything, they wanted to be honored for their commitment to eye-for-an-eye justice.

Dina Porat said in an interview in the Israel newspaper *Haaretz,*

[Nakam members] don't regret the terrible thing they planned to do. They explain that only someone who was in their place could understand them, and they want to receive recognition and appreciation for the attempt, which fortunately was unsuccessful. . . . As far as they were concerned, there was no need for warnings, arrests or trials. They wanted to take revenge—"an eye for an eye, a tooth for a tooth"—as is written in the Bible. They felt that the world was morally bankrupt, and only this punishment could settle the account and put it in order. They believed that the laws practiced at the time did not provide a suitable response to the terrible crimes that were committed.[14]

The remnants of the Avengers who did not initially seek shelter in Mandate Palestine found life in the new Federal Republic of Germany difficult. Much of the postwar chaos had subsided as the country worked to become profitable and stable. The government, through a variety of laws and regulations, made it difficult for the Avengers to achieve their goals. Some of the Avengers committed crimes to support themselves. After being arrested, many were able to escape from prison with the help of their allies, former members of the French Resistance. After 1950, the Avengers realized that they would be unable to succeed in their revenge missions and so for the next two years, several at a time moved to Israel, where they led normal lives, contributing to the growth of their new country.

While Nakam had ceased to exist, others were determined to exact revenge in the name of the 6 million Jews slaughtered by the Nazis. Between 200 and 250 Jewish assassins, many of whom were Mossad agents, killed more than 1,500 Nazis war criminals in the years after the war. At the beginning of the 1960s, Mossad agents were told they had permission to kill or kidnap any former Nazis they encountered. One of the most loathsome of the wanted Nazis was Herberts Cukurs, who had taken great pleasure in shooting Jews while mounted on his stately stallion. He had been known as the Hangman of Riga for sending many innocent Jews to the gallows. He achieved further notoriety for packing a synagogue in Latvia with three hundred Jews and then having the men under his command burn it to the ground. According to Bernard Press, "Eyewitnesses heard the people who were locked inside screaming for help and saw them breaking the synagogue's windows from inside and trying, like living torches, to get outside. Cukurs shot them with his revolver."[15]

At the time of Cukurs's death in 1965, *Time* reported that his crimes included not only the infamous synagogue fire but also the drowning of 1,200 Jews in a lake and his participation in the November 30, 1941, murder of 10,600 people in a forest near Riga.

Who was this monster? Herberts Cukurs was born in 1900 in Latvia where he was a celebrated aviator, often compared to Charles Lindbergh. He won national acclaim for long-distance solo flights in the 1930s, one of which was from Riga to Tokyo. On another occasion he flew to Palestine and back. Following his return to Riga, he gave a lecture to a Jewish group about the sites of the Holy Land, and he often associated with Jewish intellectuals, artists, and writers in Riga's cafes. He was certainly not seen as an anti-Semite. But he was drawn to authoritarian military leaders and ventures. He saw himself as a heroic man on horseback or in the cockpit of a plane. It was not surprising then that in 1939 he even designed a dive bomber known as the Cukurs C.6bis. Though he would have loved to have sold it to the Luftwaffe in 1941, the plane was not put to military use. It didn't matter, for what was more important was his subscription to Nazi propaganda. Shortly after the Nazis took control of Latvia, they published defamatory lies about Jews in local newspapers. They claimed that the Jews were the "enemy within" who had stabbed their countrymen in the back as they secretly sided with the previous Soviet occupation forces. One newspaper wrote that "no pity and no compromise must be shown. No Jewish tribe of adders must be allowed to rise again." Cukurs, though honored with various awards and trophies for his impressive aviation feats, would not be honored by history for his complete immersion in Nazi ideology and enjoyment of carrying out atrocities.

Why the rapid change? Like many Latvians, he had hated the Soviets during their 1940 occupation of his country and regarded the subsequent Nazi occupation as a liberation. And being a highly ambitious opportunist without a moral compass, and a thirst for heroics, he joined a notorious group of fascist thugs known as Arajs Kommando, which was set up at the direction of the Nazi *Sicherheitsdienst des Reichsführers–SS* (Security Service of the *Reichsführer–SS*) as the Latvian Auxiliary Security Police. Cukurs was such an enthusiastic and ruthless killer of Jews that he was quickly promoted to second in command of the group. On July 2, Arajs Kommando, led by Cukurs, unleashed a murderous pogrom on Latvian Jews. The viciousness of the Kommando attacks was celebrated by both the SS and the Gestapo for Kommando murdered more than 26,000 Jews not only in Riga but also in the Rumbula Massacre. Cukurs took great pleasure in riding through the streets of Riga and firing his pistol at scampering Jews. He once shot an infant being held in the arms of her mother. Following the Rumbula Massacre, he invited his Kommando colleagues to his luxurious villa where they got drunk, went out into the street, hauled in any Jews they could find, and Cukurs clubbed them to death as his men cheered him on. So prized were the members of Kommando that a number of them got to impose their brutality as guards at the Salaspils concentration camp. After the war, the Allies discovered the graves of 632 children, ages 5 to 9, who had been killed at the camp, either by starvation or disease.

As Germany was losing the war and retreating out of the Baltics, Cukurs retreated along with the withering Nazi army. As the Soviet advance against the Nazis relentlessly continued, Cukurs made plans for a postwar career. He knew that he would be tried for war crimes and perhaps executed if captured. Like many other Nazis wanted for war crimes, Cukurs was able to escape: he went to Brazil via the infamous rat lines.[16] With the assistance of the rat lines, Cukurs was issued a certificate of permanent residency in Brazil on December 18, 1945.

He initially settled in Rio where he operated a marina. He pretended to be a refugee from Nazi terror who had risked his life to save numerous Jews. He even befriended a few Jewish businessmen who believed his stories. He was profiled in a popular Brazilian magazine in which he was lauded as a friend of humanity. However, the truth about his past began to emerge and his business started to fail so he moved to São Paulo, where he opened a small business flying tourists and others in his Republic RE-7 Seabee, a small single-engine amphibious aircraft. He made a modest living flying eager tourists over many of Brazil's most scenic sites such as Iguazu Falls; the 98-foot-tall statue of Christ the Redeemer on Corcovado Mountain; Sugarloaf Mountain; Lençóis Maranhenses National Park; and Chapada dos Veadeiros. Unlike Eichmann and Mengele, Cukurs did not conceal his identity, he simply stuck to his story that he was a courageous refugee who had saved the lives of many Jews. He lived as a virtuous and proudly successful entrepreneur. Had he concealed his identity his fate might have been different, but his narcissism overtook his caution. He still needed to believe that he had been an aviation hero and an admired leader on horseback.

Judging from his lack of concealment, it was apparent that he did not know he was on a Mossad list of Nazi war criminals to be hunted down and executed. The plan to assassinate Cukurs began in early 1965 when the West German Bundestag was considering the approval of a statute of limitations for Nazi war crimes. There was a great outcry: for months protests took place in cities such as London, Los Angeles, Tel Aviv, and Toronto, among various others. Ordinary men and women were joined in the streets by famous writers and politicians. Future pope Benedict XVI added his voice to the protests. The commotion caused a divisive debate in Germany between those who wanted to forget the past and those who wanted to atone for it. Finally in March 1965, moved by public opinion and pressure from foreign governments, the Bundestag voted overwhelmingly to defeat the proposal that would have brought an end to the hunt for Nazi war criminals. The world was not about to forgive the perpetrators of horrific crimes.

During the debate in the Bundestag, Israeli prime minister Levi Eshkol made a decision that the world should never forget the beasts who had killed millions of Jews. Mossad should make an example of Cukurs and other Nazi war criminals who would never see the inside of a courtroom, never receive the justice they deserved. Mossad, without a courtroom in which to bring a case against Cukurs, was its own judge and jury. The spy agency judged Cukurs to be a war criminal and sentenced him to death for the thousands of Latvian Jews he had ordered killed.

According to Stephan Talty, Mossad used a skilled undercover operative named Yaakov "Mio" Meidad to trap Cukurs. Meidad, whose parents died in a concentration camp, had helped kidnap Adolf Eichmann and transport him for trial in Israel. It was his job to form an ersatz friendship with a man whom he despised. He assumed the false identity of one Anton Keunzle, a successful Austrian businessman, who would befriend Cukurs and lure him to his death. Soon after their first supposedly fortuitous and serendipitous meeting, Cukurs asked Keunzle questions designed to find out his motives. Keunzle convinced Cukurs that he was interested in investing in his various businesses. He told Cukurs had been in the *Wehrmacht* and fought on the Eastern Front. To test Kuenzle's veracity, Cukurs invited him to a shooting contest in the jungles of Brazil. Keunzle passed the test and went on to convince Cukurs that he could help him regain his wealth.

Cukurs, ever the narcissist in need of approval, showed Keunzle his medals and trophies from his days as a celebrated aviator. Next he showed Keunzle photos of two beaches that he thought should be developed as tourist sites with hotels and restaurants. He bragged that he owned two ranches and would like Keunzle to be his guest at them. Cukurs suggested that his guest wear a pair of thick leather boots to protect himself from potential snakebites. Kuenzle was not as much concerned about snakebites as he was that Cukurs might suspect him of being a hired assassin and lure him into the jungle and kill him. So Kuenzle brought along a switchblade knife for protection. Of course, it would be an inadequate defense against the pistol and rifle that Cukurs carried. On their trip to one of the ranches, they crossed the Crocodile River on a dilapidated wooden bridge that creaked under their footsteps. Cukurs surprised Kuenzle by suggesting that they take target practice with the rifle. Keunzle proved himself a fine marksmen who, Cukurs said, was no doubt a formidable German asset on the Eastern Front. That night, the two men slept in the room that was normally occupied by the ranch manager, who was on vacation.

The time at the ranch passed pleasantly and Cukurs did not seem to have any suspicions about Keunzle. While chatting over breakfast, Kuenzle suggested that Cukurs join him in Montevideo, Uruguay, where they could lay the groundwork for a new aviation company. Cukurs agreed and Keunzle gave him the address of a villa outside of the city in which they could meet. Keunzle departed, saying he had business to take care of, but would meet Cukurs later.

Cukurs and Keunzle drove to the villa and were the only ones on the street. Keunzle led the way into the villa. Seconds after Cukurs entered, the front door slammed shut behind him and three men in their underwear grabbed him, attempting to wrestle him to the ground. (Like many professional assassins, the Mossad agents did not want to get blood on their clothing, which is why they were in their underwear.) Cukurs had always worried that something like this might happen to him, but he had not considered the possibility that he would be set up by his new prospective business partner. Shouting and screaming, Cukurs attempted to break free. He was much stronger than the agents had thought he would be. *"Lass mich sprechen, lass mich sprechen* [Let me speak, let me speak]," Cukurs shouted. He ripped one of his pants pockets as he desperately attempted to get hold of his pistol. To stop Cukurs's screaming, one of the agents grabbed Cukurs's face and pressed the palm of his hand over his mouth. Cukurs bit into the man's hand drawing blood, then attempted to bite off the agent's fingers. The furious agent grabbed a hammer with his bloody hand and smacked Cukurs's head. Cukurs still resisted so another agent brought out his pistol and fired two bullets into Cukurs's brain. Cukurs collapsed like a marionette whose strings have just been cut. Agents then fitted the body into a trunk, folding his legs at the knees so the entire corpse would fit.

On Cukurs's corpse, one of the agents pinned a note stating that Cukurs had been condemned to death by "those who can never forget." The Mossad agents then sent a note to the government as well as to the media. It stated,

> Taking into consideration the gravity of the charge leveled against the accused, namely that he personally supervised the killing of more than 30,000 men, women and children, and considering the extreme display of cruelty which the subject showed when carrying out his tasks, the accused Herberts Cukurs is hereby sentenced to death. Accused was executed by those who can never forget, on the 23rd of February, 1965. His body can be found at Casa Cubertini Calle Colombia, Séptima Sección del Departamento de Canelones, Montevideo, Uruguay."[17]

Those who received the note thought it the work of a prankster until police followed up and discovered the corpse.

When the event was reported internationally, the perpetrators were thought to be Jews seeking revenge for the terrible Riga massacres. The stories were generally sympathetic to the Jewish avengers.

# 10

# The Nuremberg Trials

The American people not only sympathize with all victims of Nazi crimes but will hold the perpetrators of these crimes to strict accountability in a day of reckoning which will surely come.—Franklin D. Roosevelt[1]

If Hitler falls into our hands we shall certainly put him to death.—Winston Churchill[2]

Prosecutors at the postwar Nuremberg trials were portrayed in the media as heroes of the courtroom, of the tribunal that would bring justice to some of the worst criminals in the history of civilized nations. The prosecutors were able to do what Nakam and Mossad were not able to do. They sought justice not only on behalf of the boxers who had to fight for their lives but for all inmates who had endured torturous conditions in the Nazi-run death camps. The boxers who survived praised the prosecutors and judges for so determinedly delivering judicial punishment to those who had committed horrendous crimes.

While there were prosecutors from four Allied countries who participated in the first major Nuremberg trial, it was the American prosecutors who brought a level of judicial dispassion to their mission. They were the most dispassionate (as chief prosecutor Robert Jackson stated in his opening comments) because the land of the United States had not come under direct attack by the Nazis. Another reason for focusing on American prosecutors in this chapter is that the American government was the only Allied government to conduct a total of twelve Nuremberg trials against the Nazis.

Furthermore, the original plan, "Trial of European War Criminals," was drafted by a U.S. cabinet official, Secretary of War Henry L.

Stimson and the staff of his War Department. Then following the death of President Roosevelt, the U.S. government negotiated with its allies to work out the mechanics and the location of the trial, which the Allies agreed should be held in Nuremberg in the Palace of Justice, beginning on November 20, 1945. At what was formally known as the International Military Tribunal, the prosecutors entered indictments against twenty-four top-ranking Nazi war criminals and several Nazi organizations: the Reich Cabinet, the SS, the *Sicherheitsdienst* (SD), the Gestapo, the *Sturmabteilung* (SA), and the Nazi High Command. Included in the indictments were charges against the Nazis for "the extermination of racial and national groups, against the civilian populations of certain occupied territories to destroy particular races and classes of people and national, racial, or religious groups, particularly Jews, Poles, and Gypsies and others."

Robert H. Jackson, chief American counsel, opened the trial with an introduction that has been acclaimed in journals of jurisprudence for its clarity and high moral tone, particularly as related to crimes against humanity, such as genocide. Here are several important excerpts from his opening comments.

> What makes this inquest significant is that these prisoners represent sinister influences that will lurk in the world long after their bodies have returned to dust. We will show them to be living symbols of racial hatreds, of terrorism and violence, and of the arrogance and cruelty of power. They are symbols of fierce nationalisms and of militarism, of intrigue and war-making which have embroiled Europe generation after generation, crushing its manhood, destroying its homes, and impoverishing its life. They have so identified themselves with the philosophies they conceived and with the forces they directed that any tenderness to them is a victory and an encouragement to all the evils which are attached to their names. Civilization can afford no compromise with the social forces which would gain renewed strength if we deal ambiguously or indecisively with the men in whom those forces now precariously survive.

> These men created in Germany, under the "Führerprinzip," a National Socialist despotism equaled only by the dynasties of the ancient East. They took from the German people all those dignities and freedoms that we hold natural and inalienable rights in every human being. The people were compensated by inflaming and gratifying hatreds towards those who were marked as "scapegoats." Against their opponents, including Jews, Catholics, and free labor, the Nazis directed such a campaign of arrogance, brutality, and annihilation as the world has not witnessed since the pre-Christian ages. They excited the German

ambition to be a "master race," which of course implies serfdom for others. They led their people on a mad gamble for domination. They diverted social energies and resources to the creation of what they thought to be an invincible war machine. They overran their neighbors. To sustain the "master race" in its war-making, they enslaved millions of human beings and brought them into Germany, where these hapless creatures now wander as "displaced persons." At length bestiality and bad faith reached such excess that they aroused the sleeping strength of imperiled Civilization. Its united efforts have ground the German war machine to fragments. But the struggle has left Europe a liberated yet prostrate land where a demoralized society struggles to survive. These are the fruits of the sinister forces that sit with these defendants in the prisoners' dock.

In general, our case will disclose these defendants all uniting at some time with the Nazi Party in a plan which they well knew could be accomplished only by an outbreak of war in Europe. Their seizure of the German State, their subjugation of the German people, their terrorism and extermination of dissident elements, their planning and waging of war, their calculated and planned ruthlessness in the conduct of warfare, their deliberate and planned criminality toward conquered peoples—all these are ends for which they acted in concert; and all these are phases of the conspiracy, a conspiracy which reached one goal only to set out for another and more ambitious one.

Among the nations which unite in accusing these defendants the United States is perhaps in a position to be the most dispassionate, for, having sustained the least injury, it is perhaps the least animated by vengeance. Our American cities have not been bombed by day and by night, by humans, and by robots. It is not our temples that had been laid in ruins. Our countrymen have not had their homes destroyed over their heads. The menace of Nazi aggression, except to those in actual service, has seemed less personal and immediate to us than to European peoples. But while the United States is not first in rancor, it is not second in determination that the forces of law and order be made equal to the task of dealing with such international lawlessness as I have recited here.[3]

His summation at the end of the trial is equally admired for its judicial wisdom. Here are several excerpts.

The dominant fact which stands out from all the thousands of pages of the record of this Trial is that the central crime of the whole group of Nazi crimes the attack on the peace of the world was clearly and deliberately planned. The beginning of these wars of aggression was not an unprepared and spontaneous springing to arms by a population excited by some current indignation. A week before the invasion of Poland Hitler told his military commanders: "I shall give a propagandist cause for starting war never mind whether it be plausible or not. The victor shall not be asked later on whether we told the truth or not. In starting and making a war, it is not the right that matters, but victory.

Nor were the war crimes and the crimes against humanity unplanned, isolated, or spontaneous offenses. Aside from our undeniable evidence of their plotting, it is sufficient to ask whether 6 million people could be separated from the population of several nations on the basis of their blood and birth, could be destroyed and their bodies disposed of, except that the operation fitted into the general scheme of government. Could the enslavement of 5 millions of laborers, their impressment into service, their transportation to Germany, their allocation to work where they would be most useful, their maintenance, if slow starvation can be called maintenance, and their guarding have been accomplished if it did not fit into the common plan? Could hundreds of concentration camps located throughout Germany, built to accommodate hundreds of thousands of victims, and each requiring labor and materials for construction, manpower to operate and supervise, and close gearing into the economy could such efforts have been expended under German autocracy if they had not suited the plan?

What these men have overlooked is that Adolf Hitler's acts are their acts. It was these men among millions of others, and it was these men leading millions of others, who built up Adolf Hitler and vested in his psychopathic personality not only innumerable lesser decisions but the supreme issue of war or peace. They intoxicated him with power and adulation. They fed his hates and aroused his fears. They put a loaded gun in his eager hands. It was left to Hitler to pull the trigger, and when he did they all at that time approved. His guilt stands admitted, by some defendants reluctantly, by some vindictively. But his guilt is the guilt of the whole dock, and of every man in it.

Hitler ordered everyone else to fight to the last and then retreated into death by his own hand. But he left life as he lived it, a deceiver; he left the official report that he had died in battle. This was the man whom these defendants exalted to a Führer. It was they who conspired to get him absolute authority over all of Germany. And in the end he and the system they created for him brought the ruin of them all.[4]

Robert H. Jackson, for his role at the Nuremberg trials, has gone down in history as a judicial and prosecutorial hero who expatiated in clear language the many crimes the Nazis had committed and why they should be held accountable in a court of law. Jackson, who was an associate justice of the U.S. Supreme Court, was unlike his judicial colleagues in that he learned the law by what's known as "reading the law": while working for a lawyer (just as Abraham Lincoln had). Unlike Lincoln, however, Jackson managed to attend law school for an abbreviated time. Prior to his decision to become a lawyer, he wanted to be a writer and practiced daily for that craft. The combination of law and writerly skills may be one reason he is well known for two aphorisms: "Any lawyer worth his salt will tell the suspect, in no uncertain terms, to make no statement to the police under any circumstances," and about the Supreme Court, "We are not final because we are infallible, but we are infallible only because we are final." Prior to serving on the Supreme Court, he served in the administration of President Roosevelt as solicitor general, then as attorney general. He was nominated to and confirmed as an associate justice of the Supreme Court in 1941 and served until 1954. In 1945, President Truman appointed him chief American counsel at the first Nuremberg Trial and so Jackson took a leave of absence from his position on the court.

Jackson invited Thomas J. Dodd, an outstanding young attorney, to join his prosecutorial team. Thinking that he would serve on the team for only a few months, Dodd accepted the offer but wound up serving as a prosecutor for fifteen grueling months. Initially Jackson named Dodd a senior member of the trial board but then so impressed was Jackson by Dodd's excellent legal skills that when he had to return to Washington, he named Dodd acting chief of counsel. Though Jackson is highly regarded, Dodd is considered to have been much more skillful in his cross examinations of several of the war criminals. His efforts resulted in numerous convictions. After the trial, he was awarded the Medal of Freedom and the Certificate of Merit by President Truman.

That Dodd would achieve such renown did not seem predestined, for early in his career as an FBI agent, he bungled a planned capture of John Dillinger. However, he repaired his reputation following a successful prosecution of the Ku Klux Klan and then another against five Axis spies who had attempted to steal classified army and navy information.

The brilliance of his legal skills at cross examination became apparent not only to the judiciary, the other prosecutors, and defense counsels, but also—much to their regret—to the criminals who were sentenced to death or long prison terms after Dodd devastatingly portrayed them as moral monsters who had committed some of the most heinous crimes in the history of civilized nations.

Those sentenced to death included Wilhelm Keitel, Alfred Rosenberg, Hans Frank, Fritz Sauckel, Wilhelm Frick, Alfred Jodl, Ernst

Kaltenbrunner, Joachim von Ribbentrop, Julius Streicher, and Arthur Seyss-Inquart. Who were these men?

Upon viewing the prisoners, all members of the Nazi hierarchy, slumped and tired in defeat, William Shirer wrote,

> In the dock before the International Military Tribunal they looked different. There had been quite a metamorphosis. Attired in rather shabby clothes, slumped in their seats, fidgeting nervously, they no longer resembled the arrogant leaders of old. They seemed to be a drab assortment of mediocrities. It seemed difficult to grasp that such men, when last you had seen such men, had wielded such monstrous power, that such as they could conquer a great nation and most of Europe.[5]

The arraignment of men who created and executed acts of psychopathic criminality formed a contingent of second-rate thugs, power-mad gangsters, amoral politicians, and homicidal maniacs.

Wilhelm Keitel was a field marshal who served as chief of the Armed Forces High Command, the highest-ranking officer of the Nazi Germany armed forces. He was regarded as a loyal martinet to Hitler. He was a thoughtless sycophant about whom Hitler commented, "You know he has the brains of a movie usher . . . (but he was made the highest ranking officer in the army) . . . because the man's as loyal as a dog." Hermann Goring added that Keitel had "a sergeant's mind inside a field marshal's body" and had been promoted for his loyalty to Hitler. Behind his back, Keitel was known by military officers as "Lakeitel," a pun composed from the German word for "lackey" and his surname.[6]

At Nuremberg he was indicted for conspiracy to commit crimes against peace; planning, initiating, and waging wars of aggression; war crimes; and crimes against humanity. He was convicted on evidence Dodd showed the court that consisted of Keitel's signature on dozens of orders and memos that demanded that captured soldiers and political prisoners be killed. When given an opportunity to speak, he said he had only been following orders based upon his loyalty to Hitler. Yet he admitted that what he had done was illegal. Upon being sentenced, Keitel asked if his death sentence could be carried out by firing squad; his request was denied because the court said he had not acted as a military man but as a criminal. He went to the gallows on October 16, 1946. The trap doorway, through which he shot downward, was small, and as he descended his head swung back and forth like a silent bell, banging against the sides of the drop. Blood dripped over him as his body dangled. He fell a short distance (known as a short drop), as did the other defendants sentenced to death. As a result, his neck was not broken; instead, the rope—like a boa constrictor's muscles, slowly tightened and strangled the life out of him for twenty-four minutes.

Alfred Rosenberg was the head of the NSDAP Office of Foreign Affairs during the twelve-year rule of the Third Reich and was head of his own organization, known as the Rosenberg Bureau. The bureau issued proclamations on Nazi cultural policies and surveilled those whom it considered enemies of the state. Once war broke out, Rosenberg was put in charge of the Reich Ministry for the Occupied Eastern Territories. Following Germany's surrender, Rosenberg was arrested and soon put on trial at Nuremberg. There he was convicted of crimes against peace; planning, initiating, and waging wars of aggression; war crimes; and crimes against humanity. Additionally, he was named a principal planner of the invasions of the Soviet Union and Norway. He was further accused of plundering commodities from occupied countries. At trial it was noted that he had been a key theorist of Nazi ideology that included the necessity for exterminating Jews in Germany and all of Europe and the need for *Lebensraum*. He had also written that the Nazis should reject all aspects of Christianity; indeed, he hated Christianity almost as much as he hated Jews.

In a speech he said,

Some six million Jews still live in the East, and this question can only be solved by a biological extermination of the whole of Jewry in Europe. The Jewish Question will only be solved for Germany when the last Jew has left German territory, and for Europe when not a single Jew stands on the European continent as far as the Urals . . . And to this end it is necessary to force them beyond the Urals or otherwise bring about their eradication.[7]

While on trial, he wrote a self-justifying memoir that was published after his execution by hanging. As with all the executed defendants, his corpse was cremated in Munich and his ashes were carried by a cold October wind, scattering his remains in the Isar River.

Hans Frank, a lawyer, did not use his position as Hitler's legal advisor to benefit anyone but himself and his boss. In fact, he got Hitler to appoint him head of the government in Poland during the war. Prior to that, in June 1933, Hitler named him Reich leader of the Nazi Party, then promoted him to be a member of the cabinet with the title Reich Minister. As a war criminal, he came into his own as governor of Poland, instituting a reign of terror against the civilian population, particularly against the Jews, whom he ordered to be liquidated.

He took particular pleasure in overseeing four extermination camps where thousands of Jews were daily killed.

On December 16, 1941, in a speech to the officers under his command, he stated, "Gentlemen, I must ask you to rid yourself of all feelings of pity. We must annihilate the Jews wherever we find them and whenever it is possible."[8]

Frank was the Samuel Pepys of the Third Reich. His diary was forty-three volumes long, and he proudly turned it over to the Americans following his capture on May 4, 1945. In addition to a record of his two failed suicide attempts, the diaries are a forthright record of all of his crimes. Prosecutors, including Dodd, were able to use Frank's own words to condemn him. It may be the longest written confession in judicial history. Hearing the inevitable sentence of death pronounced by the court, Frank admitted some of his crimes then expressed remorse. To amplify his remorse, he let it be known that during the trial he had converted to Roman Catholicism. Journalist Joseph Kingsbury-Smith wrote of Frank's execution,

> Hans Frank was next in the parade of death. He was the only one of the condemned to enter the chamber with a smile on his countenance. And, although nervous and swallowing frequently, this man, who was converted to Roman Catholicism after his arrest, gave the appearance of being relieved at the prospect of atoning for his evil deeds. He answered to his name quietly and when asked for any last statement, he replied "I am thankful for the kind treatment during my captivity and I ask God to accept me with mercy."[9]

On the recommendation of the notorious Martin Bormann (Hitler's private secretary), Ernst "Fritz" Sauckel worked directly under the even more notorious Hermann Göring as general plenipotentiary for labor deployment—a euphemistic title for being in charge of slave labor. He was charged with forcibly bringing more than 4.5 million Polish and Russian workers to Germany. Concentration camp workers were regularly beaten for not working fast enough or for not achieving their production quotas. Their lives were made even more miserable by the starvation diets that barely kept them alive. Many did not survive. Sauckel made his point in a letter to Alfred Rosenberg: "All the men [prisoners of war and foreign civilian workers] must be fed, sheltered, and treated in such a way as to exploit them to the highest possible extent at the lowest conceivable degree of expenditure."[10]

He, like Frank, was condemned by his own words, found guilty and hanged like the others. Just before the hangman's noose was placed around his neck, he stated, "I die an innocent man, my sentence is unjust. God protect Germany. May it live and one day become great again. God protect my family."

Wilhelm Frick began his rise in the Nazi Party as early as 1923 when he participated in Hitler's failed Beer Hall Putsch. By 1933, Hitler had appointed him Reich Minister for the Interior then promoted him again to the position of *Reichsleiter*, the second-highest political rank in the Nazi Party. His upward rise continued, and in May 1934 he was appointed Prussian Minister of the Interior (head of the police) under Minister-President Hermann Göring. By 1935 he also had near-total control over the local government.

But his crimes against humanity were based on his drafting numerous laws against Jews (e.g., Law for the Restoration of the Professional Civil Service) and the notorious Nuremberg Laws. The laws he originated and implemented resulted in the forced sterilization of those with mental and physical disabilities and progressed to massive acts of euthanasia. At trial, he was one of only two defendants who refused to testify in his own defense. The other was Rudolf Hess. Frick was convicted not only of planning, initiating, and waging wars of aggression and committing war crimes and crimes against humanity but also for formulating the Enabling Act and the Nuremberg Laws. Those laws had been used to deport millions of people to their deaths in the concentration camps. And the very existence of those camps was attributed to Frick. Of Frick's execution, Kingsbury-Smith wrote,

> The sixth man to leave his prison cell and walk with handcuffed wrists to the death house was 69-year-old Wilhelm Frick. He entered the execution chamber at 2.05 am, six minutes after Rosenberg had been pronounced dead. He seemed the least steady of any so far and stumbled on the thirteenth step of the gallows. His only words were, "Long live eternal Germany,"[11] before he was hooded and dropped through the trap.

Alfred Jodl, a high-ranking general in the *Wehrmacht*, was chief of staff during the invasions of Denmark and Norway. His own death sentence grew out of his signing the Commissar Order of June 6, 1941, which stated that all Soviet commissars were to be shot. Another order would eventually add weight to Jodl being convicted of war crimes and crimes against humanity. It was the Commando Order of October 28, 1942, which stated that all Allied commandos, including those in uniforms as well as those in civilian clothes, were to be shot without trial if caught behind German lines.

Jodl saw himself as a strict military man who was above lowering himself to the status of a mere criminal. It was as a military officer and representative of the German high command that he signed Germany's unconditional instrument of surrender on May 7, 1945. As a top general, he was shocked that he was condemned with those who ran the extermination camps. His Commando and Commissar Orders would confirm his guilt. When presented with evidence of the shootings of Soviet prisoners of war, Jodl stated that the prisoners shot were "not those that could not, but those that did not *want* to walk"[12]—in other words, recalcitrant prisoners who had the gall to defy SS orders to march. Jodl's callousness was reflected back to him in the stern expressions of the judges. As if the two orders were not sufficient cause for him to be found guilty, he was presented with evidence of his signature on an order to transfer Danish citizens, including Jews, to concentration camps. Like many unremorseful Nazis who deemed themselves patriots of the Third Reich, he shouted from the gallows, "I salute you, my eternal Germany."[13]

As a high-ranking SS official, Ernst Kaltenbrunner was a hydra-headed criminal who had been in charge of three vastly powerful organizations: the Gestapo (the secret state police), Kripo (the criminal police), and SD (the security service). He oversaw them from January 1943 until Germany's surrender in 1945. He was as vociferous and fanatical an anti-Semite as his childhood pal, Adolf Eichmann, and as loyal to Hitler as one of the Führer's German shepherds. He was feared by many, including Himmler, who was intimidated by Kaltenbrunner's fiery temper and his imposing appearance: 6'4" and a face etched with numerous fencing scars. He was the highest-ranking SS member on trial at Nuremberg.

According to Leni Yahil, Kaltenbrunner accelerated the Jewish genocide for "the process of extermination was to be expedited and the concentration of the Jews in the Reich itself and the occupied countries was to be liquidated as soon as possible."[14]

In addition to being violently anti-Semitic, Kaltenbrunner hated homosexuals, and in 1943 he demanded that the Ministry of Justice mandate compulsory castration of all homosexuals. More than six thousand homosexual members of the *Wehrmacht* were tried and imprisoned on his orders.[15]

Following Germany's surrender, Kaltenbrunner took off like a rabbit at the sound of a shotgun. He, his adjutant, and a pair of SS officers, using falsified papers, made their way to a mountaintop cabin in Austria. He was soon captured by members of the U.S. Army Intelligence Corps and the Eightieth Infantry Division, Third U.S. Army. They had been tipped off by an assistant *Burgermeister* named Johann Brandauer. The corps members and soldiers climbed over ice-covered terrain and jagged rocks for six hours before reaching the hideout. Once there, the corps leader announced that Kaltenbrunner and his comrades were surrounded and they should exit the cabin. There was a brief standoff, but unable to escape, the quartet surrendered on May 12, 1945. Kaltenbrunner pretended to his captors that he was a doctor but as he was being led off to prison, his mistress Countess Gisela von Westarp called out his name. The jig was up. Kaltenbrunner's lover had lifted the veil that concealed his real identity. When put in the dock at Nuremberg, Kaltenbrunner, no longer inspiring fear in anyone, desperately claimed that all the decrees that the prosecution used as evidence contained only his rubber-stamped signature that was applied by his Gestapo underling. He knew nothing about it. He even claimed that he had urged Hitler to end the genocide of the Jews. Nevertheless, he was found guilty and sentenced to death by hanging, which took place on October 16, 1946, at 1:15 a.m.

As ambassador to the Court of St. James, Joachim von Ribbentrop was said by an American reporter to have the dreary, dead eyes of someone with a bad hangover. He was a hapless blunderer, the Inspector Clouseau of the Nazi foreign service who mouthed Hitler's most outrageous comments as if they were his own. They were like a ventriloquist and his obedient dummy. Hitler marveled at such loyalty. Yet Ribbentrop's buffoonery and faux pas earned him the derision of many of the Nazi top leaders. Two examples will suffice. In November 1936, while serving as ambassador to Great Britain, Ribbontrop accompanied the Seventh Marquess of Londonderry to Durham Cathedral for a Sunday morning religious service. As the organist played *Glorious Things of Thee Are Spoken*, Ribbentrop leapt to his feet and gave the stiff-armed Nazi salute. The marquess, flushed with embarrassment, grabbed his outstretched arm and yanked it down as if it were the handle on a gallows that the executioner thrusts downward dropping a hanged man to his death. Ribbentrop, a look of annoyance on his normally placid face, reluctantly sat down, his face now set in an angry grimace. The following year, Ribbentrop was invited to Buckingham Palace to meet King George VI. Upon hearing the conclusion of the formal introduction of the king, Ribbentrop again gave the stiff-armed Nazi salute: as the king approached his guest, he was nearly knocked over by an underhanded smack to his chin. He quickly backed up a few steps as Ribbontrop lowered his outstretched arm. Göring once said of Ribbentrop that he was like a mechanical soldier whose Nazi salute popped up at the most inauspicious times. Ribbontrop's own secretary said that his employer was "pompous, conceited and not too intelligent and utterly insufferable to work for." To Hitler, Göring commented that Ribbentrop was a "stupid ass." Yet Hitler was deeply appreciative of Ribbentrop's loyalty and came to his defense, saying, "But after all, he knows quite a lot of important people in England." Göring replied, "*Mein Führer*, that may be right, but the bad thing is, they know *him*."[16]

Asked how Hitler could have promoted such a fool to high office, a German diplomat stated, "Hitler never noticed Ribbentrop's babbling because Hitler always did all the talking."[17]

Yet this foolish man with an IQ of 129, the tenth-highest of those on trial, had proved to be an effective negotiator, his efforts resulting in the Molotov-Ribbentrop Pact (the Nazi-Soviet non-aggression pact) and the Pact of Steel alliance with Italy. He was so deeply involved in executing Nazi ideology and its resulting crimes that he was charged and convicted of crimes against humanity, crimes against peace, and war crimes. As an advocate for the highest levels of productivity, he had ordered that all diplomats in Axis countries speed up the extermination of Jews. Like many homicidal criminals, murder for him was as easy as swatting flies. That he supported the execution of American and British airmen who had been shot down over Germany did not strike him as immoral. He was such a devotee of Nazi ideology and Hitler that he told his guard at Nuremberg that if Hitler came to him then, he would still do what he was asked to do. However, once he knew that he faced a death sentence, he told the judges at Nuremberg that Hitler had deceived him about his aggressive intentions. On October 16, 1946, he was the first of the Nuremberg defendants to be hanged.

Julius Streicher was considered extreme even by some of the most extreme members of the Nazi hierarchy. Author John Gunther wrote that Streicher was "the worst of the anti-Semites."[18] A raving, raging anti-Semite with the heart of an insatiable entrepreneur, he became a millionaire publisher by printing viciously anti-Semitic tracts and books for adults and children that warned of the dangers of Jewry and preached the need for the extermination of all Jews. Such assaults resulted in large sales and bountiful profits. While his publishing company was raking in millions of Reichsmarks, Streicher's newspaper, *Der Stürmer*, a weekly tabloid that he began in 1923 and published until the end of the war, was also making millions from a combination of advertising and subscriptions. Its headlines screamed fabricated cases of Jewish criminality, and its news stories consisted of blood libels about Jews killing Christian children to make matzos. *Der Stürmer* also attracted readers by publishing pornographic cartoons of Jewish men raping German maidens. Its editorial screeds regularly demanded the extermination of Jews. The paper was so popular that it was read by many German immigrants in the United States, Canada, and several South American countries and had a circulation of more than 600,000; but, of course, its largest circulation was in Germany.

For Streicher's relentless incitement against Jews, Hitler appointed him *Gauleiter* in the Bavarian area of Franconia. In that position Streicher ordered that 250 Jews be arrested and forced to mow a grassy field by using their teeth to pluck up all the blades of grass. It's not surprising that Hitler declared *Der Stürmer* his favorite newspaper and made sure that Germans were able to read it in countless public venues.

Streicher was so psychopathic in his advocacy of extermination of the Jews that he proved an embarrassment to many Nazis who endeavored to camouflage their anti-Semitism with euphemisms such as "the Final Solution." Streicher's most critical enemy was Hermann Göring, who ordered his staff never to read *Der Stürmer* and never permitted a copy to be seen in his offices. In 1940, Göring helped to engineer the loss of much of Streicher's power; yet Hitler wanted Streicher to keep publishing anti-Semitic books and *Der Stürmer*. Hitler considered Streicher a brilliant journalist, and Streicher gladly accepted the evaluation, though his IQ was 106, 23 points lower than Ribbentrop's and the lowest of all those sentenced to death at Nuremberg.

Following his capture after the war, he was indicted and convicted of crimes against humanity for inciting others to exterminate millions of Jews. Throughout the trial he vehemently complained that all the judges were Jews and on that account were prejudiced against him. When the trap door opened and he dropped at the end of a rope, he descended wildly kicking and squirming, which caused the noose to loosen around his neck. Rather than quickly dying he slowly strangled to death, his legs still kicking, his body squirming, trying to escape the fate he had brought on himself.

In contrast to Streicher's limited intellectual abilities, Arthur Seyss-Inquart was the smartest of those condemned to death. He had an IQ of 141. By profession, he was a lawyer. However, being a successful lawyer did not reflect his image of himself as an important personage in the history of Germany. He began promoting himself to political importance by opportunistically joining the Nazi Party in 1938. Hitler was impressed by the man's devotion to Nazi ideology and to the Führer himself. He was rewarded with an appointment as governor of Austria, which had become a German province known as *Ostmark* following the *Anschluss* (the annexation of Austria by Germany on March 12, 1938). As governor of Austria, Seyss-Inquart ordered the confiscation of all Jewish property and later arranged for Jewish deportations to concentration camps. From his position as governor, Seyss-Inquart was promoted to *Reichskommissar* of the Netherlands. In that position, he instituted a reign of terror during which most of the Dutch Jews were deported to concentration camps. Of the 140,000 Jews who were deported, only 30,000 were still living at the end of the war.

As the Allies were closing in on a losing Germany, Seyss-Inquart insisted he would not surrender. He told General Walter Bedell Smith that no surrender was possible. In response, Smith told him that he would be shot, to which Seyss-Inquart arrogantly responded, "That leaves me cold." Smith grinned and said, "It certainly will." [19]

Not living up to his word, Seyss-Inquart was arrested on the Elbe Bridge in Hamburg. He did not offer any resistance nor did he ask to be shot. One of the two men who arrested him was a member of the Royal Welsh Fusiliers named Norman Miller, who had been saved as a fifteen-year-old by the famous *Kindertransport* that bought him to England. He was the only survivor of his family, all of whom had been killed in Riga, Latvia, in 1942.

Seyss-Inquart was put on trial and convicted of planning, initiating, and waging wars of aggression; war crimes; and crimes against humanity. One of his most famous victims was a sixteen-year-old girl named Anne Frank. When the guilty verdict was read and Seyss-Inquart was sentenced to death by hanging, he said, "Death by hanging. . . . Well, in view of the whole situation, I never expected anything different. It's all right."[20]

Two of those indicted and sentenced to death, but who escaped the hangman's noose, were Martin Bormann and Hermann Göring.

Bormann was power hungry, officious, and so sycophantically devoted to Hitler that he accompanied his master wherever he went. He was always so close to Hitler that Göring said he could have been the Führer's shadow. As expected, the Führer was delighted to have such a devoted acolyte as his private secretary. Bormann, ever hungry for authority, was rewarded for his loyalty by being given final approval over all civil service appointments. In addition, he reviewed and approved legislation, and by 1943 he had control over all German domestic matters. Bormann, as a Nazi ideologue, was not only an ardent anti-Semite, he advocated the persecution of Christian churches and clergy too. As the end of the Third Reich became imminent, Bormann did not fade in his devotion to Hitler: he followed his master to the Führer's bunker in Berlin on January 16, 1945. They could hear the pounding of Russian artillery and the crack of gunfire as the Russians closed in on Berlin. Hitler was a nervous wreck. The apocalypse was fast approaching, dooming the one-thousand-year Reich that Hitler had promised. Hitler, though possessed of a messianic view of his destiny as Germany's leader, was sufficiently a realist to know that if the Russians got hold of him, he would be arrested as a war criminal, put on trial in Moscow, and executed. Or the Russian hordes might get him first, kill him, then hang his corpse upside down, as happened to his ally, Benito Mussolini. Better to commit suicide.

After Hitler had killed himself, a rattled Bormann took off like a horse from a burning barn. He hoped to evade capture by the Russians and perhaps find a safe haven in South America via the rat lines. He was as fearful of capture as Hitler had been. He knew that Russian soldiers wanted revenge for the millions of their fellow citizens who had been murdered by the Nazis. In the end he seemed to disappear, though the Allies surmised that he had probably committed suicide. Bormann, tried in absentia at Nuremberg, was found guilty of war crimes and crimes against humanity. If he were found, he was to be executed by hanging. A body thought to be Bormann's was found near Lehrter station and was buried on May 8, 1945, though it wasn't officially identified as Bormann's until 1973. In 1998, DNA tests confirmed that it was indeed Bormann's body. He had apparently killed himself by biting into a cyanide capsule. His body was cremated and his ashes scattered in the air over the Baltic Sea on August 16, 1999.

Whereas Bormann was sycophantic, a weaselly Uriah Heep, Göring was arrogant and often spoke candidly to Hitler. And unlike all the other defendants, Göring was the only one who could boast a heroic past from his participation in World War I. He had been an ace fighter pilot, a recipient of the prestigious Blue Max award, and a commander of the *Jagdgeschwader*, a fighter group that had previously been led by the celebrated Red Baron, Manfred von Richthofen (whose daughter married the novelist D. H. Lawrence). Yet Göring was drawn to the former dispatch runner of the Bavarian Reserve Infantry Regiment, Adolf Hitler, whose oratorical skills impressed him. Göring, along with Rudolf Hess, Ernst Rohm, and Alfred Rosenberg was an early member of the Nazi Party. He participated with Hitler in the failed Beer Hall Putsch of 1923 and suffered a severe wound to his groin. He was taken to the hospital, where surgery was performed. Göring was given regular doses of morphine to alleviate the pain, and from that time until he was tried at Nuremberg, he was addicted to the drug. He would evolve to become the second-highest-ranking Nazi after the Führer.

On his way to increased power, he oversaw the creation of the feared Gestapo. He later let Heinrich Himmler run the organization. However, he was best known as the commander-in-chief of the Luftwaffe, and after the Nazi victory over France, he was made *Reichsmarschall*, head of all the German armed forces. He was also a kleptomaniac and secured vast wealth for himself by stealing paintings, sculpture, and valuable artifacts from Jews; paintings and sculpture from the museums of defeated nations; and jewelry, cash, and homes from those whom the Nazis murdered throughout Eastern Europe. However, as the war progressed and the Nazis suffered a series of defeats, Göring's star began to dim. So certain was he of the power of the Luftwaffe to control the skies over Germany that he once proudly bragged that if the Allies were ever to bomb Germany, you could call him "Meyer" (i.e., a name usually associated with Jews). As the bombardment of Germany increased, many airmen surreptitiously referred to him as Meyer. He began to withdraw from active commitment to Germany's defense not out of shame for his failures but because he wanted to devote more time to his insatiable kleptomania—and of course, the escapist pleasures of morphine. Yet he still thought of himself as the second-most-powerful man in Germany, so when he learned that Hitler intended to commit suicide before he could be captured by the Russians, Göring sent the Führer a telegram asking to be appointed head of the Third Reich. Hitler flew into a rage, frenziedly waved his arms, shouted that Göring was a traitor and should immediately be expelled from the Nazi Party. He then ordered Göring's arrest for treason, and Bormann followed up by ordering that Göring be shot. Knowing that Germany's collapse was imminent, Göring rushed to the American lines, hoping to reach them before he could be taken by the Red Army, for the Russians would have either shot him on sight or made him a humiliated figure in a show trial in Moscow. After such a trial, which would have been filmed and shown throughout the Soviet Union, execution would have been sure to follow. Instead, the soldiers of the U.S. Thirty-Sixth Infantry Division arrested him near Radstadt on May 6, 1945. He was grateful to be taken into custody and even joked with his captors as if the war had been a game badly played by the Germans. Göring pretended to be a good loser, a good sport to the end.

He remained an arrogantly proud man who felt he should have been the highest-ranking Nazi at the Nuremberg trials and not Admiral Karl Donitz, whom Hitler had appointed Reich president. Yet Göring stylishly set himself apart from the other defendants by wearing a powder-blue uniform with polished metal buttons but stripped of its array of colorful medals. The once obese *Reichsmarschall*, who once weighed more than three hundred pounds, sat in the first row of the prisoners' dock diminished by his sickly loss of weight and vaporous prestige. In earlier days he never would have been seen in such an ill-fitting uniform, certainly not like the one he now wore with its shoulder pads drooping over his upper arms and excess fabric bunched around his soft belly. He was indicted on the following charges: conspiracy; waging a war of aggression; war crimes such as the plundering and removal to Germany of works of art and property; and crimes against humanity, including the disappearance of political and other opponents under Hitler's Night and Fog Decree; the torture and ill-treatment of prisoners of war; and the murder and enslavement of civilians, including what was at the time estimated to be 5,700,000 Jews. To all charges of the indictment, Göring pleaded not guilty. He regarded his codefendants with contempt, for he stated they were not up to his high standards and historical importance. Only he should be on trial, he asserted to an army psychiatrist. Yet Göring proved to be a clever defendant and was able to outwit Robert Jackson, who was the first prosecutor to cross-examine him.

According to Airey Neave, the attorney who indicted Göring and author of *Nuremberg*,

> Jackson was certainly ill-prepared for this contest. He did not realize he was dealing with a subtle master of European affairs and the form and substance of many of his questions were an invitation for Goering to repeat his indictment of the Versailles Treaty. . . . The cross-examination had not proceeded more than ten minutes before Jackson was in trouble. It was obvious that Goering would soon be master. He saw the intention behind each fumbling question. Soon Jackson was overwhelmed by his documents and his resonant voice. Goering offered to help him.[21]

Neave goes on,

> Goering had won the first round but he lost the next decisively to the British. On the following day, Sir David Maxwell-Fyfe rose to cross-examine and he pressed Goering about his knowledge of the murder of the fifty RAF officers after their escape. Goering immediately looked frightened and ashamed. Soon with clenched fists and red with anger, he denied that he or Field Marshall Milch knew anything about it. For many in the courtroom the affair of the Great Escape sounded the death knell for Goering.[22]

It was the beginning of the end for Göring, and his defense crumbled like a deserted building under Allied bombardment.

Jackson, though failing to break down Göring's defenses during cross-examination, delivered a devastating summation that unnerved the defendant: "Goering was equally adept at massacring opponents and at fanning scandals to get rid of stubborn generals. He built up the Luftwaffe and hurled it at his defenseless neighbors. He was among the foremost in harrying Jews out of the land." Jackson added that Göring was "half militarist and half gangster."[23]

The court found Göring guilty on all counts, and he was sentenced to death by hanging. The judgment stated,

> There is nothing to be said in mitigation. For Göring was often, indeed almost always, the moving force, second only to his leader. He was the leading war aggressor, both as political and as military leader; he was the director of the slave labour programme and the creator of the oppressive programme against the Jews and other races, at home and abroad. All of these crimes he has frankly admitted. On some specific cases there may be conflict of testimony, but in terms of the broad outline, his own admissions are more than sufficiently wide to be conclusive of his guilt. His guilt is unique in its enormity. The record discloses no excuses for this man.[24]

Upon hearing that he was to be hanged he asked the court that he be executed by firing squad as befitting a soldier of his rank. The court declined his request and affirmed that he should be hanged. Confined to his cell, he committed suicide by biting down on a potassium cyanide capsule that had been smuggled to him by an American soldier.

The man who put the nooses around those who didn't escape death was Master Sergeant John C. Woods. In 1929 he had gone AWOL from the U.S. Navy and was subsequently court-martialed. Prior to his trial, military psychiatrists had diagnosed him as suffering "constitutional psychopathic inferiority without psychosis." The navy concluded that he would be of poor service and so discharged him. Then in 1943 he was drafted by the U.S. Army. He eventually was promoted from private to master sergeant and sent to the Paris Disciplinary Training Center, where he was proud to be the primary executioner, hanging thirty-four American soldiers. The army, however, reported that he participated in at least eleven bungled hangings of U.S. soldiers between 1944 and 1946. Such bungles did not halt or deter his career as an executioner. He was a man proud of his prowess and professionalism. Following the executions of the war criminals at Nuremberg, Woods told a reporter from *Time* that he was proud of his work. "The way I look at this hanging job, somebody has to do it . . . 10 men in 103 minutes. That's fast work."[25] On July 21, 1950, while repairing a lighting set, Woods managed to electrocute himself. He is buried in Toronto, Kansas.

After it was all over, the prosecutors returned to their homelands. Many Nazi criminals had been executed or sentenced to prison terms. Many more returned to their pre-war jobs as if the war and their crimes had never taken place. Back in the United States, Thomas Dodd said of the Nuremberg trials that he had performed "an autopsy on history's most horrible catalogue of human crime."[26]

# ⑪

# German Boxing before, during, and after the War

There was no athlete in Germany who was more emblematic of the sport of boxing and more celebrated than Max Schmeling. From 1939, when he knocked out Adolf Heuser in the first round, to 1948, when he lost his final bout to Richard Vogt, he tried to escape the degradation of being a Nazi pawn and of having fought as a paratrooper for a government that he held in contempt. That government even coerced him into being an emissary to the pope, for Hitler and Goebbels wanted the pope to bless their war efforts and say that he was praying for a German victory. Schmeling's meeting with the pope did not produce the results that Goebbels wanted to trumpet to the world. Here's what happened.

> Schmeling was brought to the Papal Palace and ushered past the Swiss Guards and into the pope's private chambers, where after a brief waiting period, he was received by the pope. Pope Pius XII entered the room and heartily greeted Schmeling, whom he had admired from afar. He thought that Schmeling was a marvelous athlete and had watched films of his fights. The pope, according to Schmeling's autobiography, expressed his sadness about the immense destruction of Europe and the death and wounding of people throughout the world during the war. He said that he would pray for peace. Schmeling thanked the pope for his time and departed.[1]

Goebbels was furious at the outcome and would not let newspapers in Germany report the pope's comments. His fury raged more intensely when he learned that various European newspapers had quoted the pope. Goebbels vehemently blamed Schmeling for the unforeseen and unfortunate results.

Schmeling was secretly pleased that the pope had not advocated for a German victory. It was Schmeling's modus operandi to passive-aggressively disobey the demands of Hitler, Göring, and Goebbels while never venturing to tell them that he thought Nazism was an obscenity that imposed a barbaric darkness over Germany and the conquered countries. He certainly never told them that he had hidden two Jewish teenagers in his apartment during *Kristallnacht*, but he spoke clearly and with certainty when he told Hitler he would not fire his Jewish manager, Joe Jacobs. Hitler had demanded Jacobs be fired after the manager embarrassed the Nazis. As we saw in chapter 1, this occurred following one of Schmeling's knockout victories in Germany. Jacobs had rushed into the ring to congratulate Schmeling. As the spectators stood and honored Schmeling with the stiff-armed Nazi salute amid chants of *Sieg Heil*, Jacobs—unsure of exactly what to do—took his ever-present cigar from his mouth, held it between his index and middle finger, and raised his arm straight over his head. To onlookers and in newspaper photos, Jacobs looked as if he were giving the finger to the Nazis. Hitler was furious. Jacobs must go. No, said Schmeling, who demonstrated extraordinary courage and loyalty. It's amazing that he was not penalized for his disobedience. Hitler uncharacteristically dropped the subject of Jacobs and dismissed Schmeling from his presence.

On another occasion, prior to America entering the war, Schmeling told an American reporter that he hoped Germany and America would not go to war against one another. He said it would be a tragedy, especially since he regarded America as his second home. For that breach of Nazi etiquette, Schmeling was nearly court-martialed. Goebbels had him tried before a military tribunal as a traitor. However, since Germany and America were not yet warring enemies, Schmeling had not committed treason and so he was acquitted, much to Goebbels's disgust. Goebbels then made sure that Schmeling's name and image would not be printed in any German newspaper. He would not be the subject of any newsreels. He was a nonperson, so much so that when he was discharged from the army in 1943, no notice appeared in any German publication.

Back in 1939, Schmeling had incurred the wrath of Goebbels through no fault of his own. Schmeling was signed to fight Adolf Heuser (aka "the Bulldog of the Rhine" and "the Bonn Tornado") in a bout for the EBU European Heavyweight title and the German BDB Heavyweight title. Schmeling knocked out his opponent, who lay sprawled unconscious in the ring for an unusually long time and required artificial respiration to be brought back to consciousness. Though the fight had taken place in what was then known as *Adolf-Hitler-Kampfbahn* (Adolf Hitler Stadium), a local newspaper reported that Schmeling had knocked out Adolf Hitler in Adolf Heuser Stadium. The misprint caused Goebbels, who as minister of propaganda controlled all the newspapers in Germany, to fly into a rage and accuse Schmeling of attempting to undermine Hitler's dignity. Nothing came of the accusation. It was another reason for Goebbels to dislike Schmeling.

Goebbels also disliked Heuser, for the fighter had suffered an ignominious loss to the Jewish boxer Slapsy Maxie Rosenbloom in 1933. It was not a good year for German boxers fighting Jews, for that same year Schmeling lost to Max Baer in a fight that Schmeling called a disaster. The referee had to stop the fight out of concern that Baer would kill Schmeling. Film of the fight was banned in Germany and a radio broadcast of the fight was censored once it was apparent that Schmeling could not withstand Baer's brutal attack.

That Schmeling was not sent off to a concentration camp for all his failures to please Hitler and Goebbels speaks to his enormous popularity as the premier German athlete of the 1930s. Win or lose, he was beloved not only by boxing fans but by all those who prized his exceptional athletic abilities.

Heuser, unlike Schmeling, was eager to get into Goebbels's good graces. He had more than a dozen fights during the war, emerging as both a heavyweight and a light heavyweight champion. He had a record of 88 wins, 21 losses, and 17 draws. Though the Nazis cheered his victories, their appreciation did not save Heuser from a life of clinical depression and humiliating poverty. After his house was bombed into rubble during the war, he was so traumatized that he never fought a title fight again. His fights lacked the zest and confrontational determination of his earlier battles. He continued to fight until February 1949, when he lost to Helmut Janke. He was forty-one years old and spent the next forty years in a state of unremitting depression. He was in and out of psychiatric hospitals. When outside, he volunteered in a restaurant in Bonn. But once his condition overwhelmed his ability to work, he was again hospitalized. He died in 1988, age eighty-one. Though he was an afterthought to the Nazis, a road in Bonn, the Adolf-Heuser-Weg, was named after him in 1997.

Max Schmeling's postwar life was rosy compared to that of Heuser. The war over, Schmeling decided he would return to boxing. He had no other skills other than leaping out of a plane as a paratrooper. From boxing he could still earn a living. People knew him as the boxer who had beaten Joe Louis and who had been badly beaten by the partly Jewish boxer Max Baer. He could still draw a crowd. So he arranged for a series of fights, training as vigorously as he ever had. In his first postwar fight, he knocked out Werner Vollmer in the 7th round of a 10-round bout. Less than three months later, on December 7, 1947, he beat Hans Joachim Draegestein on points in a 10-round bout. He fought Draegestein again on October 2, 1948, and this time scored a TKO in the 9th round of a 10-round bout. Draegestein did not have a great record: 23 bouts of which he won 7, lost 8, and had 7 draws. His career ended in 1950, with each of his last 12 fights ending in a loss.

Between his two bouts with Draegestein, Schmeling lost a decision to Walter Neusel on May 23, 1948. Neusel, known as "the Blonde Tiger," was a formidable heavyweight who was ranked the sixth-best German boxer across all weight divisions. Yet years earlier, on August 26, 1934, he suffered a 9th-round TKO loss after a relentless pounding by Schmeling. The fight generated a great deal of publicity for the two men fought in front of an audience of more than 100,000 boxing fans. It was the largest audience at that time for a German boxing match. Though Neusel put up a valiant defense against Schmeling, he was not able to withstand the barrage of punches that Schmeling landed. Nearly six years later, on June 22, 1940, Neusel finally won what he had aimed for since the start of his pugilistic career, the German Heavyweight Championship, by beating the formidable Arno Kolblin. However, the sweet taste of victory turned bitter when he lost the title on November 3, 1940, in a bout with Heinz Lazek. Never giving up on his ambition for a championship, he regained it on June 6, 1942, by beating Adolf Heuser, and would go on to beat Schmeling on points after the war. The end of Schmeling's boxing career was just around a few more ring corners. He had 5 postwar fights, winning 3 and losing 2, including a loss to Neusel.

By 1948, Schmeling was forty-three years old—long in the tooth for a professional boxer—but still in need of money so he agreed to participate in one more fight. It would be against Richard Vogt, who had won a silver medal as a light heavyweight in the 1936 Berlin Olympics. Before twenty-thousand spectators, Schmeling and Vogt put on a fast-paced display of pugilistic skills that did not cease until the final bell sounded. When it was over, Schmeling had lost the decision. It was his seventieth fight, his last hurrah. He would need to find another means of earning a living.

He felt no shame in losing for Vogt had been a tough opponent, regarded as one of Germany's premier pugilists. He had begun his career in 1938 and retired in 1952, having won 55 bouts, with 7 losses and 10 draws. He had won the German Light Heavyweight title in 1950. Schmeling understood that his own speed and stamina had diminished with age, that boxing was a young man's game, and it was time for him to move on. He had compiled an impressive record of 56 wins, 10 losses, and 4 draws. He was regarded by sportswriters and fans as the best German boxer of the twentieth century. A modest man, he was quietly proud of his accomplishments as a boxer.

His boxing career over, Schmeling and his wife, Anny Ondra Ondrakova, a former Czech movie star, settled in Hamburg. The couple had been married since 1933 and were still treated as celebrities. Out shopping, dining, dancing, or just strolling down a boulevard, they were often photographed and asked for their autographs. Goebbels, who had killed himself, was no longer there to block newspapers from printing photos of the Schmelings.

By 1950, the future looked bright for Schmeling: he had secured a job with the Coca-Cola Company at the firm's German offices. It was the beginning of a stellar career that would make him a wealthy man. Before long, he owned his own bottling plant and held a senior executive position with the company.

Having secured a level of comfort and security, Schmeling felt he could visit America without suffering accusations of having been a Nazi pawn. So in 1954 he decided to pay his respects to the memory of his former manager Joe Jacobs (who had died in 1939) and to former ring opponent Joe Louis.

> I flew to New York. My first path took me to a Jewish Cemetery. The caretaker, a small bent over man wearing a black yarmulke, asked me whom I was looking for. And when I told him, he said, "So you come from Germany?" Then he showed me the way. It was a beautiful spring day. Trotting on ahead, the caretaker led me through a maze of headstones.
>
> He stopped in front of a simple grave marked only by a flat stone plaque. Then he began to speak—"Joe," he said bending way over as if he wanted the deceased to understand, "Joe, here is a friend of yours! Its Max Schmeling. He didn't forget you. He came from Germany and wants to visit you. His first stop, Joe, was to visit you."
>
> As the little man spoke I stood unmoving, looking at the weathered stone. I imagined Joe, how he used to gesticulate excitedly from my corner of the ring, pulling animatedly on the ropes chattering away wildly at me in the locker room and always with the cigar in his mouth, which he really didn't smoke, but rather chewed, literally eating the cigar from one end to the other.
>
> The old man brought me out of my thoughts. "Friends always die too soon," he said, "no matter how old they live to be. But Joe here, he died much too soon."[2]

From Brooklyn, Schmeling traveled to Chicago to visit Joe Louis, with whom he had two highly publicized fights. Journalists had portrayed their encounters as battles between Nazi ideology and American democratic values.

> During the war and into the postwar years as well, journalists had sought repeatedly to play us off against each other . . . trying to put hateful or insulting words in our mouths.
>
> One day, without calling ahead, I found myself standing at Joe Louis's door. A woman answered the door, seemed startled for a moment, and then said in surprise, "Oh, Mr. Schmeling. Please come in."
>
> She told me that Joe was unfortunately not at home but out playing golf, and that she would call him right away. But Joe was already on his way home. I had only waited a few minutes when the front door opened. I heard her speak to him and then he was standing before me. For a few moment he stood there as if he had grown roots. Then he dropped his golf bag and rushed over to me. "Max! How good to see you again!"
>
> We sat there together for hours, until late in the evening, talking about the great fights and the old friends. And it was only then that I realized how much it had bothered me over the years that the hatreds of the times had managed to separate us. A short time later, Joe visited me in Hamburg.[3]

Schmeling, throughout the remainder of his life, provided financial help to Louis, and upon Louis's death on April 12, 1981, he paid for his friend's funeral. Schmeling's wife died six years later on February 28, 1987. One year short of a century of life, Schmeling died on February 2, 2005. He was celebrated throughout his native land: newspapers, television, the internet were full of stories about his life, an honorable German who followed his conscience and not poisonous Nazi ideology.

While Schmeling remained friends with many Jews from the boxing world of the 1930s, no Jewish boxers played an important role in postwar Germany. They had either emigrated or they had been exterminated in the concentration camps.

Boxing is not as popular in Germany as it once was. There was a brief spurt of great popularity soon after the fall of the Berlin Wall, and many champions excited fans who regularly tuned in on television to watch the bouts. But soon the interest died down. Very few boxers had personalities that excited the public, and boxing's popularity has always depended on the outsized personalities of its champions.

Though there has been a number of skillful boxers in postwar Germany, no one has exhibited the kind of charisma that Schmeling did.

No one, that is, until Wladimir Klitschko (aka "Dr. Steelhammer") dropped one opponent after another to the raucous cheers of rapt boxing fans. Though actually a Ukrainian, he is considered an honorary citizen of Hamburg, where he has lived for decades. According to German surveys, he is listed as one of the most recognizable athletes in Germany and one of the most marketable. He drew fans to his fights as if he were a rock star. From 2004 to 2015, the 6'5" pugilist carried the banner for what became known as the Klitschko era. He was aided by his brother Vitali, who was also a heavyweight champion and went on to become the mayor of Kyiv in the Ukraine. Both brothers earned PhDs in sports science.

Wladimir began his career in 1996 and accumulated an impressive record of 64 wins and only 5 losses. During his career he was celebrated for 24 consecutive wins, 10 by knockout. His total number of knockouts was 53. He had an overwhelming ring presence. As soon as he entered a ring, crowds roared their approval, cheering, whistling, stamping their feet, whooping and hollering. Of course, no fighter goes on winning bout after bout, and Wladamir's career wound down after two major losses, one to Tyson Fury, the other to Anthony Joshua. For the fight with Joshua, more than ninety thousand fans filled Wembley Stadium in London, and 1 million fans paid to watch the fight on pay-per-view in England. In Germany alone, more than 10 million additional fans watched their hero. So popular was he in Germany that he signed to be a spokesman for Porsche and Deutsche Telecom, and those gigs only added to his immense celebrity. By the time he retired at age forty-one in 2017, Wladimir had earned the WBO, IBF, WBA and IBO belts and was listed as one of the top 100 sports earners by *Forbes*. He stated,

> Twenty-seven years ago I started my journey in sport. It was the best choice of a profession I could have made. Because of this choice, I have traveled the world, learned new languages, created business, built intellectual properties, helped people in need. At some point in our lives, we need to, or just want to, switch our careers and get ourselves ready for the next chapter—obviously I am not an exception to this. I am expecting and hoping my next career, which I have already been planning and working on for some years, will be at least as successful as the previous one, if not more successful. I was and am still capable of doing all this because of the global appeal of sport and boxing, my own talent, and most importantly because of you, my loyal fans.[4]

By the time he retired, Wladimir had defeated twenty-three boxers for the world heavyweight championship; he had broken a record established years earlier by heavyweight champ Joe Louis. Even more impressive, Klitschko fought in twenty-nine world heavyweight title fights, more than any other boxer in history. With his PhD as a passport to teach, Wladimir became an adjunct professor at Switzerland's University of St. Gallen. One of his fans was Schmeling, and the two boxers became good friends. One German commentator stated that it seemed as if Schmeling had passed on his charisma to Klitschko, a link spanning pre-war Germany and postwar Germany.

I have asked several authorities about the future of boxing in Germany. They hope that another popular world champion will emerge. In looking for an answer, I watched a touching documentary titled *Comeback*. It's about a German boxer named Jurgen "the Rock" Hartenstein. He is an athlete of extraordinary discipline and devotion to the sport of boxing. He is determined to have a successful career but is too poor to train in a professional gym so he trains in a dark and dreary attic and in the park near his home. He is determined to make a comeback but no one in Germany will give him a match. Hartenstein regularly contacts promoters and asks if they could set up a match for him. After all, he was once the middleweight champion of Germany. But that was years ago. His record, unfortunately, is one of wins and losses. He is finally offered an opportunity to fight in Philadelphia. If he wins, it will be his comeback, his ticket to future well-paid matches. But his record does not portend a happy ending. From 2002 to 2010, he won 1 fight and lost 11 other fights. For his fight in Philadelphia, he trains with the determination of a man whose career hangs on a hinge that could open the door to success or slam it shut with a sudden knockout punch. Will he fight on as an underdog? Is his boxing career over? Does his career portend the future of German boxing? It's impossible to predict. However, Germany itself has been a nation of defeats and comebacks. I assume that there is another aspiring pugilist willing to go through the long slog to become champion, for every sport inspires young athletes to dream of being the best there is.

Though Schmeling and Klitschko were giants of the world of German and international boxing, there were exciting boxers of the 1930s who died unable to achieve possible greatness. There are no more heroic Jewish and Roma/Sinti boxers in Germany today. Harry Haft, Victor Perez, Salamo Arouch, Nathan Shapow, and Johann Trollmann are long gone, their careers destroyed by a vicious, despotic regime whose ideology sought to eliminate anyone regarded as inferior to an idealized Aryan.

# 12

# Anti-Semitism in Germany and the United States

Could the Holocaust have been prevented if the United States and countries of Western Europe had acted against Germany in the 1930s? It's a question that has often been asked by survivors and historians. Only two European countries defied the Nazi effort to exterminate their Jewish citizens: Denmark and Bulgaria, whose citizens believed there was no "us" versus "them"; all citizens were one body. Any Nazi attack on Jews was perceived as an attack on all citizens.

And what of America? Many potential refugees looked to America as "the land of the free and the home of the brave" and as a nation of immigrants. The Statue of Liberty put out a welcoming mat to all who wanted to enter the country. Inside the pedestal of the statue is a famous sonnet by Emma Lazarus, "The New Colossus." It sums up America as a land that welcomes the downtrodden and the outcasts from all other lands.

> Not like the brazen giant of Greek fame,
> With conquering limbs astride from land to land;
> Here at our sea-washed, sunset gates shall stand
> A mighty woman with a torch, whose flame
> Is the imprisoned lightning, and her name
> Mother of Exiles. From her beacon-hand
> Glows world-wide welcome; her mild eyes command
> The air-bridged harbor that twin cities frame.
> "Keep, ancient lands, your storied pomp!" cries she
> With silent lips. "Give me your tired, your poor,
> Your huddled masses yearning to breathe free,
> The wretched refuse of your teeming shore.
> Send these, the homeless, tempest-tost to me,
> I lift my lamp beside the golden door!"[1]

As Germany's oppression of Jews and of Roma and Sinti grew more and more onerous and deadly, the lamp of the lady in the harbor shone as a welcoming light. There was America, across an ocean. It was large and sprawling, populated by many people of different races and religions. There was safety and tolerance for refugees. However, the U.S. State Department and various members of Congress turned off the lamp in the harbor. For those attempting to escape the Nazis, the lamp had turned to darkness. The doors of open immigration were slammed shut and locked. The immigration policy of the United States went from welcoming to being complicit in the deaths of millions of Holocaust victims. So lacking in compassion were many Washington officials that in place of "The New Colossus" they might have written a new sonnet titled "The New Callousness" with the warning "No Jews Allowed."

Why did a nation of immigrants offer such obdurate resistance to Jewish immigration? Anti-Semitism was a virus circulating in the air. During the years before America entered the war, there were more than one hundred anti-Semitic organizations that published vile stereotypes of Jews. Henry Ford in his newspaper, *The Dearborn Independent*, railed against the Jews in every issue. So pleased were the Nazis by Ford's screeds that copies of his newspapers were bound and distributed throughout the Third Reich. Henry Ford is the only American praised in *Mein Kampf*. Many people were led to believe that Jews killed Christian children and used their blood to make matzos. During Holy Week, countless clergy preached that Jews had killed Christ. In numerous cities, young gangs of anti-Semites vandalized Jewish cemeteries and synagogues. Incitement came not only from men such as Henry Ford but also from such popular figures as Father Charles Coughlin, who preached a hateful ideology on a weekly radio broadcast that attracted millions of listeners. He referred to FDR as "President Rosenfeld." The famous aviator Charles Lindbergh claimed that American Jews were angling for a war with Germany, and they would suffer the consequences. He made his remarks while German Jews were being thrown in concentration camps. He visited Germany and received an award from Herman Göring. Another ideologue who railed against the Jews, while referring to President Roosevelt as "Frank D. Rosenfeld," was Fritz Kuhn, leader of the pro-Nazi German-American Bund.

In the 1930s and early 1940s, surveys revealed that anti-Semitism ranged from 40 percent to 60 percent of the American population. In a 1938 poll, approximately 60 percent of the respondents said that Jews were greedy, dishonest, and pushy, and they agreed with the statement that Jews "have too much power in the United States." In addition, several surveys taken from 1940 to 1946 found that Jews were seen as a greater threat to the welfare of the United States than any other national, religious, or racial group.

Though many senators, congressional representatives, and members of the Roosevelt administration paid lip service to the plight of the Jews (while omitting mention of Roma and Sinti) in Germany, they refused to permit large numbers of Jews into their country. In a report issued years later by the State Department, Undersecretary of State Stuart Eizenstat noted that the United States had accepted only 21,000 Jews, far fewer per capita than many of the neutral European countries and fewer in absolute terms than Switzerland.

Many of those in important government positions who could have lobbied to alter the country's immigration policies were passively anti-Semitic. They would never commit an act of violence against a Jew, would never even condone such an act—they would just refuse to take any remedial action. Their point of view was dramatized in the award-winning movie *Gentleman's Agreement*, in which Gregory Peck plays the part of a gentile reporter posing as a Jew in order to uncover the injurious role played by passive anti-Semites. His fiancée (played by Dorothy McGuire) tells their Jewish friend (played by John Garfield) that a man at a dinner party told an anti-Semitic joke that disgusted everyone but no one said or did anything in opposition. They just sat there, feeling embarrassed. Garfield tells her how good she would have felt if she had hit back, if she hadn't been a passive patsy. During the 1930s, America was not willing to hit back, not willing to be proactive against a growing threat to humanity. And during the years of World War II, America refused to bomb the railroad tracks on which cattle cars of condemned Jews were delivered to the slaughterhouses of Europe.

Anti-Semitism, like an out-of-control fire, not only raged in groups that admired the Third Reich but also found voice in some politicians. For example, Congressman John Rankin, a malevolent and spiteful anti-Semite, supported a visa policy that caused Jews to run a gauntlet of dehumanizing obstacles before they could gain entry into the United States. Even then, many were turned away. He vituperatively called out Jews as a threat to the welfare of the United States and referred to them on the floor of Congress as "dirty kikes."

Another defender of the anti-immigration status quo was Breckenridge Long, an assistant secretary of state. He was an expert at creating obstacles to Jewish immigration. He denied that he was an anti-Semite and thought that as a WASP member of the upper echelons of society and government, he would be safe against accusations of bigotry. He was a member of the best clubs and he had been a long-standing friend of FDR, yet in his official capacity as an assistant secretary of state, he wrote the following memorandum in 1940.

> We can delay and effectively stop for a temporary period of indefinite length the number of immigrants into the United States. We could do this by simply advising our consuls to put every obstacle in the way and to require additional evidence and to resort to various administrative devices which would postpone and postpone and postpone the granting of the visas.[2]

His efforts to obstruct the rescue of European Jewry and restrict immigration by creating large, fictitious numbers of refugees admitted to the United States were eventually exposed. He was held in contempt not only by the Jewish community but also by others who believed the United States had a moral obligation to live up to its ideals. Criticism of his actions mounted. In 1944, President Roosevelt was presented with "Report to the Secretary on the Acquiescence of this Government in the Murder of the Jews." The report was a thorough indictment of the State Department's immigration policies. It condemned the U.S. policy of complicity in the destruction of European Jewry by not only closing and locking and double-locking the doors to the entry of immigrants but also by opposing the release of funds that could have been used to rescue Holocaust victims. For example, seventy thousand Romanian Jews could have been saved if the State Department had not blocked the payment of a $170,000 bribe. The bribe had previously been approved by the president and the Treasury Department. Treasury Secretary Henry Morgenthau used the report to convince Roosevelt to establish the War Refugee Board, which was done by executive order in 1944 (and which should have been done years earlier). The order declares that

> it is the policy of this Government to take all measures within its power to rescue the victims of enemy oppression who are in imminent danger of death and otherwise to afford such victims all possible relief and assistance consistent with the successful prosecution of the war.

Government officials estimated that if Breckenridge Long had not prevented Jews from entering the United States, between 190,000 to 200,000 Jews could have been saved from the gas chambers of the concentration camps. Long's erstwhile friend, FDR, demoted him. Yet Roosevelt refused requests to bomb the railroad tracks to such infernos of horror as Auschwitz because this was not, as his executive order declared, "consistent with the successful prosecution of the war."

And what of German anti-Semitism in the years before the outbreak of World War II? From its inception, the Nazi Party required a scapegoat to further its heroic image of protecting pure-blood Aryans against contamination from the viral infection of Jewry. As a tiny minority comprising a mere 0.76 percent of the German population, Jews were an easy target. In addition to being portrayed in propaganda films as disease-carrying rodents, they were blamed for interwar hyperinflation and for conspiring with Germany's enemies to bring about the defeat of the German army in 1918. As conspiratorial traitors, the Jews had stabbed Germany in the back. They had not only engineered the country's military defeat, they had induced the government to agree to the Treaty of Versailles. The Nazis claimed that Germany's onerous reparations payments profited the Jews, who made out like bandits, laughing all the way to their Swiss banks. It didn't matter that thousands of Jews had served honorably in the military and many had been killed during World War I. The stab-in-the-back accusation became a rallying cry for the Nazis and the basis for their anti-Semitic propaganda.

Though a small minority of the German population, a disproportionate number of Jews were represented in the legal, medical, and financial professions. Their presence in those professions incensed the Nazis, who as nationalistic and jingoistic populists not only declaimed the superior virtues of Aryan man but demanded that the Jews be kicked out of all the professional classes. Only true Aryans should be permitted to practice medicine, law, and banking or any kind of financial brokerage. In their propaganda and rallies, the Nazis were able to generate envy and hatred of Jewish elites who were accused of controlling the levers of power. If given an opportunity, Goebbels claimed, the Jews would press their boots on the necks of ordinary, patriotic Germans. Soon many resorts, universities, and clubs would not admit Jews. Many churches, fearful of antagonizing the Nazis, remained timidly silent about government inspired anti-Semitism. To win favor, some of the clergy preached viciously anti-Semitic sermons. All the elements came together to create a perfect storm that led to the death of millions of Jews. As in America, most German citizens remained passively anti-Semitic. They did not join the SA, did not volunteer for the SS, and were only vaguely aware of what was being done at the concentration camps. Better to avert one's eyes and go on with one's life.

Ronnie Landau writes that the institutionalization of anti-Semitism provided "formal confirmation of the isolation and removal of the Jews from the midst of the German nation . . . The laws met with public approval because they curbed the apparently random and anarchic anti-Semitic violence, containing it securely within the framework of law and order." He adds, "The German population appears to have remained entirely consistent in their indifference towards the persecution of the Jews, even when its level was severely increased during the summer of 1938." He concludes that "the public had gradually grown used to an anti-Semitic reality and had generally taken no notice of it. Their toleration of 'mild' anti-Semitism had unquestionably paved the way for harsher measures."

One would think that after one of the most-civilized countries in Europe attempted the extermination of a portion of its population, the citizens of America would be on their guard to make sure that nothing like it would happen again. And one way of ensuring that future genocides are avoided would be knowledge of what happened in the past. Yet a 2018 survey in the United States found that 22 percent of 1,350 adults said they had never heard of the Holocaust while 41 percent of Americans and 66 percent of millennials did not know what Auschwitz was. Even worse, of course, are the professional Holocaust deniers.

And what of Germany today? According to an article in the *New York Times Magazine*,

> in the decades that followed, a desire among many Germans to deflect or repress guilt for the Holocaust led to a new form of antipathy toward Jews—a phenomenon that came to be known as "secondary anti-Semitism," in which Germans resent Jews for reminding them of their guilt, reversing the victim and perpetrator roles. "It seems the Germans will never forgive us Auschwitz," Hilde Walter, a German-Jewish journalist, was quoted as saying in 1968.
>
> Holocaust commemoration in West Germany increasingly became an affair of the state and civic groups, giving rise to a prevailing *erinnerungskultur,* or "culture of remembrance," that today is most prominently illustrated by the Memorial to the Murdered Jews of Europe. But even as Germany's remembrance culture has been held up as an international model of how to confront the horrors of the past, it has not been universally supported at home. According to a 2015 Anti-Defamation League survey, 51 percent of Germans believe that it is "probably true" that "Jews still talk too much about what happened to them in the Holocaust"; 30 percent agreed with the statement "People hate Jews because of the way Jews behave."

Now some 200,000 Jews live in Germany, a nation of 82 million people, and many are increasingly fearful. In a 2018 European Union survey of European Jews, 85 percent of respondents in Germany characterized anti-Semitism as a "very big" or "fairly big" problem; 89 percent said the problem has become worse in the last five years. Overall reported anti-Semitic crimes in Germany increased by nearly 20 percent last year to 1,799, while violent anti-Semitic crimes rose by about 86 percent, to 69.

Often intertwined with economic and social resentment, demonization of Jews was long part of Christian tradition, and, with the growth of European nationalism in the nineteenth century, it took on delusive notions of race. Now as a worldwide resurgence of racist tribalism fuels a rebellion against the liberal democratic order, Germany's renewed confrontation with anti-Semitism will say much not just about the fate of its unnerved Jewish communities but also about the endurance of any nation's capacity to build a tolerant, pluralistic society resistant to the temptations of ethnonationalism.[3]

I have wondered if Harry Haft, Nathan Shapow, Johann Trollmann, Salamo Arouch, Victor "Young" Perez, and Max Schmeling would be appalled, resigned, or optimistic about the level and knowledge of anti-Semitism in Germany and America today. In the United States, the percentage of the population surveyed to be anti-Semitic is 9 percent, a figure far lower than what existed in the 1930s and 1940s. This represents a cause for hope.

# Notes

## INTRODUCTION

1. C. P. Snow, *Public Affairs* (London: Macmillan, 1971), 195.
2. Ronnie S. Landau, *The Nazi Holocaust* (Chicago: Ivan R. Dee, 1994), 15.
3. Landau, *Nazi Holocaust*, 117–18.
4. Arthur Morse, *While Six Million Died: A Chronicle of American Apathy* (New York: Random House, 1968), 203.
5. Albert Speer, *Inside the Third Reich* (New York: Simon & Schuster, 1997), 73.
6. P. D. Smith, "The Volunteer by Jack Fairweather Review—The Hero Who Infiltrated Auschwitz," *Guardian*, January 22, 2020, www.theguardian .com/books/2020/jan/22/the-volunteer-jack-fairweather-review.
7. Stanford University, "The Man Who Volunteered for Auschwitz: The Greatest Story Never Told," Book Haven, https://bookhaven.stanford. edu/2012/06/the-man-who-volunteered-for-auschwitz-the-greatest-story-never-told/.
8. Goodreads, "Adolf Eichmann," www.goodreads.com/quotes/734647-i-will-leap-into-my-grave-laughing-because-the-feeling.

## CHAPTER 1

1. Max Schmeling, *Max Schmeling: An Autobiography*, trans. and ed. George von der Lippe (Chicago: Bonus Books, 1998).
2. Adolf Hitler, "Basic Ideas Regarding the Meaning and Organization of the SA" in *Mein Kampf* 2:9 (New York: Reynal & Hitchcock, 1939), 801.
3. David Williamson, *The Third Reich* (London: Longman Publishers, 2002), 55.
4. Gerhard Rempel, *Hitler's Children: The Hitler Youth and the SS* (Chapel Hill: University of North Carolina Press, 1989), 2.
5. Schmeling, *Max Schmeling*, 104.
6. Jewish Virtual Library, "Joe Jacobs," www.jewishvirtuallibrary.org/jacobs -joe.

## CHAPTER 2

1. Heather Pringle, *The Master Plan: Himmler's Scholars and the Holocaust* (New York: Hyperion, 2006), 41.

2. Holocaust History Project, "Heinrich Himmler's Speech at Poznan (Posen)," https://web.archive.org/web/20120507140239/http://www.holocaust-history.org/himmler-poznan/.

3. Rudolf Höss, "Rudolf Hoess, Commandant of Auschwitz: Testimony at Nuremburg, 1946." Modern History Sourcebook. https://sourcebooks.fordham.edu/mod/1946hoess.asp.

4. Peter Applebome, "Veteran of the Nuremberg Trials Can't Forget Dialogue with Infamy," *New York Times*, March 14, 2007, www.nytimes.com/2007/03/14/nyregion/14towns.html.

5. John Jay Hughes, "A Mass Murderer Repents: The Case of Rudolf Hoess, Commandant of Auschwitz," Archbishop Gerety Lecture at Seton Hall University, South Orange, New Jersey (March 25, 1998), www.shu.edu/theology/upload/mass-murderer-repents.pdf.

6. Jewish Virtual Library, "Rudolf Höss," www.jewishvirtuallibrary.org/rudolf-h-ouml-ss.

7. Robert Gerwath, *Hitler's Hangman: The Life of Heydrich* (New Haven, CT: Yale University Press, 2011).

## CHAPTER 3

1. Martin Gilbert, *The Holocaust: A History of the Jews of Europe during the Second World War* (New York: Holt, Rinehart & Winston, 1985), 792.

2. Gilbert, *Holocaust*, 774.

3. Gilbert, *Holocaust*, 792–93.

## CHAPTER 4

1. Nathan Shapow with Bob Harris, *The Boxer's Story: Fighting for My Life in the Nazi Camps* (London: Robson Press, 2012), 2.

2. Shapow, *Boxer's Story*, 6–7.

3. Shapow, *Boxer's Story*, 58.

4. Shapow, *Boxer's Story*, 70.

5. Martin Gilbert, *The Holocaust: A History of the Jews of Europe during the Second World War* (New York: Holt, Rinehart & Winston, 1985), 115.

6. Interview with the author.

## CHAPTER 5

1. Martin Gilbert, *The Holocaust: A History of the Jews of Europe during the Second World War* (New York: Holt, Rinehart & Winston, 1985), 131–32.

2. Fourteen years after the defeat of Nazi Germany, Max Merton was arrested when he visited Greece in 1959. As the Nazi administrator of Salonica who had sent 50,000 Jews to concentration camps, he was tried, found guilty of war crimes, and sentenced to twenty-five years in prison. However, the government of West Germany, which contained numerous former Nazis, protested his arrest and demanded that Merten be extradited to his homeland. Once on German soil, Merten was given his freedom by German authorities. He died a free man in 1971.

3. While the Italian Fascists had been their enemies during the invasion of Greece, the Italians had long been known for their neighborly acceptance of Jews—at least until Mussolini passed his anti-Jewish laws. Even then many Italians refused to obey the new racial laws. In fact, when the Italian army left southern France, they protected and accepted Jews who were trying to escape the murderous anti-Semitism that was instituted following the Nazi occupation of southern France.

4. Gilbert, *Holocaust*, 745.

5. Interview with the author, June 3, 2020.

## CHAPTER 6

1. Sybil Milton, "Sinti and Roma in Twentieth-Century Austria and Germany," *German Studies Review* 23, no. 2 (2000): 318.

2. Jud Nirenberg, *Johann Trollmann and Romani Resistance to the Nazis* (Iowa City, IA: KO Publications, 2016), 27.

3. Nirenberg, *Johann Trollmann*, 42.

4. While serving time in prison for his failed beer hall putsch, Hitler refused to exercise or participate in sports for fear that a non-Aryan would show him up and poke holes in his theories of German superiority. Nazis must never lose, insisted Hitler.

## CHAPTER 7

1. Alan Scott Haft, *Harry Haft: Survivor of Auschwitz, Challenger of Rocky Marciano* (Syracuse, NY: Syracuse University Press, 2006), 36.

2. Haft, *Harry Haft*, 48.

3. Haft, *Harry Haft*, 60.

4. Haft, *Harry Haft*, 78.

5. Haft, *Harry Haft*, 112–13.

6. Allyce Schwartzbart, *Las Vegas Sun*, September 5, 2001.

7. BoxRec, "Rocky Marciano vs. Roland LaStarza (2nd meeting)," https://boxrec.com/media/index.php/Rocky_Marciano_vs._Roland_LaStarza_(2nd _meeting).

8. Haft, *Harry Haft*, 153–54.

9. Alan Scott Haft, letter to his deceased father.

## CHAPTER 8

1. Józef Garlinski, *Fighting Auschwitz: The Resistance Movement in the Concentration Camp* (New York: Fawcett, 1975), 191–97.

2. In 1945 he added more details to his initial report but it was not published until 2000, when it was of interest only to historians and survivors. The English version was not available until 2012.

3. Though the Soviets were now fighting the Nazis, they had previously allied themselves with the Nazis and had attacked Poland in 1939. It was not until the Nazis launched Operation Barbarossa in 1941 that the Soviets turned their guns on their former ally. It's no wonder that the Poles hated the Soviets as much as they hated the Nazis. And the Soviets were not about to help the Poles, though the Red Army's Ukrainian division did liberate Auschwitz on January 27, 1945. During the attack, 231 Red Army troops were killed.

4. Witold Pilecki, "Full Text of 'Witold's Report,'" Internet Archive, https://archive.org/stream/WITOLDREPORT/WITOLD%20REPORT_djvu.txt.

5. Rudolf Vrba, *I Escaped from Auschwitz* (Fort Lee, NJ: Barricade Books, 2002), 13–14, 16–17.

6. Claude Lanzmann, *Shoah: The Complete Text of the Acclaimed Holocaust Film* (New York: Da Capo Press, 1995), 112–15.

7. Vrba, *I Escaped from Auschwitz*, 218.

8. Michael Fleming, *Auschwitz, the Allies and Censorship of the Holocaust* (Cambridge: Cambridge University Press, 2014), 233.

9. Alfred Wetzler, *Escape from Hell* (Oxford: Berghahn Books, 2007), 292.

## CHAPTER 9

1. Dina Porat, *The Fall of a Sparrow: The Life and Times of Abba Kovner* (Stanford, CA: Stanford University Press, 2009), 215–16, 235–36.

2. Ofer Aderet, "'An Eye for an Eye': The Jews Who Sought to Poison Six Million Germans to Avenge the Holocaust," *Haaretz*, www.haaretz.com /israel-news/.premium.MAGAZINE-an-eye-for-an-eye-jews-who-sought-to -kill-germans-in-revenge-for-the-holocaust-1.8094962.

3. Rich Cohen, *The Avengers* (New York: Alfred A. Knopf, 2000), 192.

4. During the Ponary Massacre, 100,000 people consisting of 70,000 Jews, 20,000 Poles, and 8,000 Russians were murdered by Nazi SS and their Lithu-

anian collaborators. The victims were lined up and shot with automatic and semi-automatic weapons.

5. Dina Porat, *The Fall of a Sparrow: The Life and Times of Abba Kovner* (Palo Alto, CA: Stanford University Press, 2009), 56–73.

6. War Documentaries, "Nakam Jewish Avengers," YouTube, April 16, 2018, www.youtube.com/watch?v=p_FBI_ITJtc.

7. Associated Press, "Jewish Avengers Unapologetic for Targeting Nazis after WWII," Fox News, August 31, 2016, www.foxnews.com/world/jewish -avengers-unapologetic-for-targeting-nazis-after-wwii.

8. Cohen, *Avengers*, 203.

9. Associated Press, "Jewish Avengers."

10. Associated Press, "Jewish Avengers."

11. Associated Press, "Jewish Avengers."

12. Associated Press, "Jewish Avengers."

13. Ehud Sprinzak and Idith Zertal, "Avenging Israeli's Blood (1946)," in *Toxic Terror: Assessing Terrorist Use of Chemical and Biological Weapons*, ed. Jonathan B. Tucker (Cambridge, MA: MIT Press, 2000), 40.

14. Aderet, "'An Eye for an Eye.'"

15. Bernard Press, *The Murder of the Jews in Latvia* (Evanston, IL: Northwestern University Press, 2000), 46.

16. The rat lines were supported by clergy of the Catholic Church, and according to Michael Phayer, historian and professor emeritus at Marquette University, the Vatican fully supported the rat lines, which helped numerous Nazis escape justice, particularly Adolf Eichmann and Josef Mengele.

17. *Time*, "Uruguay: Man in the Icebox," March 19, 1965.

## CHAPTER 10

1. Kevin Jon Heller, *The Nuremberg Military Tribunals and the Origins of International Criminal Law* (Oxford: Oxford University Press, 2011), 9.

2. Jonathan Thompson, "Churchill Wanted a Captured Hitler to Die 'Like a Gangster' in the Electric Chair," *Independent*, January 1, 2006, www .independent.co.uk/news/uk/this-britain/churchill-wanted-captured-hitler -die-gangster-electric-chair-6112926.html.

3. Robert H. Jackson, "Opening Statement before the International Military Tribunal," Robert H. Jackson Center, www.roberthjackson.org/speech-and -writing/opening-statement-before-the-international-military-tribunal/.

4. Jackson, "Opening Statement."

5. William L. Shirer, *The Rise and Fall of the Third Reich* (New York: Simon & Schuster, 1960), 1142.

6. Peter Margaritis, *Countdown to D-Day: The German Perspective* (Philadelphia, PA: Casemate Publishers, 2019), 26.

7. Peter Longerich, *Holocaust: The Nazi Persecution and Murder of the Jews* (Oxford: Oxford University Press, 2010), 289.

8. Antony Polonsky, *The Jews in Poland and Russia, Volume III, 1914 to 2008* (Liverpool, UK: Liverpool University Press, 2010), 434.

9. Joseph Kingsbury-Smith, "The Execution of Nazi War Criminals," International News Service, October 16, 1946, https://web.archive.org /web/20010312175414/http://www.law.umkc.edu/faculty/projects/ftrials /nuremberg/NurembergNews10_16_46.html.

10. International Military Tribunal, "Trials of War Criminals before the Nuremberg Military Tribunals under Control Council Law no. 10: Nuremberg, October 1946–April 1949," https://archive.org/details/trialsofwarcrimi02inte.

11. Yale Law School, Lillian Goldman Law Library, "Nuremberg Trial Proceedings, Volume 22: Two Hundred and Sixteenth Day, Saturday, 31 August 1946," Avalon Project, https://avalon.law.yale.edu/imt/08-31-46.asp.

12. David M. Crowe, *Crimes of State Past and Present: Government-Sponsored Atrocities and International Legal Responses* (New York: Routledge, 2011), 87.

13. Werner Maser, *Nuremberg: A Nation on Trial* (Germany: Verlag Antaios, 2005).

14. Leni Yahil, *The Holocaust: The Fate of European Jewry, 1932–1945* (Oxford: Oxford University Press, 1990), 406.

15. Richard Evans, *The Third Reich at War* (New York: Penguin, 2010), 536.

16. Laurence Rees, *The Nazis: A Warning from History* (New York: New Press, 1997), 93.

17. Peter Applebome, "Veteran of the Nuremberg Trials Can't Forget Dialogue with Infamy," *New York Times*, March 14, 2007, www.nytimes.com /2007/03/14/nyregion/14towns.html.

18. John Gunther, *Inside Europe* (New York: Harper & Brothers, 1940), 61.

19. Harry L. Coles and Albert K. Weinberg, *Civil Affairs: Soldiers Become Governors* (1964), https://history.army.mil/html/books/011/11-3/index.html; Dwight Eisenhower, *Crusade in Europe* (New York: Doubleday, 1949), 455.

20. G. M. Gilbert, *Nuremberg Diary* (New York: Farrar Straus, 1947), 433.

21. Airey Neave, *Nuremberg* (London: Hodder & Stoughton, 1978), 258.

22. Neave, *Nuremberg*, 261.

23. Neave, *Nuremberg*, 297.

24. Yale Law School, Lillian Goldman Law Library, "Judgment: Goering," Avalon Project, https://avalon.law.yale.edu/imt/judgoeri.asp.

25. "Nuremberg Trials," History.com, www.history.com/topics/world -war-ii/nuremberg-trials.

26. Chris Dodd, "Prosecuting the Peace of the World: The Experiences of Thomas J. Dodd at the International Military Tribunal, Nuremberg, Germany, 1945–46." Speech given February 15, 2005, www.senate.gov/~dodd/press /Speeches/109_05/0215.htm.

## CHAPTER 11

1. Jeffrey Sussman, *Max Baer and Barney Ross: Jewish Heroes of Boxing* (Lanham, MD: Rowman & Littlefield, 2017), 110–11.

2. Max Schmeling, *Max Schmeling: An Autobiography*, trans. and ed., George von der Lippe (Chicago: Bonus Books, 1998), 191.

3. Schmeling, *Max Schmeling*, 192.

4. Peter Kahn, "Wladimir Klitschko Retires From Boxing: No Anthony Joshua Rematch," www.forbes.com/sites/peterkahn/2017/08/03/wladimir-klitschko -retires-from-boxing-no-anthony-joshua-rematch/?sh=662096b92102.

## CHAPTER 12

1. Emma Lazarus, "The New Colossus," 1883.

2. Doris Kearns Goodwin, *No Ordinary Time* (New York: Simon & Schuster, 1994), 173.

3. James Angelos, "The New German Anti-Semitism," *New York Times Magazine,* www.nytimes.com/2019/05/21/magazine/anti-semitism/germany .htm.

# Bibliography

## BOOKS AND ARTICLES

Applebome, Peter. "Veteran of the Nuremberg Trials Can't Forget Dialogue with Infamy." *New York Times*, March 14, 2007. www.nytimes.com/2007/03/14/nyregion/14towns.html.

Cohen, Rich. *The Avengers*. New York: Alfred A. Knopf, 2000.

Crowe, David M. *Crimes of State Past and Present: Government-Sponsored Atrocities and International Legal Responses*. New York: Routledge, 2011.

Dodd, Chris. "Prosecuting the Peace of the World: The Experiences of Thomas J. Dodd at the International Military Tribunal, Nuremberg, Germany, 1945–46." Speech given February 15, 2005. www.senate.gov/~dodd/press/Speeches/109_05/0215.htm.

Eisenhower, Dwight. *Crusade in Europe*. New York: Doubleday, 1949.

Evans, Richard. *The Third Reich at War*. New York: Penguin, 2010.

Fest, Joachim C. *Hitler*. New York: Harcourt Brace & Company, 1974.

Fleming, Michael. *Auschwitz, the Allies and Censorship of the Holocaust*. Cambridge: Cambridge University Press, 2014.

Gerwath, Robert. *Hitler's Hangman: The Life of Heydrich*. New Haven, CT: Yale University Press, 2011.

Gilbert, G. M. *Nuremberg Diary*. New York: Farrar Straus, 1947.

Gilbert, Martin. *The Holocaust : A History of the Jews of Europe during the Second World War*. New York: Holt, Rinehart & Winston, 1986.

Goldhagen, Daniel Jonah. *Hitler's Willing Executioners: Ordinary Germans and the Holocaust*. New York: Vintage Books, 1997.

Gunther, John. *Inside Europe*. New York: Harper & Brothers, 1940.

Haft, Alan Scott. *Harry Haft*. Syracuse, NY: Syracuse University Press, 2006.

Heller, Kevin Jon. *The Nuremberg Military Tribunals and the Origins of International Criminal Law*. Oxford: Oxford University Press, 2011.

Himmler, Heinrich. "Heinrich Himmler's Speech at Poznan (Posen)." Holo-
    caust History Project. https://web.archive.org/web/20120507140239/http://
    www.holocaust-history.org/himmler-poznan.
Höss, Rudolf. "Rudolf Hoess, Commandant of Auschwitz: Testimony at
    Nuremburg, 1946." Modern History Sourcebook. https:/sourcebooks.ford
    ham.edu/mod/1946hoess.asp.
Hughes, John Jay. "A Mass Murderer Repents: The Case of Rudolf Hoess,
    Commandant of Auschwitz." Archbishop Gerety Lecture at Seton Hall
    University, South Orange, New Jersey, March 25, 1998. www.shu.edu
    /theology/upload/mass-murderer-repents.pdf.
International Military Tribunal. "Trials of War Criminals before the Nurem-
    berg Military Tribunals under Control Council Law no. 10: Nuremberg, Oc-
    tober 1946–April 1949." https://archive.org/details/trialsofwarcrimi02inte.
Jackson, Robert H. "Opening Statement before the International Military
    Tribunal." Robert H. Jackson Center. www.roberthjackson.org/speech-and
    -writing/opening-statement-before-the-international-military-tribunal/.
Kingsbury-Smith, Joseph. "The Execution of Nazi War Criminals." Inter-
    national News Service, October 16, 1946. https://web.archive.org/web
    /20010312175414/http://www.law.umkc.edu/faculty/projects/ftrials
    /nuremberg/NurembergNews10_16_46.html.
Landau, Ronnie S. *The Nazi Holocaust.* Chicago: Ivan R. Dee, 1994.
Lanzmann, Claude. *Shoah: The Complete Text of the Acclaimed Holocaust
    Film.* New York: Da Capo Press, 1995.
Laqueur, Walter, ed. *The Holocaust Encyclopedia.* New Haven, CT: Yale Uni-
    versity Press, 2001.
Longerich, Peter. *Holocaust: The Nazi Persecution and Murder of the Jews.*
    Oxford: Oxford University Press, 2010.
Margaritis, Peter. *Countdown to D-Day: The German Perspective.* Philadel-
    phia, PA: Casemate Publishers, 2019.
Morse, Arthur D. *While Six Million Died.* New York: Random House, 1968.
Nardo, Don. *Nazi War Criminals.* San Diego, CA: Reference Point Press, 2016.
Neave, Airey. *Nuremberg.* London: Hodder & Stoughton, 1978.
Nirenberg, Jud. *Johann Trollmann and Romani Resistance to the Nazis.* Iowa
    City, IA: KO Publications, 2016.
Pilecki, Witold. "Full Text of 'Witold's Report.'" Internet Archive. https://
    archive.org/stream/WITOLDREPORT/WITOLD%20REPORT_djvu.txt.
Polonsky, Antony. *The Jews in Poland and Russia, Volume III, 1914 to 2008.*
    Liverpool, UK: Liverpool University Press, 2010.
Porat, Dina. *The Fall of a Sparrow: The Life and Times of Abba Kovner.* Palo
    Alto, CA: Stanford University Press, 2009.
Press, Bernard. *The Murder of the Jews in Latvia.* Evanston, IL: Northwestern
    University Press, 2000.
Pringle, Heather. *The Master Plan: Himmler's Scholars and the Holocaust.*
    New York: Hyperion, 2006.
Rees, Laurence. *The Nazis: A Warning from History.* New York: New Press,
    1997.

Rotem, Simha. *Memoirs of a Warsaw Ghetto Fighter.* New Haven, CT: Yale University Press, 1994.

Schmeling, Max. *Max Schmeling: An Autobiography.* Translated and edited by George von der Lippe. Chicago: Bonus Books, 1998.

Shapow, Nathan, with Bob Harris. *The Boxer's Story.* London: Robson Press, 2012.

Shirer, William L. *The Rise and Fall of the Third Reich.* New York: Simon & Schuster, 1960.

Talty, Stephan. *The Good Assassin: Mossad's Hunt for the Butcher of Latvia.* Boston: Houghton Mifflin, 2020.

Thompson, Jonathan. "Churchill Wanted a Captured Hitler to Die 'Like a Gangster' in the Electric Chair." *Independent,* January 1, 2006. www .independent.co.uk/news/uk/this-britain/churchill-wanted-captured-hitler -die-gangster-electric-chair-6112926.html.

Vrba, Rudolf. *I Escaped from Auschwitz.* Fort Lee, NJ: Barricade Books, 2002.

Wetzler, Alfred. *Escape from Hell.* Oxford: Berghahn Books, 2007.

Yahil, Leni. *The Holocaust: The Fate of European Jewry, 1932–1945.* New York: Oxford University Press, 1990.

## WEBSITE

Jewish Virtual Library. www.jewishvirtuallibrary.org.

## MOVIES

*Auschwitz: Inside the Nazi State,* 2005
*The Boxer of Auschwitz,* 2018
*Judgment at Nuremberg,* 1961
*The Nuremberg War Crimes Trial,* 2005
*Triumph of the Spirit,* 1989

# Index

# About the Author

**Jeffrey Sussman** is the author of fifteen nonfiction books. In addition to *Holocaust Fighters: Boxers, Resisters, and Avengers,* his most recent books are *Big Apple Gangsters: The Rise and Decline of the Mob in New York; Boxing and the Mob: The Notorious History of the Sweet Science; Rocky Graziano: Fists, Fame, and Fortune;* and *Max Baer and Barney Ross: Jewish Heroes of Boxing.* He lives in New York City.